Through the Years:
My Life in Cricket

Leonard Chambers

Printed in the United States of America
First Printing, 2024
ISBN: 9798334045934
Imprint: Independently published

Interior and cover design by The Writery Ink, LLC

Dedication

This book is dedicated in loving memory of my dear beloved parents Arnold Chambers & Cecelia Phillips-Chambers

Leonard Chambers

CONTENTS

Leonard Chambers

Acknowledgments

My sincere thanks to Dr. Vivian Tennant, who was the medical officer of the Health Center at Saint Jago Park and founder of the Saint Jago Youth Club, for his recognition of my batting talent at a young age. He likened me to the Indian test batsman Vijay Manjrekar by dubbing me with the name Vijay, a name that I am regularly called to this day. Special thanks to Mickey Murdock for his stewardship as captain of the St. Catherine Cricket Club; his remarkable knowledge of the game helped our young players to have bettered our game in many respects. I would also like to recognize the support of Roy Deleon, Allan Rae, Ludlow Stewart, Tony Burrowes, Sydney Bennett, and Charleto Williams for the job opportunities they created for me while being an active player and a cricket administrator.

Thanks to the following individuals for providing photographs: Oliver Martin, Mark Neita, William Cole, Carlton Carter Snr., Courtney Daley, Jeffrey Dujon, Linden Wright, Ferdie Harvey, Maurice Chung, Monica Willams, Sasha Rhoden, Wayne Sutherland, Carol Gordon, Carlton Gordon, Andrew Greenwood, Patrick Gayle, Arthur Brown, Larry Creighton, Alton Williams, Christopher Cheddar, Ray Stewart, Kevin Reese, Peter Douglas, Vincent Dixon, Junior Hall, Kirk Forrest, Courtney Francis, Gary Neil, Christopher Miller, Orlando Baker, Dalkeith Dempster, Marlon Tucker, Horton Dolphin, Ruddy Marzouca, Gregory Brown, and Rohan Chambers. The pictures from the Jamaica Gleaner Archives and photographers Headley Delmar and Delroy Thompson were invaluable to me for inclusion in this book.

Foreword

I first met Mr. Chambers (or "Manage," as I respectfully call him up to this day!) back in 1983, as a 15-year-old schoolboy who had just been invited to participate in Jamaica's Under-19 program. His passion and love for the game was not lost on us as young aspiring players, and he became a consistent source of encouragement and support for successive generations of players who travelled through the national junior and senior programs.

Mr. Chambers was the "engine" of our age group cricket program while serving as Team Manager and Chair of the Junior Selection Panel, and he had the dubious distinction of being a member of both junior and senior Jamaica Selection Panels that selected me for debuts at each level.

Mr. Chambers eventually migrated to the United States, leaving a tremendous legacy of having served Jamaica's cricket both as player and administrator for over three decades. Since relocating, his daily conversations with longtime friend and cricket legend Lawrence Rowe have become a source of amusement for those of us who know how much he loves, and loves to speak about, the game.

The stories told in this book cover not only Mr. Chamber's journey, but give great insight into an era that is sadly gone forever, an era that predated the global commercialization of the game and was driven only by people's love and passion for cricket.

With almost all levels of the game now fully professionalized and placed under the powerful microscope of social media, I hope this book provides you with a sense of how many of today's successful careers on the field, including my own, have been positively shaped and influenced by the unseen, yet important, contributions of those like

Mr. Chambers whose efforts may never be fully recognized or truly appreciated.

Jimmy Adams

October 26, 2023

Prologue

Leonard Chambers, my father, was the reason I got involved in cricket, from being taken to watch my first Test match (West Indies vs England, 1981 at Sabina Park) to listening to my first match on radio in the early hours of the morning (West Indies vs Australia in 1981 when Jeffery Dujon made his Test debut and Dennis Lillee broke Lance Gibbs' record of 309 Test wickets). I also recall being taken to weekend Senior Cup matches at Chedwin Park, the home ground of St. Catherine Cricket Club, and scoring the book from the early age of 11 or so.

I have had the benefit of being witness to the beginning of the national careers of several Jamaican and West Indian cricketers. From the time they were first 'discovered', to being invited to trials, to finally making their national debuts, I was privy to hearing or overhearing many conversations surrounding their eventual selection. Jamaica's young cricketers were quite lucky to have the services of my father, someone who would travel across the country to ensure that hidden talent was revealed.

This book chronicles my father's involvement in cricket from his time as a youngster in the 1950's to when he left the country as Manager of Jamaica's Youth Team and selector for both the Youth and Senior teams in the mid-1990s. Since joining Facebook a few years ago, he would often post comments about various incidents which occurred over the years, and which involved many of the youngsters he managed. I mentioned to him that he should document his vast knowledge somewhere so that it does not "die" when he leaves this earth. I have heard many of his stories before but hearing them a second time (or third time) always brings out something new, or I interpret them differently now because of my age.

There are a few special moments captured in the book that I would like to mention here. The first is when I captained the Jamaican under 19 team to victory in the 1990 West Indies youth championship, which was the first victory for my father as manager in his then 9-year tenure. The second would be our 2019 trip to the ODI World Cup in England & Wales, during which both of us visited all 18 county grounds inclusive of watching three of the World Cup matches. The third and last would have been our March 2023 trip to South Africa where we watched West Indies' 3 T20 matches versus the home team which ended with West Indies eventually winning the series 2-1. To top it off, we stayed at the same hotel as the West Indies players, and my father was able to reconnect with some of the members of the West Indies management team, whom he managed during their under 19 years, namely, Director of Cricket, Jimmy Adams, Manager, Rawl Lewis, Coach, Andre Coley, and Assistant Coach, Kenny Benjamin.

I hope you find this book enjoyable seeing St. Catherine, Jamaica, and West Indies Cricket through the eyes of someone who has been around for a while, since the "good ole days".

Rohan Chambers

Introduction

From an early age, I had an obsession with reading books, especially cricket autobiographies and detective novels, after I was granted membership to the adult section of the Saint Catherine Parish Library located on one side of the Spanish Town Park Square; the other three sides were identified with the Old Kings House, the Spanish Town Courts and the Registrar Offices, respectively. My readiness to be with the grownups was queried by Miss Jones, Head Librarian. She was impressed with my keenness in wanting to read about cricket and mentioned that her brother Jackie played and loved the game. Jackie represented St. Jago High at the schoolboy level and in the St. Catherine Parish domestic McPhail competition. Miss Jones mentioned that the impact of the great Jamaica and West Indies left arm spin bowler Alfred Valentine had an influence on her love for the game and that she knew him well from primary school days. Miss Jones and Valentine were citizens of Spanish Town, the capital city of the parish Saint Catherine. Spanish Town was once known as St. Jago de la Vega, the capital of Jamaica. For several years, the parish was one of the leading sugar cane producing parishes with a strong labour force that included the legendary Alfred Valentine and a preponderance of cricketers and footballers from the farms to the offices and factories of Bernard Lodge, Inswood, By Brook, Worthy Park and Caymanas. A number of cricketers who later became national players had full employment at the eighteen Sugar Estates across the island and had their early beginning and recognition as players in the various cricket competitions organized by the sport loving producers of Molasses, Sugar, Rum, and other by-products of the Sugar Cane.

As I began to write this book, I reflected on the earlier years, years that inspired and mirrored my early beginnings, a past that prepared me for the phases of my life to where I am. There are chapters of this book that reflect what it was like for me through a life of thankfulness. It is the early beginnings that created the interest that stimulated my activity as a participant in the sports of Cricket, Football, and Table Tennis. The three sports, two as outdoors and the other indoors were very attractive to my age group and the more advanced age groups in the sport-loving environs of Spanish Town. It was a period that cricket had a wide participation of players; the competitiveness amongst the players was reflective of their sportsmanship, a quality that was taught to me at age nine as a member of the Spanish Town Boys Club and refined me along my journey as a player.

Having acquired senior membership of the Library, my first reading on cricket was from the book *Just My Story* written by the great England batsman and captain Sir Leonard Hutton. Hutton, at that time, was the top individual innings scorer in Test Cricket, with a masterful 364 against Australia at the Oval in1938. His record stood for two decades and was surpassed by another Knight, the great Sir Garfield Sobers, with 365 not out at Sabina Park against Pakistan in 1958. The majestic Sobers, who was on 219 at the beginning of play on that Saturday with a packed Sabina Park crowd cheering excitingly, the balls leaving his bat with a melodious sound to the boundaries with exquisite timing on both sides of the wicket. At the other end was cricket immortal, the mighty and huge frame of Clyde Walcott striking the ball in majestic fashion with scorching boundary drives and huge six hits. The event remains vividly in my memory; that day was my first at a test match and also my initial visit to the world-famous test ground. On completion of reading the Hutton book, it was the starting point of a belief that I held closely, that someday I would, with the requisite background, write a book on my personal experience with the wonderful game, a game I love passionately.

The encouragement from my son, Rohan Chambers, to write this book was pivotal in my decision to do so. Rohan's beliefs and valuation of my on the field and administrative acumen positioned me ideally with so much to work with. It was the inspirational backing from a son who grew up in an environment of cricket that led to his love of the sport, a love comparable to his father's passion for the game that spurred me on to start and finish this book.

Apart from Rohan, there were others whose ardent encouragement was of immense value that urged me on to recount the beginning and ending of a memorable journey that is encapsulated in this book of actuality that I experienced on the field and beyond.

The valued inspiration of individuals that impelled me to write about the game as I have experienced throughout the years as a player and administratively, included former West Indies players Lawrence Rowe and Basil Williams, Saint Catherine club cricketers, Colin Hinds, Delroy Thompson, Samuel McFarlane, Sydney Bennett, Henry Walters, Indiana Robinson an accomplished cricket book scorer from the Saint Catherine Cricket Club. She is also a writer of children books, and there was my longstanding friend Sports journalist Headley Thompson who thought I was as good as any of the young batsmen in the country during the earlier years.

Two members of the group, Colin Hinds, who was the best man at my first marriage, and Basil Williams, who was the godfather of Rohan my son, are no longer with us. They were the best of my friends; their deaths have created unimaginable emptiness that I continue to grapple with. There were episodic interruptions in the rhythm of my writings caused by my intense obsession in watching live on TV the abundance of cricket around the world twenty-four/ seven.

The book covers the inception through the early beginning and the developmental years to that of my adulthood with the great game, a game that my generation and succeeding ones played and valued with admiration.

I relied on my memory as it happened during the course of my intimate involvement at the different levels and the years of finding my way when cricket was considered the super sport of the day in my home country Jamaica. The experience of the earlier years followed ardently by a nation that was captivated with the glorious performances of the1950 West Indies tour of England is worth reliving by the many of that period.

As a preteen, from the backyards, lanes, streets, and created spaces of unconventionality to the more conservative norms of the fields at the Sugar Estates, rural parishes, and the Senior Cup as teenagers and adults was the transition experienced by so many of my generation. During those early years, I was engrossed with activity on the playing fields and as an administrator at the youth clubs and St. Catherine Cricket Club. It was a fascinating journey that led me to the boardroom of the governing body of the Jamaica Cricket Association at age thirty-one. The first two years of my twenty-three with the Jamaica Cricket Association was as the Assistant Treasurer and the following year as the Assistant Secretary. During the first seven years as a member of the JCA, I was the captain of the St. Catherine senior cup team and represented Jamaica national senior team as a player and then as manager player to Trinidad & Tobago and Guyana; I was the captain against Tobago in Tobago. I was manager of Jamaica's youth team for thirteen years during which time I was privileged to have managed the teams at the yearly regional tournaments from 1983 to 1995 and against the touring teams of England 1984, Australia 1990 and South Africa 1991.

For two years, I was the Jamaica Cricket Association (JCA) Liaison to regional teams and the touring Indian test team.

At the West Indies level, I was honoured to have been manager of the West Indies regional Shell Shield Awards team against New Zealand at Sabina Park, manager of the West Indies Youth team at home against England in 1995 and on tours of Pakistan and Bangladesh the same year, and as a member of West Indies Youth selection committee on four occasions and once as chairman.

As a player, I participated in numerous competitions starting with the Young Men's Cricket Association (YMCA) for the parish of Saint Catherine Primary Schools, Saint Catherine McPhail, the Sugar Estates (Wray & Nephew, Crum Ewing, Bustamante), and the Sunday competitions of Hamilton, Carib, Rankine, Henriques, and Noel Hylton.

There were other competitions as a player that I revered to have played, including the rural parish Nethersole, Senior Cup, Jamaica Colts, Jamaica regional seniors, England's Warwickshire in the Minors County League, Stourbridge Cricket Club in the English Birmingham League and New York's Primrose Club in the Bronx League.

My past administrative positions separate and apart from the Jamaica Cricket Association included that as President of both St. Jago and St. Johns Youth Clubs and with Saint Catherine as Assistant Secretary, Secretary, first VP, Senior Cup Captain, Senior Cup Manager, Chairman Selection Committee and Club Captain, a newly created position that I was the first recipient of.

My duties with the Jamaica Cricket Association and with that of my club in Saint Catherine, at times, were challenging and I managed through a purpose of total commitment.

As the Liaison to the Indian team, I had a wonderful relationship with the players, particularly the manager Hanumant Singh, Ravi Shastri, and the great international opener Sunil Gavaskar. The manager Hanumant Singh was very impressed with my work ethics and suggested to the Jamaica Cricket Association President Allan Rae, that I continued in that position as the team Liaison for the remainder of the Caribbean tour. His request was not practical for a number of reasons, reasons that I explained to him before he approached President Rae, that in the other islands the standard duties of the Liaisons have always been exceptional and would have been objected to by the various territories. Hanuman Singh was obdurate and continued his plea at the Cricket West Indies (CWI) official dinner at the Pegasus Hotel to no avail.

Preceding the Test Match, the Indian team had a four-day game against Jamaica at Sabina Park.

Sunil Gavaskar, who was not with the team when they arrived in Jamaica, reached a couple of days after. I was there on the tarmac at the Norman Manley Airport as the JCA representative to extend the special Jamaican welcome at plane side. I ushered him through Immigration and Customs with the customary ease that was afforded to visiting regional and international cricketers while on tour to Jamaica. Having earlier introduced myself and now on my way to the Pegasus Hotel, Gavaskar asked if I played the game and to what level. He was pleased to know that I played for Jamaica and was a national senior and youth selector and manager of Jamaica's youth team. Gavaskar had a special liking for the shirt I wore that day and enquired where to purchase a similar one. It was the first time wearing the shirt I bought in Miami and it was not available in the stores of Jamaica; he was very disappointed. Two days later, I had the shirt laundered and offered it to Gavaskar. He gladly accepted and wore it before leaving Jamaica.

The Indian team was very special. They showed civility throughout my time with them. I was privileged to have had the honour of their wonderful relationship. On the return to India, the manager Prince Hanumant Singh and Ravi Shastri wrote to me expressing their appreciation of my performance as a Liaison. As Liaison to visiting teams, I was privileged to have interacted with present and former regional and international players and a mix of the diplomatic core, high profile government and influential national dignitaries. I personally found the responsibilities to the teams time-consuming and excessively demanding. For that reason, I informed the JCA that someone else should be considered for the position.

Like most young boys of my generation before and after, playing cricket in Jamaica would have started at the backyards, streets, lanes and avenues. In my home town of Spanish Town, the backyard was the very first place for me with my sister Una bowling to me young bread fruits picked from a tree at the back of the yard. My mother was never amused with the picking of the young fruits. The breadfruit, when fully developed, was and continues to be a staple meal of the Jamaican populace after being roasted and fried.

Later, not yet nine, I spent nine months at the district Park Hall in Clarendon with two of my aunts who were sisters of my father. There I continued playing with youngsters of my age group from the Park Hall elementary school of which I was a student. Before returning to Spanish Town, Park Hall Primary had a game against James Hill Primary at their home ground. The bats used by the two teams were carved from coconut trees and the balls from the root of bamboo trees. We never had the use of pads nor gloves. The participating youngsters were well received by the students and adults looking on. I relished the opportunity to have played with my age group of youngsters, not yet ten; it was comical at times and played in a friendly manner. My first cup game while being a student at the Saint Catherine Catholic School was organized by the YMCA (Young Men's Christian Association) for the Wise Men Cup competed for by primary schools in Spanish Town and its environs. It was the beginning of a competition that was long-awaited for the age group twelve to fifteen and was embraced by the young hopefuls as the platform to have paraded their early inherent cricketing skills.

As youngsters, we enjoyed immensely the novelty of the competitive atmosphere. A number of us from the Spanish Town region were energized with the idea of forming a club with the facilities for holding meetings and an area in which to play. The mindfulness of our intent became a reality with the help of Dr. Vivian Tennant, Chief Medical Doctor of the St Jago Health Centre, and Rennie Stanley, a staff member of the well-known facility situated at St. Jago Park next to the Spanish Town Hospital. We were able to consolidate the formation of the St. Jago youth club, a club comprised mostly of teenagers. The name of our club was integrated with St. Jago relative to the site from which we operated.

As a club, our steady growth was attributed to impressive showing against established clubs from the parish. With the club growing in status, we entered the Kingston-based Hamilton Cricket Competition played on Sundays. It was, for us, the first competitively. After a couple of seasons, the name of the club was changed to St. Johns Youth Club when we moved to our new location at St. Johns Avenue. After two seasons of the very popular Kingston-based Sunday Hamilton Competition, we entered the Carib Competition that was also Kingston-based played on Sundays. During those early years, I represented Bernard Lodge Sugar Estates in the Saint Catherine intra- parish McPhail competition. The matches were played on Saturdays. Later that year was the beginning of my eight years representing Bernard Lodge in the Sugar Estates Cricket Competitions played on midweek days. The years of youth club life created and galvanized my fortitude of life's journey, a journey that presented challenges, challenges of complexities from the youth movement to that of the board room of the Jamaica Cricket Association. There were so many positives from my relationship with the youth movement within my club where I became the president, after the founder Dr. Vivian Tennant retired from the Health Services and leader Rennie Stanley's migration to the USA.

The loyalty and trust of the membership was exceptional. Led by Secretary Anthony Prince Richards, Treasurer Tyrone Byfield, and me as President, we were able to build a relationship of togetherness that bonded the members throughout the years of our club life. As the members got older, there was a decline in the membership; we were unable to attract a new generation of youngsters to hand the baton to. There was no one with the passion to continue what we started and established as an entity for the development of so many. We were left with no visible alternative and came to the inevitable decision to close the club.

As a club, we were recognized by the YMCA and Insports of Jamaica, not only for our participation on the field of sports, but also the civic duties we performed. For my contribution as a leader, I was presented with a "Citation" by Insports of Jamaica for my services to the youth club movement. I revered, like other members, the years we were together, years that prepared us to be respectful of others irrespective of the situation. It was "one for all and all for one" that unified our resolve and aspirations of preparedness for the years ahead.

I continued playing the Sunday leagues as a guest player with Ariguanabo Textile Mills in the Henrique's Competition and later with the All Indian and Jaghai's Garage team in the very intense and combative encounters of the Rankine Competition, a competition that allowed only two current senior cup players to a team. Colin Hinds, my teammate at Saint Catherine Cricket Club, joined me as the two, and with Bob Maragh, the former Jamaica and Boys Town Left Arm Spinner, we were a potent combination of spinners.

The All-Indian squad was of approximately thirty players, all of whom were worthy of selection in the final eleven. The team showed consistency in their specialty that allowed for a settled unit, a unit that valued and demonstrated the true spirit of the game. After two seasons playing as an All-Indian side, the team was renamed Jaghai's Garage with some obvious ethnic changes to the squad. After another season, the competition came to an unexpected end as the administration, for one reason or another, lost interest in the continuation of the competition, a competition that was extremely popular and very competitive with large spectator's attendance.

I was also captain of The Port Authority of Jamaica team in the Noel Hylton competition, a competition that I was instrumental in forming with the blessing of the then Chairman of The Port Authority of Jamaica, Noel Hylton. Mr. Hylton was an ardent follower of the game before joining the Port Authority. He previously held the position as Chairman of the Shipping Association of Jamaica. The competing teams were drawn from Kingston-based entities affiliated with the Shipping Industry. The early passage of my immersion in the game included my representation to the Saint Catherine Parish in the Rural Nethersole Competition and then the Saint Catherine Cricket Club in the Senior Cup. It was by consistent performances with bat and ball in the Senior Cup that led to my invitation to the National trials and subsequently to the National Jamaica colt's team against overseas touring teams.

My performances against the star-studded overseas teams including the English Cavaliers two years in succession, Worcestershire County and the Australian test squad of 1965 was of interest to the national selectors. It was my impressive performances in those games and the senior cup that influenced the selectors naming me along with three other talented young players Herman Bennet, Rudolph Cohen, and Rex Succo for a three-month development programme with Warwickshire County Club. Our stay was supervised by Derief Taylor, the former Lucas Cricket Club player. Mr. Taylor a member of the Warwickshire County Coaching Staff was instrumental in having us representing the County in the two-day English Minor County Division and the Birmingham league on Saturdays and Charity games on Sundays. The club I represented in the league was Stourbridge Cricket Club. It was an exciting period of cricket in varying unfamiliar weather conditions, conditions that we adopted admirably to. There was no doubt that the wonderful experience I had with my club was shared by my three colleagues with their clubs. Rex Suckoo was very impressive scoring a century early on and followed with other good scores. Herman Bennet did pretty well and Rudolph Cohen impressed with his fast bowling. I had a very good season picking up 7 wickets in a marathon spell of 25 to 27 consecutive overs and scoring an undefeated half century in my first Birmingham League game.

The Birmingham League was one of the most prestigious of all English Sunday Leagues. The teams were well represented by past first class and test players from different countries. Dereif Taylor, the former Lucas Cricket Club player who migrated to England years earlier, helped us significantly in adjusting to the English conditions. Derief was an excellent coach and was pivotal in the development of some big names at Warwickshire County including Dennis Amis, David Brown, Eddie Hemmings, and several others. During our three months sojourn, we were accommodated at Derief's spacious and lovely home on Cambridge Road, Kings Heath, and Birmingham. Most evenings when there was no game, we would go to the Cinema or explore the nearby Parks. There were so many attractions of interest that fulfilled our attention.

Shortly after returning to Jamaica, Bennett, Suckoo, and I participated in the Sugar Estate finals of the Bustamante Cup at Grays Inn in St. Mary. Bennett and I represented the East Zone against Suckoo's Central Zone. The East Zone were winners with me leading the way scoring 82, which was the leading score in the match. The following year 1966, the three of us and Cohen were invited to the 1966 national trials. At the end of the three trial matches, the touring squad included Bennett, Cohen, and me; surprisingly, Suckoo was not named, which to some of us was questionable. Whatever justification not to have included him in the touring squad was to my mind bothering; he was deserving of selection.

The four of us, before leaving for England, were told that the selectors saw us as an investment for future national and possible international representation. We were also required to sign a covenant not to accept County or League contracts should we be asked. The captain of my League Club Stourbridge had an interest in me becoming a professional and for obvious reasons, I declined. Selection of any national or collective regional teams was and is challenging; the balancing was and should always be a key factor added to fitness and form of the players. When I served as a selector at both the Jamaica senior, youth and the West Indies under-nineteens, my earlier and accepted belief that everyone could not be selected was vindicated. I recognized the intricacies of team selection. In most cases, it is down to two or three spots to complete the team or squad selection. On reflection, all considerations notwithstanding, Suckoo was deserving of a place in the squad, a squad that would have been more completed by his inclusion. His batting ability was assured with a solid defense and lovely stroke play on either side of the wicket, Suckoo was also a very good off-spinner and a safe fielder in any position, and importantly, a very good team player.

For the first game against Leeward Islands played at The Antigua Recreation Grounds, I was named a reserve, and in the next game against Trinidad, I made my first-class debut at the Queens Park Oval. For the next nine years from 1966 to 1975, I was in and out of the national squad, and even when in the squad, I was unable to find a regular place in the starting eleven. In 1975, I was named player manager of the Jamaica team to Guyana and Trinidad & Tobago. The team was led by Maurice Foster and included the likes of Desmond Lewis, Lawrence Rowe, Ron Headley, Herbert Chang, Sam Morgan, Uton Dowe, Renford Pinnock, Michael Holding, Arthur Barrett and Cecil Lawson, a squad of truly outstanding first-class and International players. For the Tobago leg of the tour, I led the team as Foster, Rowe, and Barrett were called to represent the West Indies test team in Barbados against England.

Later that same year, I was appointed "Player Manager" of the Jamaica team for a special tournament involving the six regional teams; the matches were played at the Bourda ground in Guyana. The event marked the wonderful contribution to Guyana and West Indies Cricket by four exceptional Guyanese stars: Rohan Kanhai, Lance Gibbs, Basil Butcher, and Joe Solomon. I was also appointed manager of the West Indies Shell Shield Awards team against the touring 1985 New Zealand team at Sabina Park. As a National Administrator, I was elected as a Jamaica Cricket Association member for twenty-three years, starting at age thirty-one. The first two in the capacity as Assistant Treasurer and Assistant Secretary, respectively. The next twenty-one years was as a member representing the Senior Cup Clubs. During my elected time with the Association, I served on several committees including Grounds, Improvement, Youth, Players Welfare, Development, Senior and Youth selection. As a senior selector, I served for twelve years, and thirteen years as the youth selection chairman. I was also manager of Jamaica's National youth teams for thirteen years at the regional youth tournaments and the matches against young England, Australia, and South Africa in Jamaica.

I was also a West Indies Youth selector on four occasions and served as manager at home in the Caribbean against England in 1995 and on tours of Pakistan and Bangladesh that same year. At the club level, it was an absolute honour to have been a member of the Saint Catherine Cricket Club from the early age of eighteen before migrating to the USA at age fifty-four. There was a two-year break of inactivity with the club during which time I represented the JDF Senior Cup Cricket team, a period of excellent team camaraderie that stood out. My active membership with the Saints as a player and administrator were contributions I revered with immeasurable satisfaction.

I was a recipient of the Carreras Award for services to Jamaica's Youth Cricket, a Citation from Insports for services to Youth Clubs, and an award for services to the game of cricket in Spanish Town and the Parish of Saint Catherine held in Queens New York. I was inducted into the International Category of the USA Cricket Hall Of Fame for services to cricket in Jamaica and the West Indies held at the Hilton Hotel, New York in 2018. The experience with the YMCA from preteen age shaped and prepared me effectively for later years, not only as a cricketer, but also administratively.

The Early Years

Growing up playing cricket and football was a given for the many young boys in and around Spanish Town and most parts of Jamaica. For me, cricket started at the home environment of my backyard with my sister Una bowling under-arm to me with very young breadfruits picked from a tree at one side of the house. For obvious reasons, my mother was not amused; she vehemently dissuaded us and suggested an alternative for the breadfruit. The breadfruit, when fully fit, is a tasty staple food for the breakfast, lunch, and dinner tables of most Jamaicans. Naturally, the respect for mothers must be upheld and we did find an alternative in the knitted ball.

The knitted balls were made with a small round stone covered tightly by layers of cloth to create a ball shape and then covered by one layer of cork from bottle stoppers and then knitted by English cord or cord from flour bags. The bat was carved from board and other acceptable materials such as coconut bough. At age nine, I was sent by my mother and father to spend time in the pleasant district of Park Hall, Clarendon with my grandmother, two aunts and three cousins, all girls. At Park Hall Primary School, cricket was the only sport played on a makeshift small area with little or no grass and visible gravel. As small boys eager to play, we were able to create an area to bat and bowl. It was during that period of the early formative years that my talent for the sport was apparent to the school Headmaster. He was watching us at play when he, surprisingly, interrupted the session while I was batting and quietly remarked, "You are so methodical when batting. Keep it up." I was perplexed by the word methodical; I was hearing of the word, not for the first time, and concluded it must have been complimentary.

As soon as I got home, I asked one of my well-taught aunts to define the meaning of the word, the definition given invigorated my interest to play as often I could. There was a game between our school, Park Hall, and James Hill played at the James Hill School, the playing area was dimensionally favorable for a game of cricket, a far cry from the inadequate facility at Park

Hall. The balls used were made from bamboo root, the bats from bamboo and coconut bough. The ingenuity of the very young, of which I was one, to have meticulously fashioned the bats and balls was remarkable. Both teams enjoyed the game; the match fittingly ended in a draw, a result that was morally won by both teams followed by handshakes and expressions of goodwill. After leaving Park Hall, I returned to Spanish Town to be with my mother, father, and sisters and resumed my schooling at the St. Catherine Primary Catholic School.

It was about that time that the great West Indian Left-Arm Spinner Alfred Valentine, a Spanish Town resident, returned home from the victorious 1950 West Indies tour to a thrilling fanfare of great jubilation. Although he was hailed as a Jamaican hero after his magnificent performances, not many outside of his hometown were aware of his cricket prowess. His splendid bowling contributed significantly to the West Indies team success, and was acknowledged and appreciated by the people of Jamaica and the broader West Indies region.

In celebrating the much-awaited homecoming of the magnificent young cricketer, the St. Catherine Parish Council headed by the likeable Custos George McGrath, positioned in place a motorcade of memorable prominence, and was extolled by the tremendous appreciation of the town folks. It was a momentous occasion for the citizenry of the old capital watching their hometown hero being driven in an open back motor car through selected streets lined with adoring fans of all ages. The delighted hometown fans showed their happiness and appreciation of his extraordinary impact on the West Indies historical success. I was, like the onlookers, engulfed in the moment of adulation for the lovable hometown hero. The glamour of the magnificent setting of a parade watched by the town folks was amazing; my adolescent presence observing the spectacular event lives on to this day. I was not the only youngster who looked on at the awesome event with admiration; there were others of my age group who were just as elated.

Before the tour of England, the young twenty-year-old Alfred Valentine was unknown to the wider world of cricket, but not so with active players of the game in Jamaica. One of his boyhood friends, Douglas Adams, the former Saint Catherine Cricket Club all-rounder who was a remarkable left-handed batsman and right-arm off spinner alluded to his early potential and his growth as a cricketer. "The mastery of his craft grew rapidly starting at his parent's backyard to that of becoming a member of the Saint Catherine Senior Cup team," remarked Adams. The amazing homecoming event was an occasion that generated and strengthened my love for the game. The names of some of the youngsters who witnessed the magnificent event included Renford Pinnock, Herbert Bailey, Samuel McFarlane, Jimmy Mitchel, and David Henry, all of whom went on to represent both the Saint Catherine Cricket Club and the Saint Catherine Parish teams. The accomplishment of the planned parade seen at different locations on the Streets of Spanish Town was a great success. The growing interest of the youngsters in and around the environs of Spanish Town was intensified on the evidence of activity at most of the schools and community grounds, and continued to be so for many years, especially at the two leading primary schools of the town, Barracks and Catholic.

The rivalry between the Barracks and Catholic schools was an attraction that stimulated enormous interest amongst the town folks of the Parish capital. In a particular game involving both teams, I found myself embroiled in the midst of a fracas with the top batsman Frankie Whareham of the Barracks team. He was first given Out, caught by the wicket keeper and refused to leave, with obscenity at the umpire Ralston McKenzie (Ralston McKenzie became one of Jamaica's foremost TV/Radio Anchors). Before the start of the game, it was agreed that McKenzie, from the Catholic School, and a student from the Barracks School would have officiated as the umpires. Frankie's reluctance to leave after been given Out, prompted me, after consultations with both umpires, for him to continue his innings. The very next ball he edged to slip and was caught by Tyrone Byfield. He showed no indication to leave, and again he was given Out by McKenzie. He then walked towards McKenzie and shoved him menacingly. I got between them and defused a situation that looked ominous and could have escalated into an uncontrollable brawl. Eventually, Frankie accepted the merit of the umpire's decision with an apology to Ralston McKenzie and then disappeared to the confines of the player's enclosure.

While still at school, many of us in and around the Spanish Town environs, including the ill-tempered Frankie Whareham became members of the newly formed St. Jago Youth Club situated at St. Jago Park next to the Spanish Town Hospital.

It was the initiative of Dr. Vivian Tennant and Rennie Stanley that got the formation of the club started on lands of the Health Clinic situated at St, Jago Park, and Dr. Tennant was the MO of the Clinic while Rennie Stanley was an employee. The club attracted a membership of approximately sixty versatile teenagers from the nearby communities of the St. Jago Park. They were truly talented with a penchant for cricket, football, and table tennis. From the inception, the members' passion for the three sports featured prominently at our newly found club facility.

Early in the club's formation, an event for the island youth clubs was held at the beautiful Carder Park in Port Antonio, the capital town of the banana producing Parish of Portland. The festivities included a cricket match with players selected from club members who were notified days before the event. My clubmate Samuel McFarlane and I were the selected ones from our club. The game was of notable significance, a game that was the beginning of long-standing relationship amongst the players drawn from the different parishes. A number of the players' growth in the game was later seen by their representation at the parish and senior cup levels. The young group included Preston Hill, Delroy Myton, Ossie Doswell, Bertram Peart, Calder Neita, Gene Holland, Owen Mitchel and Samuel McFarlane. The nine of us went on to represent our parish teams. Owen Mitchel and I progressed to national representation while we were members of Kensington Cricket Club and Saint Catherine Cricket Club, respectively.

For the event in Port Antonio, several of us travelled by rail, a mode of travel that I enjoyed during the long journey from Spanish Town. During that period of Jamaica's life style, commuting by rail was most enjoyable, particularly on a long journey through the backdrop of our beautiful countryside.

At our newly found St. Jago Youth Club, I was dubbed with the name "Vijay" by the founder of the club, Dr. Vivian Tennant. The Doctor was a fan of the Indian batsman Vijay Manjrekar who at that time was one of India's top batsmen. It was his belief that my style of batting reminded him of the champion batsman from India. As an eleven-year-old and to be likened to the Indian top batsman, I was thrilled at the comparison, and to this day most people called me by that name "Vijay."

On reflection on the early years, they were years of learning to participate competitively with sportsmanship, a guiding factor for the way the game should be played and to accept adversities without malevolence and to exercise a level of understanding. It was while at the Saint Catherine Catholic School that I was first impressed with the principle and value of respectable leadership by the legendary school teacher Mr. Kenneth Emanuel Neale.

Mr. Neale showed a keen interest in the sport of basketball. He also showed an interest in cricket. Unlike cricket, basketball was not considered a favourite with most of the young students; however, there was a group that was very enthusiastic and showed an interest in playing the sport. With encouragement from Mr. Neale, the gifted youngsters became a team on the rise and participated initially in practice matches with Kingston-based teams. The ability and popularity of the players got the attention of the Jamaica Basket Ball Association to accept their entry as a team in the national competition. The team performed consistently well with a number of individuals who were brilliant at the game, which led to their national selection.

Meanwhile, Mr. Neale's continued interest in cricket encouraged the formation of a school team which allowed our school to participate in matches with Alpha Boys School, a Catholic institution, and the YMCA. The two organizations were centered in the capital city of Kingston.

Mr. Neale's idea of the game intensified and he was very instrumental in the formation of a school competition amongst Primary Schools of the Parish.

The visionary Mr. Neale and other Principals' perception of the value of sports participation on the young minds and their early development towards adulthood was exceptional. The concept and expectation of the competition was fulfilling and vindicated the vision of those leaders and Mr. Karl Dollhouse of the YMCA, most fittingly, the competition was named Wise Men Youth Cup.

Our first-round game in the newly formed competition was against Naggo Head School not that far from the Port Henderson community, a community that was buzzing with excitement about the game. When we got to the ground, the players from the home team were practicing with the match ball on the unprepared pitch that the game was played; my teammates were unimpressed. I defused the situation and encouraged our players that our young opponents were just like us; there was so much that we would learn as we evolved. We batted first, and in reply, the opposing team was dismissed below our score. As teammates, we were celebrating the victory when the opposing captain Frank Stone claimed that it was a two innings game. It certainly was not and with no arbitrator present and the two schoolboys as umpires unawareness of the guidelines, incited moments of provocative exchanges amongst the players of both teams. As captain, I was able to soothe the tension for resumption of the game after a discussion with my teammates. In our second turn at the wicket, we quickly set them a target which was unsurmountable, thanks to the fast bowler Charlie Brown who picked up eight wickets for twelve runs with his controlled speed and accuracy that left the opposition in disarray. Egbert Chin Sang, our left-arm spinner with his big spinning leg breaks caused mayhem and was the destroyer of the opposition in their first innings by claiming seven wickets and was well supported by Brown who claimed the remaining three wickets.

Days after that game, Mr. Neale got the organizers of the competition to issue the playing guidelines to the participating schools. It was the beginning of my involvement in a cricket competition, a competition designed for the development of the very young players. There were several youngsters from that competition who went on to represent leading clubs in the Parish competing for the McPhail Cup and later represented the Parish in the Nethersole competition and the Saint Catherine Cricket Club Senior and Junior cup teams.

Figure 1 Alfred Valentine, the great Saint Catherine, Kensington, Jamaica, and West Indies left arm spinner

Figure 2 Members of Primrose Cricket Club at Van Cortlandt Park, New York 1978
Shaking hands with Stafford Young and Roy Taylor at right.

The Inaugural Sugar Estates Experience

As my development continued, there were instances of uncertainties that could have derailed my progress. My first game representing Bernard Lodge Sugar Estate was against Sevens Estate in the Wray & Nephew competition played at the opposition home ground in May Pen, the capital town of Clarendon. Bernard Lodge had two teams in the well-organized Estate cricket programme. There was the Crum Ewing team, the stronger of the two, and the Wray & Nephew, considered the second division team. Our Wray Nephew team was comprised of players, most of whom were in their late 40's but for Harold Soarez and I; we were seventeen years of age.

It was the opening game of the competition, a competition that I was determined to do well for consideration to the senior Crum Ewing team. We arrived at the ground about 9:30 AM, an hour before the start of play. The picturesque surrounding was eye-catching with a sizeable crowd eagerly awaiting the start of the game. Before heading to the dressing room, I went to the middle and had a look at the pitch. In the earlier years, the pitches at the Estate grounds were well prepared and ideal for batting and such was the pitch at Sevens on that day (Wednesday). The appearance of the pitch lifted my confidence that I would do well as a batsman. I then proceeded to our dressing room and started to unpack my bag.

To my disappointment, the boots were not among my cricket gear. I was now very tense and informed the captain, Mr. George Cohen. "If you don't play, you would have to go back to work" said the captain. He insisted that I play in my brown rubber bottom shoe that I wore to the ground. He further stated that Soarez and I were the only youngsters in the team and that we were expected to do most of the chasing on the field. There was never any thought on my part to go back to work; furthermore, I had no idea of how to have commuted back home. I had more to gain playing in the unconventional footwear, notwithstanding the discomfort.

I knew Captain Cohen would have been upset in me not playing. He was very impressed with my batting and bowling at our practice sessions and anticipated much from me starting in the opening game. Foremost in my thoughts was to do well. The diligent and purposeful training for the opening game must be rewarded with meaningful contributions with bat and ball. Not playing would be a setback to my progress moving forward; it would have caused disquiet to my many youth club friends back home. I had a very good all-round game with bat and ball that was pivotal to our successful winning start to the competition. My inspiring debut performance as an all-rounder got the acclamation of my youth club friends; they were as pleased as I was.

I performed impressively throughout the competition with bat and ball, during that same year 1958, I represented Bernard Lodge in the St. Catherine Parish McPhail Competition for clubs in the Parish with very good performances with bat and ball that never went unnoticed.

Figure 3 Collin Hinds and Len Chambers - St. Catherine Cricket Club Teammates

Progression to the Senior Cup Competition

The following year 1959 was a breakthrough for me. I was selected to the St. Catherine Parish team in the Nethersole Cup which was a happy place to be at my age and then the prize one, "Jamaica Cricket Association Senior Cup" which was considered by many as the "Flagship" of Jamaica's local competitions. My compelling performances in the earlier competitions, McPhail and Wray & Nephew, was one of the factors for my elevation to the Saint Catherine Nethersole team and later that year to the Saints senior cup team; the other was the exodus of top players from the St. Catherine Club to Inswood. The Inswood Cricket Club previously played in the senior cup competition and was impelled by the very popular and esteemed George Mudie for their return to the competition.

The departure of the top players from the Saints senior team came about as there was discontent between Bernard Lodge Sugar Estate Management and the Saints captain George Mudie. The disgruntlement dragged on without an amicable solution that led to the Saint Catherine Club most dynamic player's departure to Inswood. They were lured by the influential and popular Mudie to join forces with him as captain of a very powerful Inwood team, a team that included Lloyd Seivright, considered one of the fastest and most menacing bowlers in the country, and Ossie Doswell, a truly wonderful stroke player. Mudie, the former West Indies player, was considered one of the leading captains in the country and the players' positive response to be a part of the Inswood team with him as captain was assured. The players leaving the Saint Catherine Club were Renford Pinnock, Herbert Bailey, Gerald Charlton, Lloyd Clarke, and John Earle. They were the leading players in a very strong Saints team. The absence of the renowned players meant that there were several places to be filled, especially in the batting and for a pacer to replace the incomparable John Earle.

The opportunity for me and a group of other young talented players to play at this level representing one of the leading teams was an absolute privilege. Our opportunity came during a period when the standard of the senior cup was flourishing with exceptional talent and matching skills aplenty. The new replacement players for our team the Saint's included Herman Bennett, a player with enormous skills as a free-scoring right-handed batsman. His effortless stroke playing on either side of the wicket was classical and pleasing to the eye. Bennett was also very effective with his left arm orthodox and unorthodox spinning deliveries added to his ability as a left-arm swing bowler of known quality. The all-round prowess of Bennett extended to his brilliance as a fielder in any position on the field. His excellence in the field was recognized by the JCA when he was recommended and accepted by the CWI as the "Emergency Fieldsman" in a test match at Sabina Park. I cannot think of a more complete fieldsman at the level of Jamaica's cricket than the unassuming and loved Herman Bennett. He was an amazing cricketer.

There was Keith Pryce the opener; very exciting to watch against the fast bowlers. His timing was superb with exquisite drives on either side of the wicket, and there was Dudley Clarke, a highly competent batsman. He possessed excellent skills in his unique style to bat for long periods as the team demanded. Another debutant was Vincent McKayle, a very skillful fast bowler with remarkable control. His change of pace was artfully disguised. He consistently swung the new ball away with pace and had the ability of moving the ball both ways off the pitch effectively. McKayle was very useful as a lower order batsman and regularly produced for the team. He was at the wicket when I made my first senior cup century after joining me when I was in the sixties, Winston Thomas aka Pepson, a proportionally built young fast bowler with the natural ability to bowl at a lively pace with two-way movements off the pitch was a very good selection to the team. Pepson was very committed to the improvement of his bowling skills. He trained methodically, not only when bowling in the nets. Awareness to fitness was very important to the young pacer; he organized his fitness routine with admirably conviction that made him superbly fit on match days. When called on to bowl at different periods during a day's play, he responded with gusto. His passion to perform for the team was remarkable.

I was extremely disappointed not having Renford Pinnock in the team when I made my debut. Renford was a close friend and teammate during my preteen years with the Boys Club of Spanish Town and later as a teenager at the Saint Jago Youth Club. He, more than anyone, had the requisite experience to help me during the period of transition to the senior cup level. During those early years, a number of my St. Jago Youth Club members were selected to the Saint Catherine Cricket Club Junior Cup team with the hope that they would have progressed to the senior level and enjoy the success that Renford Pinnock, Othniel Myles, Alexander Casey, Samuel McFarlane, and I accomplished. The challenges for places to the senior team were daunting. The admirable performances and consistency of the talented Saints senior cup players somewhat closed the door that was impregnable for the several young aspirants.

Having been selected to play my first senior cup game, I reflected on my selection as TT player representing the Spanish Town Boys Club team was the confidence in my ability that I would do well. It was a certitude that I carried with me into my debut game and that stayed with me throughout the years I played the game and other aspects of life, "sureness of belief in myself."

Before my recognition as one who could play cricket, I was seen as a promising table tennis player and was good enough to be a member of the Boys Club of Spanish Town team of five. I was very surprised to have been included in the club team to play against the champion club team of Spanish Town. I believed then that my game was improving at a rapid pace, but there were older players in their teens that expected to have been selected ahead of me; however, I trusted my ability to do well and justified the confidence of my selection. I won decisively setting the stage for our team to be the winners of the five-man team. I was ecstatic to see my name along with Renford Pinnock as winners of our games in the Jamaica Gleaner Sports page for the first time. I won my match against the twenty-plus age player Smooch Manning, the then Number Two player from the Parish. It was those priceless match minutes that motivated my intent to be positive at any given task the best possible way I can. It was a narrative that strengthened my resolve through the years, years of belief on all fronts that I confidently reminded myself of that unique table tennis scenario when at age nine, my unknown fortitude prevailed and brought me ultimate success.

As I matured along with my young mates and transformed as grown-ups and stabilized our unending relationship as friends, a friendship that embraced with love, understanding and respect prepared me to transform to a place of composed contentment.

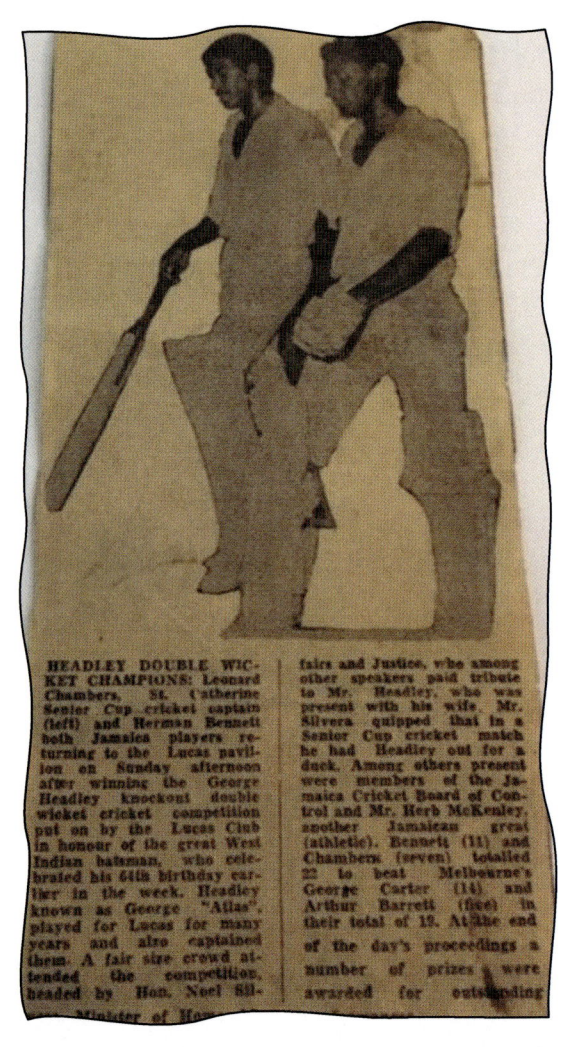

HEADLEY DOUBLE WICKET CHAMPIONS: Leonard Chambers, St. Catherine Senior Cup cricket captain (left) and Herman Bennett both Jamaica players returning to the Lucas pavilion on Sunday afternoon after winning the George Headley knockout double wicket cricket competition put on by the Lucas Club in honour of the great West Indian batsman, who celebrated his 64th birthday earlier in the week. Headley known as George "Atlas", played for Lucas for many years and also captained them. A fair size crowd attended the competition, headed by Hon. Noel Silvera, Minister of Ho... fairs and Justice, who among other speakers paid tribute to Mr. Headley, who was present with his wife. Mr. Silvera quipped that in a Senior Cup cricket match he had Headley out for a duck. Among others present were members of the Jamaica Cricket Board of Control and Mr. Herb McKenley, another Jamaican great (athletic). Bennett (11) and Chambers (seven) totalled 22 to beat Melbourne's George Carter (14) and Arthur Barrett (five) in their total of 19. At the end of the day's proceedings a number of prizes were awarded for outstanding

Figure 4 St. Catherine Double Wicket Champions: Herman Bennett & Leonard Chambers

The Impact of Estate Cricket

C ricket on the Sugar Estates was highly competitive with extraordinary, gifted players in all departments of the game. The grounds were situated not far from populated communities, communities that showed unending interest in the sport by large spectators attendances. The ground staff at each venue was adept in pitch preparation; the bounce and carry was consistent. Acknowledgement of their remarkable skills was recognized by the players as the finest to be found in the country. Although the pitches encouraged free scoring stroke play, there was assistance for the fast bowlers and spinners. The average score by teams batting first was around the 250 mark that made it very interesting for the teams chasing.

The players were privileged to have had the satisfaction of participation in an atmosphere of absolute enjoyment from the opening games of the Crum Ewing to the last fixture of the Bustamante competition. The efficiently structured competitions were spearheaded by coordinator for sports Arthur Bonito of the Sugar Manufacture Association. Arthur Bonitto was a former Melbourne Cricket Club cricketer during the period when the club was situated at Elletson Road. He was also a former captain of Jamaica's cricket team and was cousin to the brothers Colin and Neville Bonitto, two former Jamaica national senior cricketers. Arthur Bonitto showed a penchant for the development of young cricketers and footballers from the Estates. He was instrumental in Louis Williams being offered an Engineering scholarship to St. Augustine Campus of the University College of the West Indies in Trinidad.

Louis Williams was an outstanding young cricketer and footballer while he was employed by Inswood Sugar Estates. He was also a member of the All-Indian Cricket team in the Rankine competition, a team that I led for a couple of years. Later when Louis Williams was Managing Director of Matrix Engineering Company, I encouraged him to offer scholarships to two young cricketers, Roger Neil and Asonu Spencer, to the University of Technology. Neil, while attending Kingston College, represented the Jamaica National Youth team in the regional tournament and Lucas Cricket Club in the senior cup. Spencer, from Herbert Morrison High had earlier attended Cambridge High, represented St. James Parish team and later went to England on a cricket development programme sponsored by Victoria Mutual Building Society. In my request to Louis Williams for the sponsorship of the two young cricketers, he reminded me of how he was the beneficiary of a scholarship based on his cricket attributes and that he was thrilled to return the courtesy to both Neil and Spencer. It was truly a wonderful gesture by the Matrix Engineering boss.

For the Bustamante zonal competitions, the players were selected to the teams from which the participating Crum Ewing teams were located across the island. The competition was divided into four zones East, West, Central, and Northern, with the final over two days. The competition was named after the former Jamaican Prime Minister the Honourable Sir Alexander Bustamante. Sir Alexander showed an interest in the game, a sport that was played by the Sugar Estates workers from the offices to the factories to the workshops and the farms. Eligible siblings of employees were qualified to have participated in the matches. The workforces of the factory and farms were affiliated to the two major trade unions, the Bustamante Industrial Trade Union and the National Workers Union. The team East Zone that I represented included two of the top playing Estates, Bernard Lodge and Caymanas, two teams that had in their ranks players of exceptional talent.

My last game in the Sugar Estate competitions was when I represented the East Zone against Central Zone in the 1965 Bustamante final played at Grays Inn Oval in St Mary. The Central Zone team was for a number of seasons the strongest of the zones; their team for the final was an imposing one with the likes of Phelmin Nangle, Rex Suckoo, Ruel Grandison and Calvin Morgan, all of whom represented the Monymusk team in the Crum Ewing competition. The four represented the Jamaica National Colts team against the touring English Cavaliers in back-to-back years, Worcester County, and the Australian of 1965.

The East Zone was well represented by a well-balanced team that included Herman Bennett, Basil Williams, Castel Folkes, and me; all four of us went on to represent Jamaica's senior team. There were other talented players on our team including the captain Vincent McFarlane, a left arm spinner and a very good leader, and there was George Chambers, a remarkable stroke player.

Herman Bennett, Rex Suckoo, and I had recently returned from England, and despite not playing in the earlier Estate fixtures because of our stint in England, we were selected to represent our respective teams. All four Zonal teams were well represented by quality players, players that I played with and against. The players in the final aspired to do well knowing that impressive performances would undoubtedly enhance their reputation. The result of the match was a victory for the East Zone team that led on first innings with not much time for an outright result. Our team batted once with me getting 82 not out, George Chambers with 72, and Herman Bennett with a score in the 40's. George Chambers and I featured in a century partnership that was pivotal to our strong reply. At the presentation ceremony to close the Sugar Estates cricket season, the former Prime Minister Sir Alexander Bustamante was in attendance.

The presence of the imposing figure of the adorable Prime Minister was alluring. His sense of humor was appreciated by the diverse gathering, some of whom were supporters of the Bustamante Industrial Trade Union, the Trade Union he founded and headed before becoming Prime Minister of Jamaica. Sir Alexander showed his appreciation in his inimitable ways as the players received their awards. Topping the list of awardees was Ruel Grandison who was complimented by the Prime Minster on the numerous awards he received for his fantastic runs scoring during the season.

Grandison's batting at the Estate and Parish levels throughout his career was remarkable, his consistency was amazing. He took pride in batting for long periods and was considered a runs machine and deservedly so. The champion batsman from Clarendon was seen as a prospect for the national senior team but never attained that level of representation like so many others before and after him; however, he should take comfort in his selection to the Jamaica Colts team twice. For my knock in the final at Grays Inn, I was the recipient of a Gray Nichols bat. The Bustamante final was my last appearance after eight wonderful years of Estate cricket starting with my first game at the Wray and Nephew competition representing Bernard Lodge against Sevens Estates.

The Sugar Estates competitions were blessed with some of the most talented cricketers in the country. The lack of exposure prevented them being named to the national trials and they were left in the trenches of obscurity; it was a mockery to their obvious talent. For me, the Sugar Estate competition was played in an environment of amazing sportsmanship shared equally by exceptionally gifted players. I embraced the privilege of playing in the Estate competitions. The spectacular landscapes across the parishes were breathtaking and so many friends were made, not only with the players but with the officials as well.

The opportunity to have played at the Sugar Estates level opened the door of recognition for me and so many others. The camaraderie was exceptional and so was the quality of the cricket. The teams were well-served by top order batsmen and a dependable middle order and so were the opening bowlers. They were genuinely quick and very effective. It was challenging for the openers facing up to the quicks on pitches well-grassed and efficiently rolled that offered pace with bounce. The batsmen getting good scores showed remarkable skill in their productivity with attractive stroke play that won the attention of the well-learned cricket fans. It certainly was enthralling to have watched top order free scoring batsmen pulling and hooking against the hostile quicks. There were very good spinners of different varieties that had the batsmen watchful and very circumspect in their approach.

The excellence of the many who graced the cricket fields will be remembered for the entertainment provided and the valued sportsmanship exhibited on and off the field. The cordiality between teams was unmatched and extended to the team management, irrespective of the result.

Of the many competitions that I was privileged to have played, the pride of place was the Sugar Estates competitions that included eighteen teams located across the spheres of the island. The players were endowed with enormous talent, the camaraderie was excellently defined by the very best quality of sportsmanship that extended beyond the playing fields. The teams were well represented by a preponderance of undeniable talented players including Ruel Grandison, Rex Suckoo, the Nangle brothers Fitz and Phelmin, Calvin Morgan, Pat Diah, Fitz Jones, George Baker, Ransford Styles, Jumna Hamilton, Jerry Reid, Winston Bobby Clarke, Neil HoSang, Lionel Webb, George Batts, Samah McKenzie, Chester Watson, Lloyd Williams, Lester King, Silbourne Robinson, Lexford Muthra, Rupert Herah, Hume Paris, Pat McCormack, Winston Manning, Errol Northover, Vinnie

Budoo, Kirk Patrick, Barton Reynolds, the Laidlaw brothers Cliff and Roy, Herman Bennett, George Chambers, Renford Pinnock, Castel Folkes, Herbert Bobby Bailey, Basil Williams, George Miller, Sonny Miller, George Schloss, Brenton Grant, Nick Johnson, Raphael Budah, Ossie Doswell, Jimmy Mitchell, John Thompson, Horace Ennis, Lloyd Vernon, Llewelyn Thompson, Karl Morris, Headley Williams, Paul Moore, Raphael Clarke, Santin Doctor, Kingsley Smith, Stanley Goodridge, Calbert Minott, Headley Allen, Roy Buchanan, David Bernard from St. James, Wilbert Plummer, Amos Hamilton, Bim Christie, Donald Young, Colin Hinds, Don Black, Alexander Charvis, Lloyd Seivright, Vincent McFarlane, Keith Pryce, and there were others.

The majority of players from the Sugar Estates were regulars of their parish teams; the talent and performances regrettably went unnoticed by the absence of the national selectors by their rare attendance at the matches. The ongoing absenteeism provoked disquiet among fans from the rural parishes to the level of antagonism with the JCA. It was seen by the fans and players alike that the neglect to the worthiness of the players was undermined.

From my perspective having played with the multitalented Sugar Estates and Parish players over a period of eight years, it was a travesty to their exceptional skills by the obvious neglect shown by the JCA selectors. The players, all of whom but for a handful, were identified as residents of rural communities, were denied the opportunity of the lights to have shone on them; instead, many were kept in the shadows and trenches of obscurity.

No one who followed Sugar Estate Cricket and Parish competitions during the early years before the gradual closure of all but a handful of the sugar factories would, with any justification, question the undeniable talent of the cricketers. It was a travesty of justice that stifled the progress of those players. The eventual end of the competitions was attributed to the end of the once productive and flourishing factories of Sugar, Rum, Molasses, and other byproducts of the sugar cane. The closure of the many factories was devastating and disrupted the lifestyle of several players. The natural talent of the players was reflected in every department of the game; the skillset of the top batsmen was absolutely excellent; the plethora of fast bowlers complimented by spinners were special in the art and guile of their craft.

The wicketkeepers were extremely competent with extraordinary glove work, glove work that won the admiration not only of their members, but of their opponents as well. Most, if not all the keepers were very good as batsmen and batted in the upper half of the order. The teams showcased a surfeit of naturally talented players from which a minute number had the distinction of national senior representation, some of whom had their beginning at the beautiful playing fields of the Sugar Estates. The ones from my playing years who had their early beginning and identified with the talent and performances that gained them selection to the national senior team included Chester Watson, Lester King, Harold Price, Neil HoSang, Wilbert Plummer, Lloyd Williams, Errol Rattigan, and Hume Parris. Many more were just as good and through the years were deserving of the honour to have been selected. They were never extended an invitation to the trials; they were left behind frustrated and distrusting of the selection process. Having played with and observed the skills of the players, I felt it was a charade to have undermined the estimable value of so many; the lack of exposure was regrettably a barrier to their progress.

The absence of the national Selectors at Rural Parish and Sugar Estate matches was a factor that led to some players seeking recognition; they had to reorganize their way of life and made the trek to Saint Catherine Cricket Club and Kingston based senior cup clubs for attention of the selectors, selectors who were seldom seen at matches away from the senior cup playing fields.

Figure 5 Bustamante Central Zone Champions – 1960. Standing L-R: Calvin Morgan, George Baker, Othneil Myles, Lloyd Siveright, Phelmin Nangle, Rupert Hera, and Oswald Doswell. Siting L-R: Alexander Charvis, Fitz Nangle, Vinnie Budhoo, Renford Styles, Rex Suckoo, Ruel Grandison

Figure 6 Bustamante Central Zone Sugar Estate Team 1966-67. Standing L-R: Oliver Matin, Ivor Maragh, George Baker, Rex Fennel (Manager), Ronald Duncan, Franklin Quarry, Leon Brooks, Sitting L-R: Earl Gustard, Othneil Myles, Calvin Morgan (Captain), Alvin Cousins, Gladston Henry, Valencia Pennant

Figure 7 St. Mary Parish Team – 1991. Standing L-R: Bull "Gear" Samuel, Clive Garrison, Michael Mignot, Andy Morant, Wenworth Pendley, Heinsley Wilshaw, Simon Bell, Christopher Gayle, Oscar Hinds, Ossie Champagne (Manager). Front Row L-R: Garfield Silvera, Tousaint Hassan, Vincent Dixon, Keith McCrae, Winston Benain, Ralston Samuels, Raymond Lue (Assistant Manager).

Figure 8 Ruel Grandison – Sugar Estate Champion Batsman

Changing Vision for a Unified System

Anational competition encompassing the Parishes as four Zones and the Senior Cup Clubs would have been the ideal structural system for the best players to be showcased. It was the concept of a competition that would have given exposure to the long list of talented rural and senior cup players. It was a model I envisaged as a player and supported by rural and urban players I spoke with during the years I played. There was no doubt that the worth of the competition would have unearthed a plethora of players that would be better prepared for national representation.

Without a platform, I was powerless to have advocated to the ruling body of Jamaica's cricket a model of inclusiveness for the richness of rural talent. The competition as I envisaged, would have comprised the senior cup teams, Kingston, Kensington, Lucas, Saint Catherine, JDF, Police, Boys Town, Melbourne and UWI and the Zonal teams East, West, Central and Northern. The Zonal teams would be selected by a committee named by the parishes. The matches would be of two days duration, Saturday and Sunday, with a starting time at 10: AM to 6:30 PM, inclusive of 40 minutes for lunch and 20 minutes for tea.

Importantly, the JCA would have provided the resources for the selectors establishment of a comprehensive roster system for watching the games. The competition in the earlier years would have enhanced the standard of the game and a more rapid development of the younger players. There were sporadic fixtures of insufficient matches involving the Senior Cup Clubs divided in two Zones identified as Kingston East and Kingston West against rural parishes divided into four Zones as East, West, Northern, and Central. The competition helped in seeing a few players, but limitation to the number of matches mitigated a wider exposure of players who needed to be seen for more than a game or two. A competition with the four Zones and Senior Cup

Clubs with each team playing twelve matches would unquestionably corrected the imbalances of the system. It certainly would have created a level of intensity, not only by the players, but for the fans from the cricket fraternity. The motivation would have been endless, the stimulation of the rural players would have been enormous, and so many would have been inspired knowing that their performances would have opened the doors of opportunity as a pathway to the national trials. I embraced intently the day when I could have framed the narrative of my idea to the Jamaica Cricket Association for a national competition that would have augmented the development of the game in a big way.

It was of fundamental importance for those in charge of the sport to have made the necessary changes, changes that would have created opportunities for the better players, especially the many from the island rural parishes. When I became a member of the JCA at age 31, I was still an active player at the senior cup and last represented the national team at age 33. While being a member of the ruling body, I made exhaustive representation at our Cricket Improvement committee meetings for the new look competition. Members were supportive of the idea, but the JCA lacked the commitment to have garnered the sponsorship that would have had immense value to the multitude of cricketers from the Urban and Rural fields of a cricket crazed Jamaica. The funding could have been attempted through multiple sponsors. There was absolutely no palpable evidence of approaches to corporate Jamaica for patronage. It was a missed opportunity to have created a comprehensive pathway for the development and stabilization of a "Flag Ship Competition for Jamaica's cricket."

Rewinding the Clock

The Jamaican kid at preteen age fashioned imaginable areas to play the game; the creativity of the knitted balls and the carving of the bats from bamboo and coconut boughs demonstrated the ingenuity of the young ones. The experience I had at a very young age in the district at Park Hall, the agricultural district and sport-loving parish of Clarendon, was exceptional. The resourcefulness of the young minds was amazing. Not to be undone by our rural counterparts, the youngsters of a similar age group in my hometown of Spanish Town progressed from young oranges and young breadfruits to knitted balls made from a small, rounded stone, wrapped tightly to an acceptable size by layers of cloth and covered neatly by corks from bottle stoppers and knitted meticulously with English cords. When hit by any of the balls it was often time excruciating, especially without the protection of pads, batting gloves, boxes etc. Players learned from an early age the fundamentals of following the trajectory of the ball with eyes focused to determine the line and length whether to play forward or back and to play or not to play. As young boys in Spanish Town during the holidays, we played matches against each other on designated streets, vacant land areas, and the very popular Barracks School ground situated centrally in the town.

It was around that period our young minds were focused on the formation of a youth club with a playing area away from that of the centralized and overused Barracks school ground. Appreciation to Samuel McFarlane, Anthony Prince Richards, and Copeland Duke Savage, three cousins not yet twelve years old just like myself. Their relatives were caretakers of the Health Centre Complex at St Jago Park next to the Spanish Town Hospital. They identified the area with little or no grass heavily laden with gravels and weeds. It was a piece of wasted land that needed intensive effort to have it playable. After being given permission by the Chief Medical Officer Dr. Vivian Tennant for the use of the area, we were provided the tools that got us started in the reconstruction of the ground. With amazing zest, we accomplished our task in having the ground playable for both cricket and football (soccer) in record time.

We worked assiduously Mondays to Fridays after school hours and all day on Saturdays to accomplish our objective. There were special days of the week and on Saturdays that Sam McFarlane and Son Gardner prepared boiled dumplings with ackee and salt fish cooked by wood fire to the eastern side of the field where there were several trees, some of which were laden with the tasty ackee fruit from which we picked. The salt fish, flour, and additional ingredients were provided by one of our member's uncle who operated a grocery shop across the road from the entrance leading to the Health Centre Complex. We were extremely appreciative of member Thomas's uncle's valued contribution to our youth group.

Having completed the monumental task of having the ground in readiness with a pitch and an outfield in superb condition was testament to our commitment to play ball. Dr. Tennant provided us with wicket keeping gloves and pads, batting pads and gloves, bats, new and used balls, stumps, and bails. He deployed Rennie Stanley, an employee of the Centre to be our leader. Rennie was an experienced cricketer and footballer at the club level. His attentiveness to our wellbeing was marvelous throughout the early formation of the club. He was undeniably an exceptional leader.

As a club, we entered three football competitions, of which two were administered by the Saint Catherine Football Associations. The Hume Stewart league and Edwards Knock Out played midweek and on Saturdays; the other was based in Kingston played on Sundays. The club over a four-year period entered two cricket competitions; the first of the two was the Hamilton Cup for two years to be followed by another two years in the Carib Cup. Both competitions were Kingston-based teams. The St. Jago youth team was the first team outside of the Kingston-based competition to have participated in the Hamilton Cup.

For both football and cricket, we trained and played practice matches at our pride of place club ground at St. Jago Park. As much as we wanted to have played our home cup matches at our club ground, we chose instead the popular school ground Barracks, centrally located in Spanish Town. The school ground was proportionally acceptable for both sports and for that reason we stuck to that popular venue. We later used the Lime Tree Oval for all our cricket cup matches. Like our club cricketers, several of the footballers represented the Saint Catherine Parish team. They were well-known for their football skills. Our top footballers were Copeland Savage aka Duke, Vincent Brown aka Liba, Roy Thompson aka Tota, Donald Smith aka Cracka, and Delroy Russell aka Lucky. Savage, the speedy outside right, was considered one of hardest kickers of the big ball in the parish of Saint Catherine.

In 1967, Copeland Savage, for his artistry with the big ball, was voted the parish footballer of the year. From preteen years, he was a natural ball player. He represented the Saint Jago Youth Club at both cricket and football. Football was his preferred sport, a sport that he excelled at and was considered one of the parish leading players. His excellent football skills was acknowledged when he was selected by the Jamaica Football Federation for training supervised by National football coach George Penna. Copeland Savage currently as of December 19, 2023, resides in the state of New Jersey, USA.

Delroy Russell was very crafty as a midfield player and featured consistently in creating goal-scoring opportunities for our team. After the closure of our club, he migrated to the USA where he continued playing the game and later became a schoolboy coach at schools in the Philadelphia area of the USA.

In the earlier years, our entry in both the Hamilton and Carib Cricket Competitions competing against teams with seasoned and more advanced players was significant in our development. The popularity of our youth club with so many talented youngsters attracted great support to our home games, especially when the games were played at the centrally located Barracks school ground. During the second year of participation in the Carib competition, Crystal United, a newly formed club, became the second team from Spanish Town to have played in the very popular Kingston based competition. The club had in their ranks players of known quality to followers of the game in the cricket loving township and its neighborhoods, with champion batsman Renford Pinnock, fast bowler Claude Lawrence, the all-rounders Anthony Gaynor and Renford Cooke, a quartet of seasoned campaigners to lead their challenge against the very popular youth team. The Spanish Town fans eagerly awaited the much talked about fixture with the two exciting home teams.

The match was played at the Lime Tree Oval. Fans from Spanish Town and neighboring districts turned out in significant numbers with amazing support for both teams. The game was understandably gripping and had the fans cheering throughout with periods of dominance shared evenly by both teams. The contest certainly lived up to the anticipated expectation. The youth team emerged victors with me leading the way with a century. Claude Lawrence, the lanky fast bowler, thought he had me LBW before scoring, and after many years maintained that the Umpire did not give me out because the "Umpire was my Uncle." For the record, the Umpire was not my uncle. Joseph Gaynor, who bowled off spin was also of the view that the other umpire should have given me Out LBW before I got to ten from one of his deliveries. He jokingly contemplated having the umpire arrested after the game. Gaynor at the time was a Police Officer. Notwithstanding their banter, Lawrence and Gaynor complimented me on my century. At the time of writing June 6, 2023, Claude Lawrence resides in the Bronx not far from my home in Mount Vernon, and Gaynor in Saint Catherine, Jamaica.

After two seasons of the Hamilton competition, our club founder Dr. Tennant retired from the Health Service and club leader Rennie Stanley migrated to the USA. We were very grateful to both for their leadership and marvelous contribution that impacted our lives in so many ways. By their judicious leadership, we became a cohesive unit symbolic of respectability entrenched by "team work as one for all and togetherness as one." Before Rennie's departure, he arranged for us to have meetings in the garage at his home situated at St. Johns Avenue in Spanish Town. His unending kindness and devotion to the wellbeing of our members was irrefutable, he helped significantly in shaping our lives during the formative years, years when it was so important to have a mentor who exemplified civility, a trait that guided me through the years. After two seasons of participation in competition, we changed our club name from St. Jago to St. Johns. St. Johns was derivative of the avenue our club was located.

The Hamilton competition was very popular with strong community spectatorship and was given extensive media coverage, and so was the Carib competition. Our participation in both competitions was received with acclamation by the other teams and their adoring community-based fans. Most of the matches were thrilling with close finishes. The teams were represented by very talented players, some of whom had national experience. The competition allowed for the clubs to have had a maximum of two present senior cup players in their team. Our eye-catching brand of cricket and sportsmanship was appealing to the spectators of the different communities; they embraced our participation with gusto.

Teams batting first and looking for a win, if not bowled out, the timing of a declaration must be thought through methodically against certain teams. In our mid-season fixture against Magnet Club in the Carib competition at the Lime Tree Oval, we were given a lesson in power batting that lived in the memory of our players for years. The Magnet team included several explosive shot-making batsmen in Lloyd Rubber Cameron, Lloyd Burrowes, and a couple more known and feared for their attacking style of batting. We batted first starting at 1: PM and at Tea Time 3:40 PM we were 150 for 3. Our players argued strongly that a declaration be made.

As captain, I reminded my teammates about the explosiveness of known batsmen in the opposition ranks and that we would continue batting after the tea interval. We resumed batting at 4:00PM and declared twenty minutes later after adding another 20 runs, which meant that our opponents needed to score 171 runs in 90 minutes with the game scheduled ending time at 6: PM. The opening batsmen Lloyd Cameron and Lloyd Burrowes started their reply, and in the first over bowled by the Saint Catherine paceman Alexander Casey to Burrowes, sixteen runs were scored. Surprisingly, Burrowes was chided by his opening partner Cameron "for only scoring 16 runs in the over when the team required brisk scoring." Burrowes asked Cameron if he could have scored quicker. Cameron replied, "Watch me in this over to be bowled by Miles." Miles, who bowled off spin, was quickish and economical with a good line and very difficult to score quickly off. Cameron played the first ball quietly back to the bowler. The next four balls went for sixes and the last for four. After that expensive over of twenty-eight runs from the usually controlled deliveries of Miles, there was no stopping the two batsmen; they were in rampage mood.

There was a particular shot by Cameron from a Miles delivery over extra cover. Miles, the off spinner who rarely flighted the ball, operating from the Northern end pitched a quick delivery on the middle stump and with little or no room because of the length, Cameron unbelievably stepped back slightly towards the leg and struck the ball in the direction of deep cover. We watched the ball sail high out of the ground, across the marl road, and land deep, very deep in an area of the cane field that was not discernable; the ball was never recovered. The batsmen were unstoppable. Our bowlers were put to the sword. Balls from the bats of both Burrowes and Cameron raced across and over the boundary with velocity rarely seen up to that point of our young careers. There was no stopping the two. We were stunned. The runs were knocked off with ten minutes to spare. It was sustained savagery and left us dazed. The pair was overpowering.

The Hamilton Cup as a community-based competition with strong support from the residents whose passion of love for the game was unquestionable; the attendances and enthusiasm of the Green Grove and Cockburn Pen fans was habitually riveting.

There were a number of quality quicks in the competition, including Neville Brown and Logan from Green Grove, and Alvin Rose and Jeremiah Young from Cockburn Pen. They were fast and accurate with clever change of pace. Neville Brown and Alvin Rose played senior cup cricket for St. Catherine Cricket Club and Railway Cricket Club, respectively. Logan, who was called "Pacey," was truly quick and created problems for most batsmen with the bounce he extracted from deliveries not that short off a length.

While playing in the Carib and Hamilton competitions played on Sundays, I represented Bernard Lodge in the Sugar Estates on week days and Saint Catherine Club in the senior cup on Saturdays. Before my entry at the senior cup level, I represented St. Catherine parish team in the Nethersole competition played on week days.

As a senior cup player with St. Catherine, I had a very good run with bat and ball. My debut was against Melbourne Cricket Club at Lime Tree Oval. In that game, I batted once starting at number six in the order scoring 19 runs, which was third top score in a low scoring game, and picked up 3 wickets for eight runs bowling off spin in a one innings game. As an eighteen-year-old on debut in the accepted domestic top cricket competition, I was heartened by the presence of several members from my youth club; they were there to lend support. My young friends were as keen as I was and backed me to have a good start at this level. As youth club members, one of our basic tenets was the binding principle to support each other and that was absolutely in evidence when I walked to the wicket to face my first ball. The cheering was uplifting.

The friends, all of them I knew from the years when we were clad in short pants included Tyrone Bayfield, Roy Thompson, Egbert Chin Sang, Samuel McFarlane, Joseph Gayle, Donald Smith, Anthony Richards, Samuel Gardner, and Copeland Savage. After the game, in the company of my friends, we went to the open-air Crystal Cinema to watch the movie, *The Defiant Ones*, starring Tony Curtis and Sidney Poitier. It was a movie about two convicts chained together when the truck they were in with other convicts crashed. Initially, they hated each other but were inseparable being chained together. It was enthralling watching the two, one a black man and the other a white man, trying against the probabilities for self-sufficiency to succeed and eventually they did. As youth club members we were not chained; we were confronted with obstacles and yet bonded by friendship to overcome the odds, odds that we encountered and gradually overcame by support for each other. I was heartened watching the movie and at the end, McFarlane remarked, "They succeeded together just like us when you were batting today. We faced up to every ball bowled at you. Well done, Skip."

In the early years growing up in Spanish Town as ball players, most of us were proficient at cricket and football. Each sport had its season. There were several groups in the town and nearby districts; we were all friends and had fun playing amongst ourselves representing specific groups. The opportunity was there for the youngsters seeking in their own way to attract the attention of the Parish Associations for cricket and football and the Saint Catherine Cricket Club for cricket. A significant number from the group were of my age. They exhibited individual versatility at both sports that was quickly recognized by influential persons in the Town capital. The recognition of their sport prowess was an asset that effectively influenced job and employment to the nearby Sugar Estates of Bernard Lodge, Inswood, and Caymanas. The list of beneficiaries included Renford Pinnock, Herbert Bailey, John Earle, Lloyd Clarke, Anthony Mah-Lee, Clive Ogilvie, Copeland Savage, Kingsley Smith, Jeffrey Downer, Jimmy Mitchell, Alton Matthews, Keith Pryce, Herman Bennett, Samuel McFarlane, Bruza Thomas, Terry Roman, Bertram Roman, Colin Hinds, Delroy Thompson, Dudley Bonello, and many others.

Of the illustrious group, the following are still around as of May 20, 2023: Bruza Thomas in England, Dudley Bonello in Florida, Sam McFarlane in Jamaica, Anthony Mah-Lee in Jamaica, Jeffrey Downer in Jamaica, Delroy

Thompson in Florida, and Kingsley Smith in Florida. Smith was a member of our young group at the St. Jago Youth Club before migrating to England where he resided for several years. He became Mayor of Lambeth during which time he was instrumental in formalizing the twinning of his birth place Spanish Town with his adopted city of Lambeth. Additionally, Mayor Smith's benevolence was beneficial to several institutions in and around nearby areas of Spanish Town. As an All-rounder who bowled medium to fast, he was likened to Gulabrai Ramchand, the Indian All-rounder. He was so effective, especially with his bowling, that he was dubbed with the name Ramchand. Kingsley Smith aka Ramchand "A Spanish Town Legend."

Before the start of my senior cup career, I represented the St. Catherine Parish team in the Nethersole competition. The Nethersole was one of four Zonal competitions structured among the rural parishes by location, and St. Catherine, St. Mary and St. Thomas were of the same Zone. To many aspiring cricketers from the Parish, it was an achievement to be a member of either the Parish or the Saint Catherine Cricket Club senior cup team; the club team was considered the stronger of the two. My last match for the parish was against St. Mary in St. Mary. It was a memorable last appearance for me with bat and ball. I had a five-wicket haul and scored a half century.

Before the game started, there was a supporter of the St. Mary team who put out a challenge to the St. Catherine team, that should any player from our team score fifty or had a five-wicket haul, the individual or individuals would be given agricultural products. Just after I got to my fifty, the man was seen leaving the ground. Like my teammates, we anticipated that he would have returned with the promised products. He never returned. I also had a five-wicket haul when we took to the field. After the game and the usual after-match fraternizing by both teams, we jovially chided members of the home team about the broken promise of the man with the cart.

On our way home, we stopped at a popular Jerk Chicken Centre where we spotted the man standing by his mule harnessed to the cart. A couple of the players questioned him on his false promise and why he reneged. With an apology he said, "I never thought any St. Catherine player capable of scoring a half century or pick up five wickets against the strong St. Mary team." He then presented me with oranges and a bunch of green bananas. I thanked the gentleman most graciously and then shared the products with my team-mates.

As club President of the St. Jago/St. Johns Youth Clubs, I benefited administratively. The regular biweekly and emergency meetings of both the Carib and Hamilton Board enhanced my level of parliamentary protocol. The exposure prepared me adequately for the years I spent later as a cricket administrator at Saint Catherine Cricket Club and the Jamaica Cricket Association. The scheduled monthly and emergency meetings of the Carib and Hamilton competitions were held at the Henriquez Building on Church Street, the eastern side of the Kingston Parade Park, and Hyatt Drug Store off Spanish Town road, respectively. There were times when I asked for the meetings to be concluded by 11:00 PM that allowed me to travel on the last bus "Western Flyer" leaving Kingston for Spanish Town.

The Carib Competition was represented by a number of business entities and clubs with very strong following. Each team was allowed not more than two senior cup players for any one game. Our club was the first outside of Kingston to have competed in the very popular competition. The following season, the newly formed Crystal Club of Spanish Town became a new entrant to the efficiently organized Kingston-based competition, a competition that was well-organized with a very competent Secretary Hylton McIntosh. McIntosh was exceptional in his capacity as secretary, a role that was the hub of the organization that he competently structured and strengthened. Hylton McIntosh, in later years, became secretary of the well-established Kingston Cricket Club.

The teams in the Hamilton competition were represented by very "Cricket smart players" a competition that tested our resolve. Most of the teams, while on the field, demonstrated perceptible intent of derision towards the batsmen, especially the younger ones of which our team was mostly comprised. The players, most of whom were as good as the many who participated in the Senior Cup, were truly exceptional.

The last year of our club's (St. Johns) participation in the Hamilton competition, Cockburn Pen emerged as champions and deservingly so. Their batsmen were consistent in imposing totals that allowed their powerful bowling attack led by fast men Alvin Rose and Jerimiah Young to defend. The two were very good at their craft and so often very threatening to opposing bats-men with lethal deliveries on pitches very helpful to their style of bowling. The Cockburn Pen team was very dominant season after season, and after our last year as a club, a year that they emerged champions, Renford Pinnock and I from the St Johns Youth team were invited to represent a team named by the Hamilton Board to oppose the champion team in a presentation match at Cockburn Pen in Kingston.

Close Call

The last season of our participation in the Hamilton Cup won by Cockburn Pen, Renford Pinnock, and I as members of the St. Jago Youth team were named to the Hamilton Board Eleven for the presentation match against the champion team at their home ground.

We arrived at the ground for the anticipated game with the champions, and the Hamilton Board secretary, Mr. Harrison, advised me that I was appointed captain of the rest team and handed me a list of the players selected. I had a short meeting with the team and offered my congratulations on their selection, all the players were known to me and I was aware of their specialty. Cockburn Pen won the toss and elected to field, a decision that I would have made had I won the toss.

The grassless pitch was uneven and very helpful to the fast bowlers, we lost our openers early to menacing deliveries from the fast bowler, Alvin Rose, who was bowling with a lot of pace. Rose was a member of Railway's senior cup team and was considered one of the fastest and most fearsome of the fast bowlers on the senior circuit. Renford Pinnock, at his customary number four position, joined me at the fall of the second wicket. We met so often and featured in very good partnerships over the years and relished batting together. Notwithstanding the pitch condition that favoured the opening fast bowlers who were generating exceptional pace and unusual bounce, we had a quick chat and agreed that we would be very circumspect in our approach against the vaunted pace attack.

The first delivery to Pinnock was pitched at a length that he had to come forward to; the ball bounced awkwardly and hit my Saint Catherine Cricket Club teammate and very close friend just above his proboscis. He fell with blood running profusely from his nose, his eyes closed, and his body visibly trembling. He was helped off the field and taken to the car of the Secretary of the Hamilton Board, Mr. Harrison. I retired out, gathered our gear, and accompanied Pinnock to the Kingston Public Hospital. While being driven to the hospital, Pinnock was motionless lying in my lap on the back seat of the car with blood continuing to flow from his nose. The rolling of his eyes scared me into a state of nervousness, with tears visibly running down my cheek. I tried not to think of the worst but was fearful that he would die. With blood running all over my pants, I did my very best with a towel to halt the flow.

When we got to the hospital, he was helped to a bed at the emergency room with no signs of movement from his body. We waited agonizingly for a nurse or a doctor to administer assistance to the motionless champion batsman whose eyes remained closed. Mr. Hamilton and I were uneasy and expressed our anger vociferously as there was no urgency from the medical aides to render assistance. I remember asking irately, "Do you want him to die? Why the delay in offering help?" Amazingly, Pinnock opened his eyes and said, "I am not going to die." I was naturally relieved and said, "Pinnie, thank God you are talking." The many who knew Renford Pinnock would not be surprised at the cheery reaction in spite of the seriousness of his injury. On our way to the hospital, I had abysmal feelings of his survival and how, if the worst occurred, would I be able to handle the acute situation to members of his family. Pinnock was eventually attended to after a long wait, a wait that created epochs of apprehension for Secretary Harrison and me.

While Pinnock was attended to, Mr. Harrison and I prayed together quietly for his survival, it was a period that rattled my thoughts of mixed emotions. I dreaded the hours at the hospital; it felt unending and I was relieved at his remarkable recovery, a recovery that allowed him not to have been admitted. After leaving the hospital, we headed, not to the ground where I had a couple of awards to receive for scoring most runs and as the top All-rounder in the competition, but back to Spanish Town.

Pinnock was now asleep lying with his head on my lap and snored heavily which meant that he was deeply asleep. Throughout the journey, I contemplated the most comforting means by way of an explanation to his family members the circumstances of his injury. I was apprehensive and consoled myself that I knew the family very well and whatever I said to them must be comforting, and to reassure them of the help that would be forthcoming from the Hamilton Board as promised to me by Secretary Harrison.

On arrival at his home not knowing how his family would react to his condition, with his face partially covered with bandages, his sister Blossom who was soft spoken, quietly asked, "Leonard, what happened to my brother?" I calmly responded with chosen words of comfort the circumstances of his injury. His mother, father, sister Blossom, and younger brother Joe were saddened without any sign of anger. They were grateful that I was there as a friend and for Mr. Harrison's support.

I lauded Mr. Harrison for his extraordinary help and to be there with me during those long and distressing hours of waiting, a wait that caused anguished moments with the medical aides. Mr. Harrison and I stayed with the family for some time before leaving. When I got home, which was not far away from the Pinnock's home, I told my mother and sister Una what had happened. They were saddened, and shortly after went to the Pinnock's home to offer their sympathy and to help in whatever way, if needed.

As President and Captain of St. John's Youth Club, I wrote a letter of appreciation to the Hamilton Board for their continued help in the period of Pinnock's recuperation. The messages of best wishes from the Jamaica Cricket Association, Clubs, and Parish Associations for Renford Pinnock to our youth club and to the Saint Catherine Cricket Club was immeasurable. Renford Pinnock was extremely special to the cricket fraternity.

On that unforgettable Sunday afternoon, it was excruciating to have witnessed a near fatality of a teammate and friend flattened on a cricket pitch and losing consciousness with blood flowing profusely from his proboscis. I was traumatized by the incident; the sadness permeated through those present at the Cockburn Pen playing field. I am forever thankful for the miracle of his survival. The injury to Pinnock was perceived to have been lethal on that day, a day of sadness, a day that left the players and spectators numb with hearts hurting.

Figure 9 Renford Pinnock

The First Phase of My Senior Cup Years

My debut season as a senior cup cricketer was with the Saint Catherine Cricket Club as an eighteen-year-old. It was a year that the club was subjected to replacement of its most established players. The team was relatively young in age and lacked established players to provide the stability and the necessary motivation for improvement to the younger players. The captain, Clifford Harris, was returning to the game after an absence of nearly sixteen years. He was not worthy of a place in the team as a batsman or as a bowler and lacked basic leadership acumen as a cricket captain. Harris's age (he was on the upper side of forty), was a deterrent to his mobility in the field; it was an issue that hindered him throughout the season. His inclusion, and that as captain, created confusion within the mindset of the players from the first game to the last.

The calamitous situation was created when the former Jamaica and West Indies player and respectable leader of the Saints, George Mudie, and a segment of Bernard Lodge Sugar Estate management were unable to solve a deadlock over improvement of amenities for the players. The impasse prompted Mudie to successfully negotiate with Inswood Cricket Club for its return to the Senior Cup. The popular former Jamaica and West Indies player George Mudie as captain was influential in the departure from the Saints of established and match winning players Renford Pinnock, Herbert Bailey, John Earle, Lloyd Clarke and Gerald Charlton to represent Inswood Cricket Club.

Harris, as a Senior Staff member of Bernard Lodge Sugar Estates, was given the task of rebuilding the team. It was a task beyond his capabilities. He was unbelievably obstinate, a propensity that baffled, and he lacked assertiveness in construing the game. His ineptness showed areas of tactical weaknesses, weaknesses that placed the team, at most times, trying to catch up.

Away from the game for so long and left without having had a known impact on the game during his earlier playing years was disadvantageous in the process of rebuilding our team. The job was assigned to him because a certain group from the Bernard Lodge hierarchy was not for the more established Dermot Crooks. Crooks was the captain of the Saints Junior Cup team and The St. Catherine Parish Nethersole team the year before (The Nethersole matches were played on midweek days). Crooks was certainly best positioned for the captaincy and was expected to be appointed, but was overlooked to the detriment of the team. Harris was coerced into the leadership by a number of Crooks sceptics, sceptics who never considered his age and long absence from the game to have been a consequential factor of ineptness. The players gave him all the support they could and sympathized woefully with his lack of valued quality as a leader.

Inswood's return to the Senior Cup was short-lived and after one year away from the team, the return of Renford Pinnock, Herbert Bailey, and John Earle bolstered our take the field eleven. For many years through the late sixties to the ending of the seventies as a club, the Saints had in their ranks a plethora of valued cricketers. Thanks to the knowledgeable Mickey Murdock, who succeeded Harris as captain, was instrumental in lifting the individual standard of the player's game. The quality of his captaincy on the field and his articulated skills at team meetings was amazing; he spent time on what was needed by each player to improve on their specialty to become better.

In Captain Mickey Murdock, we had a very good leader, a captain who understood the game infinitely; he understood the players well. His handling of our varied attack with decisive bowling changes was a factor of our winning habits. In our team were a number of players with amazing ability, players that enhance our reputation. The likes of Renford Pinnock, Herman Bennett, Herbert Bailey, Keith Pryce, Geethan Williams, Myron Wolfe, George Chambers, and I were the main batsmen and in the bowling department, the pacers led by the evergreen and incomparable John Earle ably supported during different seasons by Neville Brown, Castel Folkes, Vincent McKayle, Livern Wellington, Lester King, Frank Farkquson, and the spinners Roy Deleon, Colin Hinds, Bobby Hall, and myself.

Apart from St. Catherine's set days for practice, a number of the St. Catherine players who were living in close proximity to the Barracks school ground practiced at this venue on Mondays and Fridays. The Barracks school facility was the central and most used venue in and around Spanish Town for the many young aspiring cricketers. Apart from the main pitch that was situated in the Centre, there were two other areas of the ground used for practice; the areas were known as little pitches situated at two of the four corners of the ground. They were heavily used as much as the center pitch where the most advanced players practiced. The center pitch would be brushed with improvised brooms and then rolled without being watered, whereas the corner pitches were swept only. Along with Renford Pinnock, Herbert Bailey, young Myron Wolfe age 17, we trained regularly for two hours on the mornings of match days starting at 7:00 AM on a concrete area close to the main school building. We worked attentively on the improvement of our batting skills during those concentrated sessions. Unlike today, we the players were our coaches and our natural style of batting served us well with minimal changes. Throughout the period of Jamaica's cricket then, the talent pool from the parishes and senior cup clubs was blessed with an abundance of skilled players. As an active cricketer, you were likely to pick up a job from one of the many Sugar Estates, Bauxite Companies, and other Industrial Entities. The goodwill of employers extended after retirement for many players including me; such were the fortunes then for cricketers.

The local standard of the game at the Senior Cup, Sugar Estates and the Parishes were highly competitive and attracted wide following by adoring fans.

I enjoyed a wonderful run as a batting all-rounder at both the Sugar Estate and the Senior Cup that led to my inevitable selection to the national trials. Following a number of good batting scores in the senior cup, culminating with 194 not out against St. Georges Old Boys at Emmet Park, the commendations from leading followers of the game, including Esmond Kentish and George Mudie, both former Saint Catherine, Jamaica and West Indies players was encouraging; their messages to me were inspirational and strengthened my resolve as a player to do well. The innings of 194 was hailed by my teammates and the St. Georges players as a wonderful knock laced with attractive stroke play. The St. Georges bowling attack was a formidable unit led by Louis Teape, the medium to fast bowler, Vinnie Binns, the right arm leg spinner, and Frankie Lewis, the Jamaican off spinning all-rounder.

National Senior Trials

To be called to the National trials was symbolic of a player's performance at the senior cup and parish levels. Regrettably, the number from the parishes was infinitesimal. The focus of attention showed a bias with the emphasis on the players mostly from the city senior cup. The disparity was attributed to the lack of a national competition, a competition that would have embraced the city and rural players. Such a competition would have given exposure to the national selectors. As it was during that period of our cricket, a national selector was rarely or not seen at rural competitions which was a mockery of fairness.

Having played at the senior cup and parish levels, players with similar experience as mine were impressed with the enormous talent seen at rural competitions, and yearned for a national competition that would have recognized and embraced the island's top players.

My first year at the trials was not a success. I failed to impress with a big score and my bowling did not show the returns I had hoped for. However, my second appearance showed remarkable improvement with a string of good scores backed by impressive off spin bowling, culminating with a good all-round performance in the final trial match at the beautiful Caymanas Park cricket ground. Representing Jackie Hendricks eleven vs Easton McMorris eleven, Herman Bennett and I resurrected the innings with a wonderful partnership of 93 runs after our team lost three early wickets for 17 runs to the hostile bowling of the then West Indies fast bowler Wesley Hall (Hall was on a coaching assignment with the Sugar Manufacturing Association and was allowed to play in that trial game), and the tall and lanky speedster Rudolph Cohen. Both were bowling and getting the ball to swing at alarming pace on the well grassed pitch that offered encouragement to the pacers. The two tested us with deliveries that were at times awkward to have handled causing blows to our bodies. Our watchful approach allowed us to have withstood the guiles of the two and we settled comfortably in a wonderful partnership against a very good fast bowling attack adequately supported by the spinners.

We were very watchful in our approach, delivery after delivery. Bennett, a resident of the Caymans Estate Community and familiar with the pitch, shared with me his knowledge of the batting conditions. He was a very stylish batsman with classical drives on both sides of the wicket. His shot making was selective and crisp in execution, be it on the front or back foot; his defensive play was a model of perfection.

As teammates at Saint Catherine Cricket Club, we shared several productive partnerships together at the senior cup level. That Sunday, the last day of the trials to select Jamaica's senior and Colts teams for matches against the touring English Cavaliers and with a large gathering of spectators looking on, we assured each other of winning the battle against the potent pace attack and we did. When the spinners were introduced in the attack, we took control and consolidated the partnership and against the run of play, Bennett was dismissed for 43, I was dismissed for 72 by a very quick delivery from Cohen when he was brought back for a second spell. My dismissal was from a square cut to backward point caught Renford Pinnock by a blinder of a catch. The ball was moving away from his left when he dived with the ball travelling speedily downward and heading for the boundary; it was a stunning catch by Pinnock that had the crowd applauding with admiration and me in disbelief.

Both Bennett and I were complimented for our batting by the fans and were acknowledged by the players of both teams as brilliant considering the quality of bowling that we withstood, especially in the early part of our innings. My significant knock of 72 provoked discussion for my selection to the senior team against the English Cavaliers touring team of past and current England test players. I was not selected to the senior team but was rewarded by my inclusion to the National Colts squad, a selection that pleased me with utmost satisfaction.

Striving for National Selection

To be selected to a national team is an achievement to be cherished. The cheerfulness of players, especially on debut, gives credence to their selection. This was in evidence as personified by the Jamaica Colts squad of thirteen at the end of the trials at Caymanas. The players apprehensively awaited the announcement of the team by the chairman of the selection committee. Each player listened intently for his name, and when called, the pleasant smile confirmed the moment of joy. We were all first-timers at the national Colts level. The selected players were considered to be on the periphery of senior selection and that was encouragement for the young Colts selectees.

For me, it was the first of my four appearances for the National Colts team, twice against the touring English Cavaliers in successive years at the beautiful Monymusk Staff ground in Clarendon, Australia's test team of 1965 in St Ann's Bay and Worcestershire County at Sabina Park. The dark blue caps issued to the players when I first played had an embroidered emblem depicting the map of Jamaica in blue with the words Colts. My selection to the team for the first time was celebrated with gusto by my family members, friends, and teammates of Saint Catherine Cricket Club. Their compliments were heartwarming to me as a young aspiring cricketer trying to find my way in a sport that had the attention of the nation.

At the first of the four matches against the English Cavaliers, the spectators were buzzing with excitement to see how the young Jamaicans would perform. The Colts team was led by Gladstone Robinson, a batsman of tremendous ability and who as a captain was very good. I consider Robinson as one of the shrewdest of captains at the local level. There were several young talented players looking to make an impression. Players like the openers captain Robinson and Ruel Grandison were batsmen very consistent with their run scoring, Herman Bennett, a very attractive right-handed batsman and very useful as a left arm spinner, Clinton Johnson, very sound in defense and very attractive with his array of strokes on either side of the wicket. Robert Scarlett, a unique type of left arm spinner, did not spin the ball viciously but just enough with good controlled and variations that baffled the best of batsmen. Lawson Matthews, a very talented leg spinning all-rounder, Fitzroy Nangle, the wicketkeeper batsman with an attacking style as a batsman; his batting was as good as his wicket keeping, and Owen Russell, the off-spinning all-rounder and there were others that complimented the team well.

We batted first and after the fall off an early wicket that of our skipper Robinson in the second over to the fiery fast bowler Freddie Truman, I walked to the wicket full of confidence, knowing that a solid knock against the strong bowling attack would have me under the radar for possible selection to the senior team later that same year. The first delivery I played comfortably into the covers for a single, Grandison who opened with Robinson, got a single from the next delivery. I was now facing up to the fourth ball of Trumann's first over, a delivery that I caressed majestically (according to the world admired cricket commentator John Arlott who was one of the commentators on the game) to the cover boundary that was applauded by the fans occupying almost every conceivable area of the ground. The great English fast bowler Freddie Truman was now riled up and gave me a tongue lashing with expletives that I never heard on a cricket field before. The very next delivery was a very quick bouncer and I ducked hurriedly and again more expletives from the fiery fast bowler. I hardly saw the next delivery that knocked out my off stump, bowled for five and again expletives from the belligerent fast bowler in waving me off to the Pavilion.

The following year against the touring English Cavaliers on their second visit to the island, my performance stood out, especially with the bat. I had a well-played sixty plus and was very impressive with the ball. The third appearance was against Worcester County at Sabina Park, a game that I performed with excellent bowling figures of five wickets in two spells of the opposition first innings and was superbly supported by Juma Hamilton, the proportionally and athletic built fast bowler from Holland Estate in St. Elizabeth. He bowled exceptionally quick and was menacing with his bouncing deliveries that the English batsmen found very difficult to have handled. He was deservedly rewarded with a four-wicket haul. In tandem, we bowled effectively and restricted the visitors to a modest score well below what they envisioned.

My performance against the touring 1965 Australians which was the last of my four games as a Jamaica Colts player, I had a pleasing knock of 39 and was batting well and looked assured of a half century before my unexpected dismissal. My bowling deserved better returns as the batsmen were tested by my controlled off spin and over spun deliveries, as mentioned by the Aussie batsman Grahame Thomas. The big game against the Australians at St. Ann's Bay was a testing assignment for the Colts team of young aspirants and former senior nationals who were eager to impress with good performances. The former senior nationals included Maurice Foster, Ferdinand Harvey, and Winston Davis. The trio were bent on doing well to regain favour with the selectors whilst the rest of us Hume Parris the wicketkeeper batsman as captain, Victor Fray opening batsman, Louis Yearwood opening batsman, Rex Suckoo batting all-rounder, Lawson Matthews right arm leg spinner, Owen Russell off spinner, Ossie Guy fast bowler, and Phelmin Nangle fast bowler, learnt a lot from the hardened Australians.

Maurice Foster, a specialist batsman with enormous talent, was dropped from the senior team. He was bent on doing well for a return to where his exceptional talent deserved for him to be. Foster later became one of the most prolific run getters in the annals of Jamaica's cricket. Winston Davis, omitted from the senior team, was exceptionally talented and admired for his repertoire of lovely stroke play on both sides of the wicket. Davis, a close friend, was determined to have had a good performance for a recall to the senior team where he rightfully should have been for a long stay, instead of the in and out appearances that so many of us experienced during our careers.

Ferdie Harvey was also a good batting all-rounder and was bent on returning to the senior team, which he did the following year just like Foster. During the playing of the Australian game, as team members, we talked about the in and out appearances that aggrieved and created uncertainties in the minds of players being recalled to the national senior team. I hope with the mindset that once selected, I would not be subjected to a scenario that plagued so many before me. Unfortunately, I was a victim like so many past players throughout my checkered career of nine years with only eight appearances in the final eleven, starting with my first game against Trinidad in

1966 at the Queens Park Oval and ending in 1975 at the same venue where it started. The subsequent years from my debut season in 1966 to 1975, I was in and out of the squad, and as a member of the squad was not selected to the starting eleven on a number of occasions. In 1973, I returned to the starting eleven after an absence of six years by playing in one game against Guyana and followed with appearances in 1974 and 1975.

For the 1975 matches away from Jamaica, I was appointed manager player, an appointment that was met with approval from many, including the Jamaica Gleaner Sports writer Freddie Smith and JBC Sport Journalist Headley Thompson, both of whom expressed to me their personal congratulations. I was overwhelmed by the confidence of the selectors and the JCA members in my ability to have performed the dual duties. The last player to have acted in that capacity was the great Jamaica and West Indies Left Arm Spinner, Alfred Valentine. It was an honour to have been player manager of the talented group of players including Maurice Foster as captain, Lawrence Rowe, Ron Headley, Sam Morgan, Herbert Chang, Desmond Lewis, Renford Pinnock, Arthur Barrett, Hylton Gordon, Uton Dowe, Cecil Lawson, and Michael Holding.

On tour, the match against Trinidad at the Queens Park Oval was my last appearance in a regional four-day game. I top scored with 52; it was the highest individual score by a Jamaican batsman in the match. After the Trinidad match, we played a two-day game against Tobago in the beautiful twin island of Trinidad and Tobago. Before leaving Jamaica, I was named captain for the Tobago leg of the tour, as Foster, Rowe, and Barrett were expected to be named and were named to the West Indies test team in Barbados that overlapped with the first two days of the Tobago match.

I certainly enjoyed playing at the Colts level, starting with that first game at the Monymusk ground against the galaxy of international stars representing the English Cavaliers to the last at Sabina Park against Worcestershire County. The three games away from Kingston attracted large crowds, crowds that were in touching distances of the players. They were very animated and the close proximity to the players allowed comfortable access for signing autographs, not only of the visiting international stars, but also the young Jamaican players. The signing of autographs and the adulation shown by the diverse age group for the matches played at Monymusk and St. Ann's

Bay gave us the Colts players a sense of recognition that was unique to us. The cocktails the evenings before and after the games allowed the inexperienced Colts players the opportunity to meet and interact with famous international players.

I recollect with relish talking with several of the visiting players including Colin Cowdrey, Jim Laker and Fred Titmus; all three were with the Cavaliers and themselves former England test players. They gave me hints that was comforting to my batting and bowling. Colin Cowdrey, one of the great test batsmen, was impressed with the way I batted, especially in that innings when I scored a half century. He encouraged me to continue playing the off spinners the way I did, not allowing the ball to do much by getting on top of the delivery when driving on either side of the wicket. Jim Laker and Fred Titmus were impressed with my delivery action and advised me how to effectively use the drifter and the over spin deliveries. Laker described the drifter as "Spin Swerve."

The interaction we the Colts players had with Grahame Thomas, a member of the Australian team, was riveting. Thomas, an Aborigine, was remarkably courteous and was at ease relating his indigenous background. He pleasantly enunciated the honour of representing his country and the importance and impact of his selection to the people of his ethnicity. He was complimentary with the marvelous interactions he had with the young Jamaican players throughout our four-day stay in St. Ann. I was happy for the honour of representing the Colts team. The camaraderie with my teammates was heartening. The opportunities afforded to our Jamaican cricketers in the earlier years to have represented not only the Jamaica National Senior and Colts teams against touring International test teams. There were regular-known teams with international and first-class players from England in particular, that toured the island and played additional matches against the combined parishes. The early exposure on the field and off, interacting with the more advanced players at cocktail events the evenings before and after matches helped immeasurably in the development of our players.

I continued performing consistently in the Senior Cup and the National Trials but could not persuade the selectors in getting their support for inclusion to the starting eleven.

There was no doubt in my mind that to be included depended on loss of form of one or two established batsmen, batsmen who were at the time performing consistently. There were others who experienced similar situation and it was up to me to wait my inevitable inclusion. I thought that having been selected to the Colts team, and was told by one of the selectors that I just missed out on being selected to the senior team after my top score of 72 against the likes of Wes Hall and Rudolph Cohen and my proven ability as an off spinner, would have accelerated my elevation to the senior squad much earlier.

Figure 10 Jamaica National Colts Team v. Australia Test Team - St. Anns Bay, Jamaica 1965 Standing L-R: Ferdie Harvey, Leonard Chambers, Winston Davis, Maurice Foster, Victor Fray, Ossie Guy, Louis Yearwood. Front Row L-R: Lawson Matthews, Phelmin Nangle, Hume Parris, Owen Russell, and Rex Suckoo.

England Bound

On a sunny Monday afternoon while at my desk as an employee of the United Fruit Company Shipping Department at 40 Harbour Street in Kingston, I heard my name called from behind. It was a familiar voice and as I turned around to respond, I saw it was Headley Thompson, my very good friend from Spanish Town. Headley was a sports journalist with the Jamaica Gleaner. As he got closer, he said, "Len, I am coming from a press conference. Congratulations. You are one of three young cricketers chosen to go to England on a cricket playing scholarship sponsored by Esso Standard Oil Company." Thompson mentioned the other two players Rudolph Cohen from Melbourne Cricket Club and my Saint Catherine teammate and close friend Herman Bennett. I was thrilled at the wonderful news and so was one of my co-workers Raymond Mair who was sitting not far from my desk. Later that evening, I was contacted by the Jamaica Cricket Association Secretary Bobby Nunez about my selection and that of Bennett and Cohen. I recalled Mr. Nunez commented, "Leonard, the selectors were unanimous in their belief that you and Herman Bennet were two of the better young batsmen in the country and that the exposure of playing in England would be of immense value to your game." I was obviously pleased and thanked Mr. Nunez for the confirmation of my selection and contractual arrangements as outlined by the JCA.

Shortly after the official confirmation by Mr. Nunez, I shared the good news with Roy Deleon and Mickey Murdock, both of whom were my co-workers at The United Fruit Company and teammates at Saint Catherine Cricket Club. The time to leave work at 5:00 PM could not have come earlier. I was exceptionally thrilled and was in a hurry to leave for home and share the wonderful news with my mother Cecilia, father Arnold, sister Una, and two nieces Melody and Dainty. They were obviously delighted and happy for me and so were my friends who I checked with later that night at our regular rendezvous the tailor shop of Donald Smith aka Cracka and Roy Thompson aka Tota. I contacted Herman Bennett the same night. He was also informed of his selection; he was extremely happy as I was.

The following day I woke up and before leaving for work, one of my neighbors who had gotten hold of the *Jamaica Daily Gleaner* for that day showed me the sports page with the pictures and the caption reading "Chambers, Bennett Cohen for England." I then left for work and when I got to the Bus Terminus to await boarding the Western Flyer bus, there were several fellow passengers who travelled with me daily on the same bus waiting for my arrival. There were some looking at copies of the gleaner sport page. They offered congratulations and expressed best wishes for a safe flight and to enjoy my sojourn in the country that gave birth to the wonderful game of cricket. When I got to my workplace, I was greeted with handshakes and congratulatory hugs. I was commended by the staff and embraces by the women with kisses on the chin. At the expense of management, I never paid for lunch the next ten working days before my departure for England. I was told by my boss, Egbert Lee, that on my return, I would be given full restitution for the thirteen weeks away from the job. Rex Suckoo of Monymusk Sugar Estate, who was a young talented batsman and an effective off spinner was selected to join the three of us on the historical visit; it was now "Four for England."

 St. Catherine Cricket Club had a reception for both Herman and I before we departed. Several of our Saints club mates were in attendance and graciously expressed best wishes. The trip to England had so many firsts for me, I was now in possession of a passport, never been on a plane, never been to New York or England.

My father, mother, sister Una, nieces Melody and Dainty accompanied me to the Norman Manley Airport. I looked forward, anticipating a flight of comfort and enjoyment to England after a stopover in New York. The first leg to New York was uncomfortable for me after the plane took off from Jamaica. I was nauseated throughout the flight to the Kennedy Airport.

Before touched down at Kennedy Airport, it was fantastic viewing from the air, with bright lights illuminating the beautiful surroundings of the Borough Queens. The setting was an attraction that continued to be so each time I returned to New York from an overseas or domestic trip at nights. After arriving and settling in a nearby hotel, we dined and looked around before returning to the confines of our hotel. After breakfast the following morning, the four of us had an extended tour of the airport complex which we found very interesting. We departed New York early that night and arrived early morning at Glasgow Airport in Scotland and then flew to Manchester. After the flight discomfort I experienced from Jamaica to New York, I adjusted and settled comfortably during the longer flight across the Atlantic.

After arriving at Manchester, we then journeyed by coach to Kings Heath, Birmingham, the permanent address of our stay in England. Driving on the M1 was captivating; the beauty of the countryside was breathtaking for me, a first timer in that part of the world. On arrival at our intended address, we were greeted by Mr. Dereif Taylor, his wife Elizabeth, and son John.

Mr. Taylor, the former Lucas Cricket Club opening batsman, was a teammate of the legendary Lucas, Jamaica and West Indies super star batsman George Headley and was now a member of Warwickshire County Cricket Club Coaching Staff. Coach Taylor's exceptional training of youngsters at the Edgbaston facility was instrumental to their development with a number of them progressing to the Warwickshire County and England International teams. Coach Taylor prepared for us a comprehensive programme for net training and participation in the Birmingham Saturday League, Warwickshire Minor County division mid-week two-day matches, Club and Ground fixtures on Fridays and Charity games on Sundays. The full use of the Warwickshire nets indoors and outdoors were utilized extensively throughout a season of personal gains for the four of us. I relished batting at the indoor net pitches, each one played differently; one was a turner and the other two were of varied bounce and pace. Coach Taylor was very attentive when we were in the nets and guided us expertly on the basics and pitch conditions we experienced during a packed calendar thirteen weeks of cricket in the country that gave birth to the great game.

After our first outdoor net session, the pacers swung the ball appreciably and there was also exceptional movement off the pitch which was very testing for Bennett, Suckoo, and I. The following day, Friday, we had our first taste of a game at the world-famous ground Edgbaston. It was a match of relatively young members of the Warwickshire County Club and the Ground staff; the popular fixture played on Fridays at different times of the cricket season was a feature of the county cricket programme. The four of us had satisfactory performances. Suckoo got a half century; Bennett and I were dismissed after scoring reasonably well, and Cohen the fast bowler with his pace was very impressive. As batsmen, we found the pitch to our liking. Our English teammates commended us for our batting and bowling skills. It was the type of start that augmented our pleasing performances on the varying match conditions of cold and unsettled weather throughout the season.

Earlier before the game started, the four of us were presented with sweaters and batting equipment including bats, pads, and gloves that served us admirably through the season. In that opening game representing the club team was a fellow Jamaican Syd Bennett from the neighboring district of Sydenham just outside of Spanish Town in Jamaica. Syd Bennett spent his early boyhood years attending the McCook School not far from the Inswood Complex at Chedwin Park before migrating to England at age fourteen. He showed a liking to the four of us and was very helpful during our Birmingham sojourn. Syd moved back to Jamaica and became a member of the St. Catherine Cricket Club. Our friendship flourished through the years and continued to be so after he migrated to the USA. Syd returned to Jamaica for the purpose of getting married, with me as his best man. He currently resides in Florida while making frequent visits to Jamaica where he maintains a lovely home just outside of Spanish Town.

After the Warwickshire club and ground game that Friday, I eagerly awaited my first game in the Birmingham League that got underway the following day, Saturday. Arriving at the ground, I was received by the Stourbridge Cricket Club Secretary. He introduced me to the members of the club executive and then ushered me to the team dressing room. The formality of my introduction as a new member of the team followed with handshakes of welcome. Shortly after, it was now game time. The opposition batted first on a cold day, a day that I wore two sweaters.

After four overs, I was introduced in the attack somewhat earlier than I expected. The first over of my lengthy spell of twenty-seven consecutive overs got me the first of my impressive spell. The right-handed batsman came forward playing for what he thought was an off-break which went with the arm and edged to slip for a comfortable catch. I got two other batsmen in that manner. It was a spell of bowling that I never experienced before. The very long spell was unusual for me. The returns was rewarding on a very cold day, a day that I adjusted remarkable well in the gripping of the ball for control with my variations. My impressive bowling allowed me the honour of leading the players off the field to tumultuous applauses from my teammates and the spectators. As soon as I sat down and was handed a refreshing drink of lemonade by the dressing room attendant, the captain told me that I would be batting at number three.

I looked up at him and smiled with a nod.

"You did exceptionally well with the ball and you are going to get a good score with the bat Leonard," said the Stourbridge captain.

I was thrilled and embraced the opportunity to bat at the important and coveted number three position. We lost an early wicket and walking to the middle, I reminded myself to "stay focused on every delivery and the runs would come. Get to ten and another and just keep going in that manner." I batted with extreme confidence before being dismissed for a half century. It was an innings of complete control in defense and attacking shots that won the admiration of the fans and my teammates.

The opposition bowling attack was a varied one. Their two opening bowlers, one right-handed and the other left-handed, and two other medium pacers bowled a tight line on a pitch that was to their liking. There was also the legendary England leg spinner Rolly Jenkins who was a jovial character. At times, he complimented me when I hit a four from his deliveries. I was determined to make it count batting in the top order and was rewarded by pacing my innings as I wanted. We won the game convincingly and for my match performances, a collection was done around the ground and handed to me. I was told by the captain that it was an established tradition that whatever crowd collection was handed to the top performer was shared amongst team members but that I would be exempted seeing it was my first game. It was a wonderful beginning for me in unfamiliar conditions, conditions that I adjusted to in remarkable fashion with the help of my seasoned teammates. Rex Suckoo was a member of the opposing team in that opening fixture. He had a good start to the season with his classical stroke play, and bowled successfully with his crafty off spin. It was a very good start to the league for both of us.

The English weather fluctuated in the first couple of weeks, with sporadic rainfall and a mix of cold and colder days. During the periods of unstable weather, I adjusted remarkably with continued good match performances in the league and reasonable returns in the limited appearances of the Minor

County games I played. There were a number of young talented players in the Warwickshire Minor County team that moved on to the county first team. Eddie Hemmings was one of the players who graduated to the senior team while being a medium pace bowler. He eventually changed his bowling style to that of an off spinner with rewarding success. So successful was his cleverly controlled off spin bowling it led to his selection to the England test team.

During the English Cricket season, charity matches for communities were played on specific Sundays in Warwickshire and the neighbouring County of Worcester. I played in a couple of the matches that were well-supported by large attendances. To be on the same team that included the likes of International players Billy Ibadulla, Dennis Amis, David Brown, and Bob Barber, and against International stars, was inspiring. The pleasant exchanges was advantageous to my understanding and acceptance of the cricket world. The charity matches were played at village grounds with large spectator attendances. During the game and in between innings, the players would mingle with the spectators and sign autographs. I certainly enjoyed those games; the financial returns to the charitable entities was just rewards for the efforts of the players.

The English county second division circuit was of immense value. It offered the opportunity of playing and rubbing shoulders with experienced players many of whom were past Internationals. As a batsman, the varying conditions presented challenges, challenges that I never experienced back home. Facing up to controlled deliveries from the medium pacers with the ball wobbling in the air and movement off the pitch consistently, required absolute watchfulness and deep concentration. The conditions tested my resolve. During the first week at the Edgbaston ground, knowing that I needed to learn more on how to handle tough batting conditions, I had a conversation with Billy Ibadulla, the Pakistan batsman who was at the time contracted to Warwickshire County as a professional. He gave me useful hints on how to approach batting in the English conditions, hints that imbued me with confidence that served me well.

"To see the controlled ball movement off the surface calls for uncomplicated thinking. Watch the ball all the way, in defense play with soft hands and be

Figure 11 Leonard Chambers in the nets with Heman Bennett padding-up – Edgbaston Ground, Birmingham, England, 1965

Figure 12 Rex Suckoo & Leonard Chambers Birmingham, England 1965

purposeful in attack," said Ibadulla, the Pakistan-born stroke player.

When playing with or being in the company of International stars, I usually seek their advice on the game such as when Jim Laker and Colin Cowdrey gave me hints on bowling and batting respectively during the Colts matches against the touring Cavaliers in Jamaica. The thirteen weeks of intense cricket in England was invaluable to my development as a cricketer. I relished just about every day while playing the game. The odd days that there was no cricket, I visited relatives in London and Wales, and found time to visit the beautiful setting of Cannon Hill Park nearby the Edgbaston cricket ground and the eye-catching Bull Ring Shopping Centre in Birmingham.

The scheduled cricket programme was of vast value to our development. Collectively, the four of us were appreciative of the Esso Standard Oil and WISCO in providing the sponsorships, the first of its kind in the annals of Jamaica's cricket, the Jamaica Cricket Association for the opportunity to have been beneficiary of the massive exposure to the country that gave birth to the game. The four of us Cohen, Bennett, Suckoo, and I were grateful to the selectors for the confidence placed in us; we were chosen from a group of other young, talented batsmen and bowlers, a testament of our skills recognized by the governance of Jamaica's cricket headed by the remarkable President Allan Rae.

We were exposed to some wonderful players in the Birmingham League and the Minor Counties. Players by their performances, demonstrated a level of absolute professionalism that had an impact and our game. I was very pleased with my personal performance and very grateful for all the help by Warwickshire and the Stourbridge Cricket Club. Individually, we were mindful of our responsibility to uphold the values aligned to the game on and off the field; to this end, we succeeded.

We were appreciative to the Taylor family for the hospitality extended during our stay at their lovely home and a very special thank you to Mrs. Elizabeth Taylor, the coach's wife. Her scrumptious dinners, particularly on Sundays, her cooking reminding us of back home in Jamaica. The Taylor's son John, a wonderful youngster, engaged us regularly in cricket conversation and of Jamaica's traditional way of life. John was sociable and accepted us with maximum respect from the country of his parents, parents who inculcated the best principles that were evidently grasped by their young son. The skilled veteran cricket Coach Derief Taylor regularly reminisced on the game in the earlier years when he played at Lucas Cricket Club with the great former West Indies batsman the immortal George Headley.

After thirteen weeks of intense cricket and the joyous experience garnered by our travel to historic places of interest, we left England with wonderful memories that would forever be with us.

Selection to the National Squad

I recalled with innermost happiness my debut selection to the Jamaica National Squad in 1966. The squad was named while I was at the wicket on the last day of the third and final trial match played at Sabina Park. It was during the last session of play just after the tea interval on a warm and sunny Sunday afternoon that the names were placed on the big scoreboard situated in the far corner of the ground towards South Camp Road. After an announcement was made that the selected squad would be placed on the board in alphabetical order, my sight on the big board was intense, hoping for my name to be among the ones inserted in white letters on black rectangle-shaped tin sheets. For me, it was a phase of trepidation. I saw when Kenneth Barnett and my teammate Herman Bennett's names went up and knew that my name, if selected would follow.

I was on strike at the South Camp Road end and with the bowler running in when I heard a shout from one of the stands "Chambers, you are in!" The bowler, Lawson Matthews my teammate in three of the four Jamaica Colts matches I played, stopped in his run-up. It was then I turned and saw my name. The letters were as big as a soccer ball. It was then I turned and saw my name. The letters were as big as a soccer ball. At the end of Matthews over, I was now at the end he bowled, with a smile he said, "Congrats Len, I paused in my run-up knowing that you heard the holler from the stands and did not want you to swing your bat in elation."

"Thanks, Lawson," I replied.

I was naturally overjoyed to have seen my name on the board. I was extremely apprehensive and more so after seeing my Saint Catherine teammate and very good friend Herman Bennett included. I wanted to be there with him. I knew that Renford Pinnock was certain to be selected and it would be good for our club Saint Catherine to have the three of us in the national squad.

The squad comprised of several members from the Jamaica Colts teams that I played with including Maurice Foster, Lawson Matthews, Ferdie Harvey, Robert Scarlett, and Herman Bennett, and there was Rudolph Cohen who was with me and Bennett to England the year before. It was a very good feeling to have had those players as members of the squad. Their inclusion inspired confidence among us to do well in the tournament. At the end of the trial game, chairman of the selection committee Allan Rae confirmed the names as posted in addressing the squad of 13 followed by congratulatory exchanges among the players.

Back in my home town, my mother, father, sister Una, nieces Melody and Dainty were extremely pleased with my selection. A couple of my friends dropped by my home much later to offer congratulations. Having been selected in the squad of thirteen, I anticipated selection for the first game against the Combined Islands in Antigua. At net practice the day before the commencement of the game, I batted and bowled with confidence and anticipated to be in the starting elven, but was overlooked. I was extremely disappointed not to have been selected and wondered, *if not now, when*? What if everyone had a good game, how long a wait would it be for my debut appearance, would I be selected for the next game days after the Antigua fixture?

As disappointed as I was, my presence in the squad would be required if necessary to do duties as an emergency fielder and to give unwavering support to the team. I offered congratulations to my Saint Catherine teammates Pinnock and Bennett, and wished for them and the team to do well. My consolation coming from the disappointment of not being in the eleven was that I took the field as an emergency fielder a number of times. My first field of the ball happened whilst at mid-off from a throw by Bennett at point. As it was the last ball of the over, I held the ball for a while before throwing it to the wicketkeeper and captain Jackie Hendricks. Hendricks jokingly asked, "Would you like a bowl, Len." I replied, "Sure. From the next end." At the conclusion of the game, we left for Trinidad where we played the twin Islands Trinidad and Tobago.

On the eve of the first day's play, the squad had fielding practice and net sessions. An indication that I would be included was when I batted after the two openers Easton McMorris and Teddy Griffiths had their knocks followed by Ron Headley and Maurice Foster and mine was an extended one that added credence to the notion that I would be a starter in the eleven. At the end of the session, we returned to the Queens Park hotel for a team meeting later that evening. Preceding the meeting, Pinnock and Bennett assured me that I would be included in the eleven on the evidence that I was given an early knock. I concurred with their notion.

At the team meeting, the eleven was announced by manager Allan Rae with me included in the eleven. I was delighted and unaware of the non-selection of Pinnock. I thought that his place in the team was guaranteed and that there was no way he would be the one to be left out to accommodate my inclusion. Pinnock never allowed the disappointment of his omission to deter him reaching out to me with his laudatory reaction to my selection. I knew that Pinnock would be more than happy for me; we have been teammates representing different teams over a long period and most of all, we were very good friends. I expressed my disappointment not having him in the team and he replied, "We will be on the same Jamaica team soon." It took another nine years for us to be in a Jamaica team together.

As was to be expected, I was overjoyed by the selection to the national team. I anticipated for that day to come when I would be wearing the national cap as a player. My debut match never went the way I expected it to. I was unsuccessful in my attempt to do well; with the bat, my contribution was negligible. In the first innings, I was given out LBW for 5, having played the ball on to my pads. The second innings was again a failure for me. My bowling was steady with little success.

On our return to Jamaica, I was retained for the Guyana game played at Sabina Park. Again, I was not able to produce with the bat, but my bowling was impressive against their top order batsmen, including Rohan Kanhai who had difficulty reading my deliveries and was finally caught by Herman Bennett from a delivery that drew him on the front foot. He was deceived in flight for his expansive cover drive. Clive Lloyd was dropped early at short midwicket by Owen Mitchell from a delivery that I held back. Lloyd went on to savagely plunder our attack with a big hundred. Roy Fredericks was very watchful and was kept quiet when facing my bowling that was never mastered, as was alluded to by wicketkeeper and captain Jackie Hendricks.

For the next and last game of the season against Barbados at Sabina Park, I was left out of the team, I was not the only player who suffered a similar fate in Jamaica's regional cricket. The selector's policy was as a batsman on debut, you had to do well in the first couple of matches to guarantee your place in the team. I was in and out of the team on a number of instances. There were occasions when I was selected to the squad and was never named to the starting eleven. It was a policy that I disagreed with when I became a national selector. My view was that a player by his proven performances at the senior cup and trials that led to his selection to the national team, be allowed a numerical number of three to four games to prove his worth.

Figure 13 Jamaica vs. Guyana 1965: Rohan Kanhai beaten outside the off stump from Leonard Chambers delivery. At slip is Teddy Griffiths and the wicketkeeper is Jackie Hendricks.

Figure 14 Jackie Hendricks – 1950. Jamaica and West Indies remarkable wicket keeper

Figure 15 Ferdie Harvey

Passiveness of Teammates

I became a member of the Saint Catherine Cricket Club at age of seventeen. Most members of the club were from Spanish Town and the neighbouring communities and well known to me. Before becoming a member of this outstanding cricket club, I had an early beginning at age twelve scoring the board handling tin plates and later as the book scorer using pencil and pen recording balls bowled and runs scored. I was now one of the main players in a successful team that had the admiration of the parish folks. The sport of cricket then was embraced by the sporting fraternity with remarkable adulation.

After a very impressive senior cup season as the top run getter and leading wicket taker for Saint Catherine Club, my imposing performances placed me in the top categories of leading run getters and wicket takers for the season. My impressive accomplishment was recognized by the *Sports Life Magazine* as one of the top five senior cup players of the season.

As the Vice-Captain, I fervently anticipated the following season to be another good one for the club and that I would have an important role to play with bat and ball. Before the Saints training got underway at the Lime Tree Oval, I trained extensively on weekends, Saturdays and Sundays at the Barracks School ground in the company of teammates Renford Pinnock, Herbert Bailey, Dudley Clarke, Clive Ogilvie, Colin Hinds, and other club members who were living close to the Barracks venue as the six of us were. As it was in the earlier years, the regular practice days at the Lime Tree Oval were Tuesdays, Wednesdays, and Thursdays. At practice sessions, the top six batsmen from the senior team usually had a net each day with the junior cup batsmen slotted in the mix.

During the last week of training for the opening game, I expected, like the other top batsmen, to be given a knock at each net session. I never batted during the period that meant so much to my preparation. As one of the top batters, for me it was an unusual occurrence and I needed to know from the captain Mickey Murdock why I did not bat on those days. I reminded Murdock of my performances the season before, and to be denied batting was an affront to me. He responded that it was his "prerogative to determine who bat and bowled at each net session" and that no further explanation was needed. The club selection policy was that the captain and vice-captain of the senior team, along with junior cup captain, were the ones designated to select the senior and junior teams on Thursdays before each game. The teams for that weekend were selected without my input as the senior cup vice-captain. I was obviously hurt and concerned and reported the matter to the club secretary.

Our opening game for the new season was against Railway Sports Club at the Railway Oval. The Railway team was a formidable one with the likes of the former Jamaica and West Indies batsman Ken Rickards and the big names of Patrick Blair, Winston Davis, Aston Sheerwood, Arthur Barrett, Gilbert Chang, and Ronald Tomlinson. The Railway team batted first, amassing a challenging total close to three hundred. Surprisingly, I was never used as a bowler, Colin Hinds and I were the preferred spinners for a number of years along with Roy Deleon. In the absence of Deleon, I expected that Hinds and I would have been the ones the captain turned to as the front-line spinners. The captain, Murdock, had other ideas; preference was given to part-timers Basil Williams and Silbert Robinson, both of whom had two spells each.

Before starting our reply, Murdock announced the batting order. I listened attentively as he mentioned the names in order of the batting positions and was dumbfounded with my name at eight. For the Saints, I never batted lower than six and that was on my debut against Melbourne some nine years before.

We lost to a very good Railway bowling attack led by spinners Gilbert Chang off spin, Ronald Tomlinson left arm spin, and Arthur Barrett right arm leg and googly. The three were very effective and never mastered.

I was surprised by Murdock's injudicious handling of a player of my status; a player who was the team leading run scorer and leading wicket taker the previous season; a player who was the team vice-captain; a player who was a recent national representative; a player who by his all-round performances was selected by *Sports Life Magazine* as one of the top five senior cup cricketers the season before. Throughout the two days of that game, I kept my equanimity, a characteristic of self-control that prepared me effectively to deal with adversities such as what I endured during the passages of two Saturdays of unprecedented agony.

At the end of the game, Murdock arranged a team meeting and surprisingly, I was replaced as the vice-captain. I was disappointed with the outcome and let down by my teammates, teammates most of whom I grew up with in Spanish Town and considered as friends. Captain Murdock's decisions not to have me batting in the nets and my inaction as a bowler and batting at the bottom end of the order during the opening game of the new season against Railway was unrelated to the game. Whatever reason he concocted and presumably conveyed to the players was convincing to have influenced their decision to strip me of the vice captaincy.

The true story behind this sordid episode started the second week before the opening game of the season while we were at net sessions, Murdock and I had an heated argument concerning a lady friend who was a loyal fan of the Saint Catherine Cricket Club. She took a liking to me and apparently he had an interest in her and jealousy got the better of him. A number of the players overheard the exchanges but were not able to have followed with certainty the source of what was going on. A couple of the players asked what was wrong. I let them know it was an issue that would be dealt with at a later date.

I grappled with the enormity of a development that was consequential to me in pursuit of regaining a place in the Jamaica team. While I contemplated the best way forward, it was absolutely clear that I could not have been comfortable with a captain who had no regard of my presence in a team that I deservedly should be a part of.

I was perplexed by the passiveness of a number of the senior players, players who I played with for a number of seasons, not only at the senior cup level, but players who I shared a lot with away from the playing fields. To have continued playing under Murdock's captaincy and the indifference of certain players who I expected to have been more thoughtful about an issue that derailed my progress was untenable to me.

I was extremely disappointed with Murdock's assertiveness in a situation that caused the acrimony that should not have been. Throughout the years from my debut senior cup appearance at age eighteen, Murdock was extremely helpful to my development as a player. His support for me was inspiring. He recognized my knowledge and passion for the game by having me confirmed as his deputy once he became captain. We were co-workers at the United Fruit Company and along with Roy Deleon the Saints left arm spinner who was also an employee with the Shipping Company, we became friends. The relationship among the three of us was amiable and revered respectfully on the field, beyond the boundary to our work place. As the neophyte in the group of three, on the odd day we had lunch by the nearby Myrtle Bank Hotel, I was the one to pay the bill including the tips. According to the two, it was an aspect of my initiation at the workplace where they were employed years ahead of me the rookie.

The unexpected turn of events made it unsustainable for my continuation as a player with the Saints. I took a two-year break from the Lime Tree based club at Bernard Lodge approximately six miles from the main region of Spanish Town.

The Rankine Years

I was very disappointed to have played only one game of the senior cup season, which was the opening fixture against Railway Sports Club. Though disconnected from the playing fields of the Senior Cup, my interest in the game never diminished. I played in several friendly games across the island on weekends and public holidays.

On a day while at work, I got a call from Henry Jaghai, the dynamic Kingston based entrepreneur who had a love for race horses and cricket. He was the owner, manager, and captain of the All-Indian cricket team. Before Jaghai became owner of the team, there were previous owners including Bertie Smith, Arthur Singh, Jadlyn Singh, and Samuel Singh. From the inception of the Indian team at the Rankine Cup level, there were players of exceptional gifts, most of whom were well-known to the cricket fraternity. The affable Jaghai wanted a conversation with me after work that day at his Rosalie Avenue home nearby to his business place in Kingston. We had a very private one-on-one talk that included the captaincy of the All-Indian team for the Rankine cricket competition. As captain, I was offered a match fee and other benefits. The offers were rewarding for me in multiple ways. I never expected the captaincy or any financial favours and to be remunerated handsomely was like a dream, a dream of charitable proportion.

Later on, Jaghai's benevolence extended to my wedding day with gifts including that of a motor car for a period of three weeks and contemporary household items.

The charismatic cricket enthusiast, race horse owner, and garage operator was also interested in having Colin Hinds, my long-standing friend and teammate at Saint Catherine Cricket Club, be a member of the team with an attractive match fee. Hinds was exuberant with the invitation to play and the financial offer was an incentive that sealed the deal for his participation. Jaghai advised that we should never mention the financial offers to anyone; we conformed to his instruction. The former Boys Town and Jamaica left arm spinner Bob Maragh, a mainstay of the All-Indian team for a number of years, was also a recipient of the lucrative offers of Jaghai and to have him in the team would be an invaluable asset as told to me by Jaghai. I was aware of Bob Maragh's prowess as a cricketer. He was an exceptional left arm spinner, comparable to the great West Indies left arm spinner Alfred Valentine.

Bob Maragh playing for Boys Town against Saint Catherine Cricket Club at Charley's Oval, in a devastating spell of controlled spin bowling mesmerized and humiliated the Saints batting line up with the remarkable returns of eight wickets for approximately forty runs. If it were not for the presence of Alfred Valentine, Bob Maragh would have been a mainstay in Jamaica's national team. So many from the cricket fraternity lamented his limited appearances at the national level; he was that talented. There were other aspects of Bob Maragh's resourcefulness that made him an integral member of the powerful Jaghai's team. He was a captain dream player. Bob Maragh and Colin Hinds bowling in tandem unsettled the batting line up of most teams. Their contribution as team members was excellent and pivotal to the team as a cohesive unit that led to our remarkable accomplishments.

Jaghai's magnanimity was felt by other team members in circumstances of dire need; as manager of the team, he did a very good job in communicating regularly with the players on non-match days. Jaghai loved batting. He was sound in defense and played the spinners skillfully. He had a flowing cover drive and pulled downward in remarkable fashion and featured in several match winning knocks. While I was the captain, a position he handed to me, I wanted him to have played more regularly. He was never keen on playing in every game but selective in playing against the more fancied and stronger oppositions.

Jaghai attracted a number of very good players to the squad that often times posed questions in selection of the final eleven. The team had phases of participation in the Rankine competition when I played, first as the All-Indian team and then as Jaghai's Garage. As the All- Indians, the group of players included Jaghai as manager, me as captain, the Maragh brothers Bob and Joe, Colin Hinds, the Rhyman brothers Aston, and Baby, Keith Singh, Bobby Mignott, Louis Williams, Kenneth Beepot, John Tai, Les Brown, Maurice Rambana, Joe Spencer, Alvin Thompson, Danny Lewis, and Adolphus Arjun.

As Jaghai's Garage during the last year of the Rankine competition, the team was bolstered by the presence of batsman Neville "Larger" Reid and Winston Manning the fast bowler who bowled at a lively pace. At the end of a day's play, Jaghai invited the team and other squad members to regular Indian festivities, especially in the Cockburn Pen area of Kingston, a community with strong East Indian population. The Indian dancers were spectacular; the food and beverages left us with memorable satisfaction.

There was a very special occasion when Jaghai invited the team members and friends to his goat farm located at a rural area outside of Kingston. The scenery was a spacious countryside of greenery. The secured acreage of farmland with a couple of hundred goats in spacious enclosures protected by barbed wire fencing was ideally situated for what followed. The setting was spectacular and a most enjoyable place to have been on a Sunday afternoon with friends in jovial mood, conversing and reminiscing on light-hearted witticisms while consuming assorted choice of beverages.

Meanwhile, the aroma from large aluminum boiling pots of "Manish Water," well-seasoned goat meat, green bananas, and white rice was mouthwatering. The scrumptious curried goat was prepared by a renowned chef of the day. I was filled with two servings of over flowing plates by the server. Each time he served me quietly he said, "After that wonderful hundred and as captain you should eat a lot." He was referring to a century I made the week before representing the All-Indian team against Jacks Hill Cricket Club played at the Machado playing field situated a couple blocks up the road from the famous test match ground Sabina Park.

The Jacks Hill team was formidable with a number of good young players including Winston Alsol, Devon Barnes, and the Gordon brothers Carol and Hylton. Hylton represented both the Jamaica national youth and senior teams. He was a very special cricketer. In that memorable knock against the Jacks Hill aggregation with me batting at number seven instead of my regular spot at number three was attributed to my displeasure with certain team members who callously challenged my decision to have Neville McKoy's inclusion to the West Indies Paper Products team when he was not declared in the starting eleven. I made it clear to Jaghai, the manager of the Indian team that McKoy was a regular member of the opposition, that there was a misrepresentation of his name to the team, and at the request of the opposing captain Arthur Barrett I agreed to the change unreservedly. I further explained to Jaghai that the disparaging response of the members was disconcerting to me and that I would not be available for the next game. I stuck to the decision and stayed home.

Surprisingly, Leslie, a staunch supporter of the Indian team, turned up at my home with a message from Jaghai asking me to play in the game that was already in progress and that the team was struggling. I responded positively and within half an hour I arrived at the ground. We were precariously placed, having lost four early wickets for a total bellow forty runs. At the fall of the fifth wicket, I went out to bat with the mindset of attacking the bowling. The onslaught was blistering and in quick time I got to a century. Hylton Gordon, with his accuracy and variations was the only bowler that kept me in check on a day of carnage for the bowlers. The Chef at the Farm event was a follower of the Indian team, and according to him, being present at the game, he was thrilled with my batting.

Unexpectedly, at the Rankine Cup season presentation ceremony, an announcement was made by the chairperson that the founders would no longer continue the competition. No apparent reason was given, which left those of us present aghast at the announcement.

The Rankine Competition was very competitive. The teams had several known players who played the game with aggressive intent to secure victory. The approach was similar to the very popular and community-based Hamilton Cup competition. Their brand of sledging augmented their aggression. It was an attitude with the notion to unsettle the opposing players, especially the younger ones, including Lawrence Rowe, Herbert Chang, and Hylton Gordon all of whom were under the age of sixteen. The early initiation at this competitive level strengthened their resolve not to be intimidated by the hardcore brand of cricket permeated in a competition that was one of the two most competitive city Sunday competitions during that period of Jamaica's cricket. The tenacity of the three youngsters was identified in their mental approach to bat for long periods, despite the chattering to upset their young minds. Their skills were sharpened and made them stronger as they progressed to National and International status.

Hylton Gordon was age fifteen when I first saw him in that game against Jacks Hill. His performance with the bat and ball was encouraging. Herbert

Chang represented West Indies Paper Products led by Arthur Barrett the former Jamaica and West Indies player and included Neville Mckoy, one of the most dynamic local batsmen. McKoy was also a former national player; the help of the two was significant to the growth of young Chang. The Jaghai's team acknowledged the quality of the gifted Chang. He was diminutive in stature and batted like a senior campaigner. He was absolutely impressive.

It was in the Rankine competition that I first saw the immortal Lawrence Rowe at the wicket. We were engaged in a cup final match against Cement Company at the Lucas Oval. The game had been postponed twice before because of inclement weather. The Cement Company's team led by Desmond Lewis, who later became a West Indies player, had in their eleven a sixteen-year-old youngster that most of the Jaghai's players were seeing for the first time. I was introduced to Rowe months before by Lewis who was a regular senior cup player with Kensington Cricket Club. Lewis introduced young Rowe to me as a talented young batsman with the prospect of becoming a future star, a prediction that was vindicated.

The Cement Company team batted first and during their innings, Hinds an off spinner who spun the ball prodigiously, had two balls to complete an over in which he had taken a wicket off the fourth delivery when Rowe walked to the wicket. The first delivery to Rowe was driven spectacularly through the covers and the next ball he got a single. Bob Maragh, the left arm leg spinner bowling from the opposite end first delivery was driven majestically to the long on boundary and the second imposingly to the midwicket boundary. Before bowling the next ball, Maragh called me for a talk. As captain, I thought that he wanted an adjustment to the field placing. To my surprise, he wanted to know the name of the youngster Rowe. He went on to predict that he would go on to represent the West Indies at an early age. He continued by describing the exquisite cover drive played by the young stroke player off the bowling from the crafty off spinner Colin Hinds, and the two majestic driven fours from his, Maragh's bowling were shots of perfection, shots against the spin on a pitch where the ball turned extensively.

"The youngster is batting like a seasoned batsman," continued Maragh.

As it is well documented, Rowe went on to represent Jamaica and had a string of three-figure innings before his debut test match, including an innings of a double century in a regional game against Guyana and another double of 227 for Jamaica against the touring New Zealand team days before his debut Test Match for the West Indies against New Zealand at Sabina Park in 1972, with scores of 214 in the first innings and 100 not out in the second. Rowe's performances during a three-week period culminating with his debut test appearance was phenomenal. His occupation at the crease during a period of dominance left him with discernable scorched lips. Rowe went on to charm the cricketing world with his majestic stroke play, including his masterclass triple century of 302 for the West Indies against England at the Kensington Oval Bridgetown, Barbados.

The Rankine competition paraded several talented players; the results of the matches were usually decided during the last half an hour of each game. Usually, the competitive nature of the matches offered keen interest amongst adoring fans, fans who understood and appreciated the passages of the games.

The comradery of the Jaghai team was excellent from the first game to the last but for that infamous game against West Indies Paper Products. The take the field eleven played as a unified group. There were some exceptional talent in our team including Kenneth Beepot a wicket keeper batsman; he was among the very best in the competition. My assessment of his capability was that his glove work was superb and that he was among the top keepers in the country. His proficiency behind the stumps was breathtaking and won the admiration, not only of his teammates, but also the opposing teams and the usual large spectators at the matches.

I tried like others did by persuasion for him to consider playing senior cup cricket. He was receptive to the encouragement but his family business on Saturdays would not have allowed him the time.

Unfortunately, his untimely death in a motor vehicle crash robbed the local cricket fraternity of an amazing talent, a wonderful person loved and respected enormously by so many. There was also the talented stroke player Maurice Rambana, a young player who was pleasing to the eye and was good enough to have been playing in the senior cup but for reasons similar to that of Beepot, he was confined to his family business on Saturdays. The Rankine competition was very competitive; games were hard-fought by combative individuals who were exceptionally passionate in their quest for victory.

All Chinese vs. All Indians

The end of the All Indians as a team was treasured with memories of great satisfaction. For me, it was a wonderful experience never to be forgotten culminating with the playing of the All Indians All Chinese game at the Melbourne Cricket ground. As players, we were privileged to have rekindled our relationships on a day with an extraordinary team of cricketers from an ethnic background that previously adorned the cricket fields locally. In earlier years, there was a regular fixture set aside for a game featuring the two teams of Asian background: Indians and Chinese. For whatever reason, the celebrated calendar fixture was put on pause for several years. On the initiative of two charismatic sporting personalities from either side of the ethnic dichotomy, the multitalented Johnny Wong Sam and Henry Jaghai's collective efforts were able to have rejuvenated the interest of business entrepreneurs for the staging of the once must-see glamorous contest. The match played at the Melbourne cricket ground previously owned by the Chinese and went by the name Chinese Athletic Club (CAC). As the CAC, the club in previous years participated in the JCA Junior Cup cricket competition. The location of the ground was centrally positioned and attracted a membership of exceptionally talented young Chinese cricketers and footballers who were well- known and respected by the sporting fraternity

For many years, the players of both groups and the local sporting fraternity enjoyed with remarkable satisfaction the friendly rivalry in a sport that had the support of so many. The match generated extensive media coverage, printed and electronic, and attracted a gathering of hundreds of avid fans to the centrally located venue.

With a jam-packed crowd cheering their favourite players for every ball fielded and runs scored, the setting was enthralling and appreciated by the well-informed fans.

The memorable game with players recognized for their talent lived up to the anticipated competitiveness. The enthusiastic multiracial gathering reveled in the joyous atmosphere of an event that the players made possible by the wonderful entertainment provided. Most fittingly, the game ended in a tie, a result that was received by the players and fans most gracefully.

From the player's perspective, the interaction reminiscing the golden years of friendly rivalry between both teams was riveting. The renewed exchanges bolstered profound and lasting relationship throughout the years after. It was gratifying to see the interaction between the fans of different age groups; the imagery portrayed a setting of attachment, a symbol of Jamaica's moto "Out of many one people."

In earlier years, the preponderance of well-known local Chinese players included Gilbert Chang, Tom Young, Bruce Lyn, Johnny Wong Sam, Melvin Cooke, the Lowe brothers, John Tai, Egbert Chin Sang, Anthony Mah-Lee, and Vincent Lyn, and from the Indians Henry Jaghai, Arthur Rhyman, Aston Rhyman, Adolphus Arjun, Leonard Mullings, Joe Maragh, Bob Maragh, Rex Suckoo, Les Brown, Kenneth Beepot, Keith Singh, Bobby Mignott, the Budhoo brothers Vinnie, William, and Emanuel, Lexford Muthra , Lascelles Collesso, Raphael Buddha, and there were others from both groups.

Having played with and against players from both sides, I am compelled to recognize the impact of Melvin Cooke. Cooke, short in stature, represented St. Georges Old Boys in the senior cup. He was adept to every pitch condition and bowlers that he faced. He was a prolific accumulator of runs with admirable consistency. The quality of his batting was comparable to the top senior cup batsmen of the day, and he was considered an exceptional stroke player with credentials fitting of national representation.

A settled Jamaica batting line-up made it difficult for Cooke's inclusion, but he had the support of pundits who strongly argued for his inclusion. Unfortunately for selection to the national team, Cooke, like other good players particularly the batsmen, had the door closed when he was on the fringe. As one who was privileged to have served as a national and regional selector and conversant with the intricacies of the selection process, I am of the view that Melvin Cooke must have been considered a probable starter.

The Jamaica Defense Force Experience

A fter a year of inactivity as a senior cup player, I was invited by my very good friend Major Abe Bailey of The Jamaica Defense Force to the Officers Club at Up Park and introduced to a small group of the rank and file members. Among the Officers was Captain Linton Graham who at the time was a member of the JDF senior cup cricket team with Major Bailey as the skipper. In our conversation, Major Bailey talked about my inactivity as a senior cup player and offered me the opportunity of a place in the Army's senior team. I graciously accepted the offer and advised the Major that I would play for two years as I intended to resume playing for the Saints. The Officers present gave me their blessing to be a member of the team, a team that I was extremely happy to be a part of.

My relationship with Major Bailey began in the early 1950's when we were members of our respective youth clubs May Pen and Spanish Town. At that time in Jamaica, the youth club movement was very proactive in the presentation of collective events across the island.

The Army team was very formidable with the likes of Abe Bailey, Donavan Ferguson, Neville Walker, Neville McKoy, Junior Powell, David Bernard, Vester Constantine, Linton Graham, Lloyd Ross, Kingsley Wright, Stafford Shand, Bernard Chris, Horace Bonner, Charles Simpson, and Gene Hamilton The players were extremely fit. The agility in the field was demonstratively superior to most teams; the suppleness was derived from the discipline inculcated in their fielding sessions that exemplified the excellence of their fielding capabilities and also bolstered the mindset in other areas of their game. Our batting was superb with the likes of Donavan Ferguson, Neville Walker, Neville McKoy, Kingsley Wright, Abe Bailey, Lloyd Ross, me, and there was always good support coming from the lower order. I had some very impressive innings including a century and an innings of 95 and other half centuries. The innings of 95 was against Kingston at Up Park Camp, I attempted a big hit at a delivery from Reggie Scarlett the former Jamaica and West Indies off spinner and was bowled. Stafford Shand, who was at the wicket as the non-striker when I attempted the atrocious shot was not impressed. He expressed disappointment that I lacked confidence in his capability with the bat and reminded me that not because he came in at number ten, he was no novice with the bat. To this day, more than half a century since that dismissal, my longstanding friend Shand has been unable to comprehend the terrible attempt of that shot that caused my dismissal. Shand was no novice with bat; he had a compact defense and for that reason he was annoyed by my injudicious attempt to clear the field with him at the other end. With the presence of Mckoy, Ferguson, and I as batting allrounders, Shand was rarely called upon to turn over his bowling arm; he was indispensable in the field and considered the best of our fielders.

The team training sessions were conducted Monday to Thursday starting at 12 noon to 3: PM. I was allowed time off from my workplace, The Port Authority of Jamaica, with the understanding that I return to the workplace and put in a couple hours after the practice sessions. I was very fortunate to have had a boss like Mr. Taylor, an Englishman who was a member of the Warwickshire County Club based in Birmingham. He showed an interest in my performance at the senior cup and was very critical of me when I did not perform to his high expectation. Mr. Taylor considered himself a very good fast bowler at school and club level growing up while he was in England.

The team spirit of the Army players was exceptional. There was the usual team drink shared by both teams at the end of each day's play; there was a group of us that widened our socializing at locations away from the Army compound after the day's play.

The team was led at different times by two very good captains: Abe Bailey the first year and Donavan Ferguson the following year. Their astute leadership style contributed significantly to the team standing as one of the strongest in the senior cup. The bowling changes were decisive, complimented by strategic field placings; the batting of the two showed consistency with productive scores. Ferguson, a batsman of known quality and dependability, had a penchant for scoring big. When batting at training, he was well measured in facing up to each delivery as if it were match time, such was his selectivity. Donovan Ferguson was among the top local batsmen and there was no limitation to his runs scoring capability as an opener. His dependability for scoring heavily was marvelous; he could bat anywhere in the order from one to six and still be successful. He stuck to his preferred position at top of the order with astounding success. Ferguson's splendid batting and consistency in compiling big scores got him into the national trials.

As JDF teammates, we spoke about what it was like to be one of the twenty-six invitees from hundreds of aspirants across the country and how privileged we were. This was Ferguson's initial outing to the trials and he was prepared to have showcase his enormous ability and preparedness for the matches ahead.

The first of the trial games played at Sabina Park was for the naturally gifted Jamaica Defense Force batsman to unleash his prowess as a wide range stroke player of exceptional quality that he consistently demonstrated on the fields at the senior cup on weekends. The expectation of seeing the gifted Ferguson on show was thwarted. He did not walk to the wicket as a batsman and he was callously pushed to a position of despair with no impetus to have continued after an act of injudiciousness.

On the opening day while fielding at backward square leg half way to the boundary, a ball was hit in his direction, bounced awkwardly, then deviated from him to the boundary (So many of us who have played the game for anytime would have had that type of misfortune). The on-field captain Easton McMorris, surprisingly, shouted contemptuously at him, an act not worthy of any captain, especially one of McMorris' prominence. It was obvious to us on the field that Ferguson was rattled by the skipper's reaction that had a demoralizing effect on his movements in the field throughout that Saturday. It was a day of agony for the easy-going Donavan Ferguson on his debut at national trials. At the end of the day's play, he hinted to me that he would not be returning the following day, Sunday. I jokingly asked, "Will you be at church all day?" He replied, "I have had enough of McMorris." I encouraged him to reconsider his position and finish the game and things would be sorted out later on but it was to no avail; he never returned. The Army champion batsman was traumatized. His close friends and admirers of his cricket skills were disappointed by the indefensible reaction of McMorris that dampened the aspiration of one so gifted.

Ferguson runs scoring in the senior cup was spectacular. His aggregate positioned him as one of the top run getters over a two-year period. Days after McMorris' ham-fisted handling of a trivial misjudgment on the field, Ferguson told me that was it for him at national trials. He was no longer interested. He would never again be subjected to the embarrassment he experienced on that day, a day of sadness, a day that he was dazed and was incapable to have grappled with.

The Army's other skipper Major Abe Bailey was himself extremely respected by the players. He saw himself a cricketer amongst cricketers and never at any time did the players, especially the other eight or nine rank and file soldiers overawed by his rank. Abe was unquestionably a team player whose contribution on and off the field was extraordinary throughout. I was deeply indebted to him for the opportunity given to me in representing the Army; it was an invitation of immeasurable benefit that I grasped appreciatively. My consistent performances in the two years as a JDF player kept me in contention for a place in the national team. I continued to revere Abe's friendship dated back to our earlier teen years at the youth club level when we first met. Abe was very consistent with the bat and more than useful with his medium pace deliveries, deliveries that yielded important wickets. Abe Bailey, the former St. Jago Sunlight captain and Manning cup player, was in later years a member of the Jamaica Cricket Association and manager of both the Jamaica youth and senior cricket teams; he was a very special ball player and cricket manager.

The passing years away from the game have not diminished our love and respect for each other. We communicate regularly, reminiscing on the wonderful years of our lives in our beautiful island in the sun. Abe currently lives in Miami where he was a practicing Lawyer before retiring in 2020.

There was a period when the Jamaica Defense Force celebrated a week of festival activities that included cricket matches against team's representative of the Police, Fire Brigade, Jamaica Cricket Associations, and former members of the JDf senior cup team. I was selected to the team of past players, most of whom by then had no affiliation with the Army. Before the start of play, a very close friend of mine Dave Roberts, a former Saint Catherine Cricket Club Secretary and JCA Assistant Secretary residing in Miami was spending a couple days in Jamaica. On the day of the match, he asked if I could take him to the Norman Manley International Airport at a specific time while the game was in progress. I promised him that the practicality of it happening would be evaluated during the course of the game.

The JDF past team batted first in the thirty-five overs contest and at the fall of the second wicket, I started my innings on a batting paradise that was to my liking. The pitch at the Army's number one ground was always good for batting, thanks to the competence of Darby the curator. He was very good in pitch preparation and was considered one of the best in the country. At the first water break with my score in the 30's, my nine-year-old son Rohan Chambers, who was one of the two book scorers, came on to the field at the first water break with a note from Roberts reminding me of the airport arrangement. I reassured Roberts not to worry and if not dismissed, I would have retired at an appropriate time to fit in with the plan. I was scoring freely and in full control enjoying the flow of my innings and got to a half century when another note came from Roberts suggesting that I get out, but my son insisted that I should bat on. When I got into the seventies, there was another note from Roberts and again Rohan urged me to bat on for a century. I told Rohan, who had the keys to my car, to ask an Army friend Delroy Greene aka Baller Greene who was at the game to use my car and drive Roberts to the airport. Greene agreed and left with my friend Roberts for the airport. In the meantime, I was having fun with the bat and I certainly enjoyed that moment when I got to my century and was undefeated at the end of our innings to the delight of Rohan.

While I was on the field during the opposition innings, I saw my car returning with Roberts and Greene and later learnt that Roberts missed the flight. The game was attended by present and former soldiers of different ranks and fans of the sport. They were treated to a wonderful day of reunion amongst themselves while enjoying the run of play. For me, the reunion with my former teammates was enthralling; the togetherness on the field of play and the socializing after the game brought back the joy I had during the two wonderful seasons I spent as a player with the Army.

Dave Roberts spent the night at my home and was given a detailed description by Rohan of how I got to my century and how well I batted.

"You certainly love batting. I enjoyed your knock before leaving for the airport and sorry to have missed the final stages of your batting," said a smiling

Roberts.

The following day, I drove my fiend Roberts to the airport; this time he never missed the flight to Miami where he was a USA citizen.

Figure 16 Easton McMorris - Jamaica's outstanding batsman

Back to the Saints

My return to the Saint Catherine Cricket Club was inevitable. I knew when I left after playing in the opening game and sitting out the remainder of the season that someday I would have returned.

To be back with the Saints was most comforting, and as captain, I was assured of total support from the players. On the initiative of Dave Roberts, Secretary of the Club and players Herman Bennett, Colin Hinds, and George Chambers, I accepted the captaincy of the club senior team when I was nominated and confirmed without being challenged.

I settled in nicely with seasoned players Renford Pinnock, Herbert Bailey, Herman Bennett, Colin Hinds, George Chambers, John Earle, and Castel Folkes. They were my teammates before l left to play for the Jamaica Defense Force. For the next seven to eight years as captain, there was a significant number of new players attracted to the club, some of whom established their position as regulars to the senior squad after representing the junior team or Mid Island team or both. During my tenure as captain, I was privileged to have led the extremely talented new players Owen Allison, William Haye, Gregory Brown, Errol Chambers, Steve Wint, Othniel Miles, Errol Brown, Calverton Brown, Carl Henry, Esward Thomas, Ali Thomas, Ephraim McLeod, Orville Mitchell, schoolboys Stumbo Tummings, Wilfred Cameron, Barrington Whitely from St. Jago, Dereck Azan and Odelmo Peters from Vere Technical.

After my retirement, Steve Wint and Odelmo Peters left the Saints for the Melbourne Cricket Club and there was George Heron who did not play while I was captain but started with the Saints when I was manager of the team. He later left for the Kensington Cricket Club where he showcased his batting skills that gained him national senior selection. Heron became captain of his new club Kensington and impressed with exceptional leadership quality, a quality that defined astuteness that led his team to championship honours in 1990. The Saints junior team was led by Calvin Ogilvie for a season, and succeeded by Hopeton Robertson who held the position for several seasons and there was the Mid Island team captained by Sydney Bennett. Both the junior and Mid Island teams were well represented by talented players such as Ewart Gayle, Samuel McFarlane, Errol Webley, Neville Glanville, Newcomb Miller, Wilber Robertson, Barington Bartley Snr., Derick Azan, Robert Harley, Vincent Harris, Delroy Thompson, Henry Walters, Anthony Mah-Lee, Binsworth Robinson, and there were others including the champion bowler John Earle after his retirement from the senior team. The youngsters Stumbo Tummings, Wilfred Cameron, Barrington Whitely, Danny Thompson, and Orville Mitchell who were all regulars of the senior team, left the game for different reasons. Tummings and Whitely who were former Jamaica Youth Players, migrated to the USA for educational studies. Cameron, also a former National Youth Player, on religious ground was unable to continue playing on Saturdays; Mitchell and Thompson the fast bowler also migrated to the USA.

There was also Milhando Barker, a truly talented wicketkeeper batsman who could not hold a regular place in the senior team because of the magnificent Renford Pinnock's presence; Henry Walters and Delroy Thompson two very good wicketkeeper batsmen also had similar experiences. Barker went on to represent the Saint Catherine Parish team in the Nethersole competition and became captain; he later ascended to the Presidency of the Saint Catherine Cricket Association.

Unlike my first tenure with the Saints, there were significant changes to the senior cup competition; St. Georges Old Boys, Inswood and Railway Sports Club were no longer participants. The Jamaica Public Services, Police (The Jamaica Constabulary) returned after a lengthy absence and the All-Bauxite team complimented the existing participants. Unfortunately, but for the Police team, the other two Jamaica Public Service and All Bauxite were short-lived. The performance of Jamaica Public Services team was considered well below the standard expected of a team at the senior cup level. It was predictable that they would have performed poorly. Their batsmen lacked any semblance of solidity; the mindset was wanting and needed help. The Captain John Nesbit was a good leader who understood the game well but could not say or do enough to improve the standard of a team that needed quality players worthy to be a participant of Jamaica's Flagship competition. In the

JPS team was John Thomas, a medium to fast bowler who was very good, good enough to have been a candidate for any of the existing senior cup teams and so was Edgar Hibbert, a very good batsman. The team needed to make several changes towards improvement. It was my view that The JCA should have been more resolute in their defense of the Light and Power team's continued participation with the proviso they enlisted, for a start, a minimum of two to three school-leaving youngsters of known quality from the Headley/Sunlight competitions, preferably the Headley or locally organized rural competitions within close proximity to their main cricket ground.

The youngsters would have been attracted by job offers to JPS at locations reachable in specific time to the Sports Club for training after work. There were so many youngsters that I knew that by their inclusion would have been an asset to the team. Additionally, invitation to one or two senior cup players with the right job offer would have improved the standard of the company's team. At a period when the Sugar Estates were vibrant, they employed individual cricketers and footballers to strengthen their teams; the JPS organization could have had a similar system which would have made their team a formidable one.

I was a beneficiary of a job offer by the Bernard Sugar Estates for similar reasons, and like so many I knew, who not only strengthened their respective teams but became national and international players. When I became a member of the JCA with responsibility as manager of Jamaica's Youth team and chairman of the youth selectors, I was asked by individuals in supervisory positions at different work places to recommend young players for employment. One such supervisor was Robert Taylor of West Indies Paper Products. I recommended four young cricketers for employment that bolstered the company's team in the Rankine Cup Cricket Competition; the four were employed in quick time. I was also asked by Phillip Keane Dawes of the Bank of Nova Scotia and Michael Gibbs from another bank, to help with the recruitment of school-leaving youngsters for job opportunities for the purpose of bolstering their respective team in the Banks competition. There were other Banks and Industrial Companies that facilitated that concept.

The All-Bauxite team, a team of talented and experience players was led by the Saint's Renford Pinnock. The very popular Pinnock showed loyalty to his employers Alcan Bauxite, a company that provided his financial livelihood, by representing the Giant Bauxite Mining Company team instead of continuing with the Saints. After the withdrawal of the All-Bauxite team from the senior cup, Pinnock resumed playing for the Saints with his usual proficiency.

The standard of Jamaica's cricket for years had a collection of excellent players representing the senior cup clubs. The leading players of the country were most times available, unless they were doing national duties in the regional tournament or representing the West Indies. The teams as they had been for several years were very competitive with quality players that were adored by the cricket-loving fans. The talent pool was adequately served by a cadre of players waiting to be selected when the opportune time was presented. It was not a given that exceptionally talented players who were performing consistently would automatically be selected to the national team when players in a settled team were seen immovable and rightfully so by their proven consistency.

So many were never chosen to the national team; they performed admirably in the senior cup and rural competitions but had to wait hopefully their turn, a turn that never came for many.

Unpredictability of the Selection Process

As I continued my regular appearances at the trials, except for the year when I took a break from the senior cup level after playing in the opening round, I was imbued with confidence after a good local season with both bat and ball. Like so many through the years, I ardently awaited announcement of the trial invitees.

Selection to the national trials at both the youth and senior levels should be considered an exceptional honour; the pool of aspirants for each group across the sphere was enormous. At the youth level, hundreds from the rural and city schools and outside of the school system from which only twenty-six or twenty-eight were named for the camp/trials and at the senior level similar numbers were selected from the Senior Cup, Parish Associations, and school boy competitions for the national trials.

It was heartening to the cricket fraternity, especially followers of the Saint Catherine Cricket Club when the names for the senior trials were announced that Herbert Bailey aka Bobby was included. Bailey, for years, performed enough to have been a regular at the senior trials and was never invited. He could no longer be denied the honour to participate and challenged as an aspirant for national selection, he joined Renford Pinnock, Herman Bennett, and I as the Saints selectees. Bailey was a batsman of amazing talent; the consummate ease in which he played his shots, he was a superb hooker and puller, his pulling off the front foot was exceptionally, his majestic drives down the ground and through the cover and square cuts off the front foot had him among the best of our local batsmen. Many followers of the game considered Bailey as one of the better batsmen in the country who never had the opportunity to have represented the national team. The question was often asked why was he never called to the trials despite his consistency at the senior cup. For Bailey, it was an agonizing wait, too long a wait to display his wide range of stroke play. He vowed to do well at the trials. The four of us trained diligently at the Barracks school ground with the help of selected bowlers from the Spanish Town area. Unlike later years, it was a period when there were minimal days of organized training by the Jamaica Cricket Association.

From the very first of the four trial matches, Bailey addressed the selectors to tick the box as a probable for the thirteen-member squad when he scored a majestic century of total dominance against a varied bowling attack, it was a signal that he should not be overlooked. Bailey followed up with another century that made it unlikely for the selectors not to now tick the box of confirmation in his favour. In the final of the trial matches played at Sabina Park, Bailey again had another excellent score that should have been considered as a closure for his inclusion to the squad. His performances outshone all the batsmen with an aggregate and average confirming his superb quality; he was absolutely magnificent.

At the end of the trials, while the players apprehensively sat and waited in the visiting player's dressing room at Sabina Park for the chairman of selector's entry, Bailey's best friend Renford Pinnock encouragingly said to him quietly, "Hombre, start packing your bag for Guyana." I am sure that Pinnock's reassurance to Bailey was shared by every player in the dressing room.

Usually when the squad was announced, the player listened for his name without concentrating on the name of others. After the names were announced, there was the usual disappointment for those not selected, including me, but it never prevented us from congratulating the chosen ones. All the players thought and with justification that Bailey was named. It was after one of the players offered his congratulations that Bailey said, "My name was not called." He was unquestionably dejected. There was silence; a pin falling to the ground would have been heard. Then there was the reaction from some of the players, "unjustified, unreasonable, irrational, illogical and ridiculous." For me, I was saddened by his non-selection. He performed splendidly and without question and should have been among the first to have been named by the panel of selectors. The prevailing gloom in the dressing room after the earlier expressions of disbelief, left us dumbfounded for several minutes; among the ones not selected was the young teenager

Linden Wright. Wright and I later became National Youth and Senior Selectors and served as members of the Jamaica Cricket Association for a number of years at different periods during our respective tenures. Wright, the brother of the former legendary West Indies cricketer Collie Smith in later years ascended to the Presidency of the JCA. Both of us by our experience as National Selectors are cognizant of the complexity of the selection process. Herbert Bailey's non-selection continues to baffle us after 55 years from 1967 to 2023.

As the players left Sabina Park that evening going their different ways, we the Saint Catherine quartet were still smarting from the shock of Bailey's non-selection. We travelled back to Spanish Town in almost silence throughout the journey; a journey that is usually forty minutes seemed to have been hours. We were deeply saddened, with a feeling of hollowness for Bailey.

Pinnock was the only one among the four of us that was selected and there was no reason to have expected him not to have; he was well established as a Jamaica batsman.

Bailey's interest in playing with natural zest slowed down. He was never interested in going back to the trials. Herbert Bailey, one of the better batsmen in our local competitions that missed out as a national representative was obviously disappointed and after another season of the senior cup he retired from the game.

As teammates, we were extremely sad to see him leave the game. He was a young man with so much to have offered to the development of the younger players in the Saint Catherine Cricket Club. Renford Pinnock, his best friend and I implored him unremittingly not to walk away from the game he loved and played so well. The three of us from the city of Spanish Town, through the years before becoming and while playing for the Saints trained with the intent of being in the Jamaica team together. It was a setting that we talked about often times; regrettably, it never happened. He left the local playing fields dejected. His Saint Catherine Club teammates and the cricket loving fans of his home town Spanish Town were left distressed at his retirement from the game, a game he loved passionately.

The failure of the selectors not to have selected Bailey to the national team could be likened to the misfortune of John Earle, the Saint Catherine pacer. Earle, who season after season was among the top bowlers locally was never invited to the trials, which I considered at the time a travesty to the system. He frequently mesmerized our local batsmen with his change of pace. He was a clever exponent of three variation of slower deliveries; he was not a chucker and his delivery action was extremely flawless. Whatever the reason for Earle's non-inclusion to the trials continued to be a talking point by fans during the 1960s to the early 1970s. The magnificent and loved John Earle was obviously disappointed but as a true champion and his tremendous love for the game, he continued playing with his magical deliveries that mesmerized the best of our local batsmen at the Sugar Estate and Senior cup competitions.

As the uproar continued, rightly or wrongly, of the perceived partiality in the selection of players to the trials and the national team, such was the case of the magnificent Herbert Bailey and John Earle.

Consequential Changes

After years of courtship, I got married to Merville Morgan from my home town of Spanish Town. Our relationship started from our teen years while she was a student at the St. Jago High School. Two years after marriage was the birth of our first child, a baby boy christened Rohan Vijay Chambers, born October 2, 1972.

It was a new beginning to my life. The birth of Rohan brought immense joy; his lovely smiles were frequent and pleasing to the eyes.

I recalled early in my role as captain of the Saints, Rohan who was just about a year old and looked visibly unwell; my wife Merville and I were very concerned and rushed him to the pediatric department at the Nutall Memorial Hospital in Kingston and waited agonizingly for attention to be rendered as there were other kids in line ahead of him. It was a senior cup match day and with time getting closer to match time on that Saturday and without a cell phone, a rarity or nonexistent to many at that period in time, I left my son in the capable hands of his mother and a very caring helper and took a taxi home. Fortunately, we had two cars, and my wife's younger brother Hugh, who was spending holidays with us, accompanied me in the other car on our way to the ground.

While we were driving on a newly constructed back road about three miles from the ground, the left front wheel was detached and running ahead of the vehicle. By this time, the car was zigzagging from one side of the road to the next before I was able to have it under control. It was a terrifying experience and when I finally did get it under control, perspiration was running profusely from different areas of my body. We were very lucky to have escaped without a collision. The road being newly constructed was not yet fully utilized and that worked remarkably in our favour. No vehicle was visible in front of or behind us.

It was now getting pretty close to match time and I realized that to retrieve the wheel and nuts and have them fitted would not have allowed me to be at the ground on time for the spinning of the coin. As the captain of the Saint's, I was deeply concerned that I would have been late and that my teammates would be worried. Hugh apologized for the awkward situation we found ourselves. The day before, I had asked him to change that particular front wheel that had a deflated tyre. In changing the wheel, he did not tighten the nuts as he should have; his negligence was the reason for the wheel detachment. While I was deep in thought accepting the possibility of not being at the ground for the spinning of the coin, fortunately, a friend heading in the opposite direction recognized me standing by the car, stopped and realizing my predicament, readily offered help by driving me to the ground. Before leaving, Hugh retrieved the wheel and was now searching for the nuts. I told him that once he found the nuts and fitted the wheel, he should go back home and await the return of my wife, son, and helper. Appreciatively, I expressed my gratitude to the friend for getting me to the game on time for spinning of the coin.

Before the end of the day's play, Hugh returned to the ground of the renowned Lime Tree Oval, the home ground of the Saint's with the news that my wife, Rohan, and the helper were back home.

When we got home, I was particularly concerned that Rohan appeared to be in discomfort. He visibly looked even worse than earlier when he was taken to the Hospital; his body temperature was a worrying experience. I was terrified if he would make it through the night without medical attention. It was now approaching 9:00 PM. His mother and I, with worrying thoughts, took him to the University Hospital. I recognized one of the doctors on duty. His name was Ford. He asked what brought me to the Hospital and I told him of my son's situation. He immediately summoned other doctors and nurses to a room for an examination and removed every piece of clothing that Rohan was draped in and had a couple of electric fans directed on the young frame of my son for the purpose of reducing the high body temperature he was experiencing.

Knowing Dr. Ford, an ardent cricket fan on duty that night was a blessing in disguise. As the senior doctor, he was able to mobilize his crew with diligence and sustained monitoring of Rohan's condition. Merville and I stayed through the night and left with a chirpy Rohan the following morning. It was a night of agonizing moments for us. We were very thankful to the medical staff, as there were periods of trepidation, and thank God our fears were alleviated as the hours passed. As the days went by, Rohan's condition improved and that brought relief, joy, and contentment to his mother and me.

Two years later, my wife Merville gave birth to a beautiful baby girl christened Roxanne Chambers. I was later blessed with another son Terron Chambers, born 1986; all three children are currently living in the USA. In 2002, I married Marie Daley in Jamaica and presently we reside in New York.

Requisite Decision

For many years, the Saints senior cup team was plagued by absenteeism, a problem that was irrefutable and caused disquiet amongst team members. My views then was that our captain Micky Murdock should have been more assertive with the guilty players and that would have bridled the regular occurrences.

When a team played short at the senior cup level, it provoked uncomfortable comments, not only by their fans, but also within the ranks of the club membership and the Jamaica Cricket Association; it was intolerable and plagued our team for a number of seasons. The nonappearance of two players was an embarrassment to the Saints after we were humiliated in a fixture at the Charley's Oval against Boys Town. Like the other eight players, I was deeply embarrassed and reminded me of our team innings closed with nine wickets fallen and me stranded on 194 not out against St. Georges Old Boys at Emmet Park. In the match a Charley's Oval, we were bowled out, losing eight wickets, all to the remarkable bowling skills of Bob Maragh, the wily left arm spinner. The match was a home fixture for Boys Town; the pitch square at their regular ground on Colie Smith Drive at the time was being rebuilt. Charley's Oval was once a lovely and popular cricket venue situated off the Spanish Town Road. The sport facility no longer exists. In its place is the J Wray & Nephew Complex.

In that disastrous game for the Saints against Boys Town, we were bowled out for a measly total by an exceptional bowler, a bowler of genuine quality. The champion Boys Town and Jamaica spinner Bob Maragh mesmerized the Saints batsmen with his cleverly controlled variety of leg breaks, arm deliveries, and straight ones.

In our next game, our devoted supporters were outraged and wanted to know if any justifiable reason was given by the players who failed to show up for the Boys Town game. The two players were apologetic to captain Murdock, team members, and the leadership of the club administration.

When I became captain of the Saints, my aspiration to have had a settled team was dependent on the most senior player of the team, John Earle. The champion bowler rarely attended practice and was habitually late at the start of a game. I knew I had to address the issue that led me to have had a one-on-one talk with the champion bowler who was an inspirational team player but for his tardiness on match days. I asked of Earle to be present for at least one practice session, preferably on Thursdays, the last of the training days leading into match day. Earle admitted his late arrival on match days was not good for team cohesiveness and pledged to make amends. The expectation that a change was imminent did not materialize. The frustration became a talking point within the team. It was intolerable and as captain it was incumbent on me to make the inevitable decision. In consultation with senior players Renford Pinnock, Herbert Bailey, Herman Bennett, Colin Hinds, and George Chambers, I concluded that Earle's responsiveness as a player was waning and in the interest for cohesive team spirit, it was obligatory on me to have advised Earle amicably that he was no longer considered for selection to the team.

For many years, Earle was overlooked for the Jamaica trials. He was not given the recognition that was deserving of one with his obvious talent and achievements. Perhaps, this was a contributory factor that affected Earle for his indifferent approach during the last years with the senior team. As to be expected, Earle was most tolerable and very respectful of the decision to leave him out, which came as no surprise to players of the senior team. We acknowledged the wonderful contribution he gave to the team throughout the years. He was always a team player and very helpful to the new players, especially the fast bowlers. His guiding influence was essential to their development and was accredited fervently by so many individuals, including Castell Folkes, the Jamaica fast bowler, and young Calverton Brown who earlier represented Jamaica's youth team. Earle's wide knowledge of the game was of immense value and that made him an integral member of the team for several years. For days before advising Earle of the decision to leave him out, I grappled with the thought of how best to handle a player of his stature, a decision that brought an end at the senior cup level to one of the most loved local cricketers of his generation. The club members and supporters understandably were saddened at Earle's parting with the senior team and conversely were in agreement with the decision taken. Earle continued playing for the Saints Junior cup team and contributed significantly to the team success in winning the junior cup led by Hopeton Robertson that included remarkable players in Binsworth Robinson, Henry Walters, Delroy Thompson, Anthony Mah-Lee, Neville Glanville, Errol Brown, Vincent Harris, Newcomb Miller, Barrington Bartley, Samuel McFarlane, Ruddy Brown. and Aeron Daley.

Figure 17 St. Catherine Cricket Club Junior Cup Champions 1976; Standing L-R: Dave Roberts (Club Secretary), Delroy Thompson, Neville Glanville, Henry Walters, Errol Brown, Binsworth Robinson, Vincent Harris, Newcomb Miller, Cliff Lashley (President).
 Front Row L-R: John Earl, Barrington Bartley Sr., Anthony Mah-Lee, Hopeton Robertson, Samuel McFarlane, Ruddy Brown, and Aaron Daley.

The Trials

As a player, I continued doing well in the senior cup as a batsman and as an off spinner and was again called to the national trials. As was my custom, I prepared purposely with the confidence that a good showing could have influenced a return to the national team. In the first two of the three trial matches, I had what is considered reasonable returns with bat and ball and just needed to do as well in the last game.

Towards the end of the first day's play, I was introduced late in the attack to bowl the last over, and with the third delivery I got a wicket and play was halted to be continued the following day.

Traditionally at the trials, each player would have evaluated his performances as the game progressed; the emphasis was on your personal contribution and not so much the result of the game. You thrived to do well at your specialty as a bowler or as a batsman or both and to be efficient as a fielder.

At the start of the second day's play, I anticipated the continuation of my over and a longish and successful spell. Surprisingly, after completing the over the following morning, I was taken out of the attack and replaced by another bowler who bowled forever that day. He had two spells, not his fault. I am sure he relished the extended opportunity given to him. Added to my woes, I batted at the bottom half in the batting order.

At the end of the game, I expressed privately with Maurice Foster the captain that he ruined my chances of a return to the national team. The limitation of my stint as a bowler and where I batted in the order was a factor. We were members of the Jamaica Colts team that played against the touring Australian test team in 1965. We were members of the senior Jamaica team when I made my debut in Trinidad 1966 and we were captains of our respective Senior Cup teams. He knew my attributes as a player, and one-to-one, we respected each other and for that reason I found it very comfortable expressing to him my feeling of disappointment. For whatever reason, Foster listened without a response. Sometime later that evening, he apologized to me with the words, "Sorry Vig, you were under bowled and batted out of position."

It was obvious to a number of players and the usual ardent fans who were regulars at the trials that I was under bowled and batted out of position.

Despite how I felt before addressing my disappointment with Foster, his response was genuine and since that day our friendship strengthened through the years. On two tours away from Jamaica when I was manager player of the Jamaica team with him as the captain, the approximately twenty years when he became a member of the Jamaica Cricket Association, we served on several committees including both the Senior and Youth Selections, Player's Welfare, Youth, Grounds, Improvement and ad hoc committees such as senior cup player of the round etc.

After my migration to the USA and as a member of the USA Cricket Hall Of Fame Organizing Committee, it was on my recommendation that led to his 2019 Induction to the USA Cricket Hall Of Fame.

We continue to update the happenings in our lives related to our siblings and the cricketing world and humorously the idea of him at age 78 emerging from retirement to help the fading fortunes of Jamaica's cricket with his customary run glut and shrewd off spin. Maurice Foster was a versatile sportsman; he was a Jamaica table tennis champion from his preteen years and was also good at hockey and football, two sports in addition to cricket that he excelled at while attending Wolmer's Boys School. Maurice Foster was undoubtedly Jamaica's number one batsman leading up to Easton McMorris' retirement and the emergence of Lawrence Rowe. Foster was prolific with the bat; he was also a cunning off spinner with very good control. At our local senior cup, Foster was a runs machine; he dominated all types of bowling with consummate ease. The Jamaica cricket fraternity was disappointed with the selectors' decision to have left him out of the Jamaica team after he gave up the captaincy and was available to play. The selectors were subjected to a barrage of criticism from all quarters and justifiable so. Leading up to his omission from the Jamaica team, Foster was considered along with Lawrence Rowe, Jeffrey Dujon, Richard Austin, Herbert Chang, and Desmond Lewis as the mainstay of our batting. Later that same year after giving up the Jamaica captaincy and left out of the national team, Foster reminded the selectors of his quality with the bat in the senior cup by topping the senior cup runs aggregate at an extremely high average per innings. From my perspective, there were other batsmen who dominated the local season but none as compared with the consistency of Maurice Foster year after year.

Figure 18 Maurice Foster

Rookie Executive

While at Chedwin Park training in preparation for the beginning of the senior cup cricket season, I received a letter delivered by Dave Roberts, assistant secretary of the Jamaica Cricket Association. The letter was written by the President of the JCA Mr. Allan Rae, requesting my acceptance for the position as assistant treasurer of the JCA at the upcoming annual general meeting of that year. I was surprised to have been considered to serve at the highest administrative level of Jamaica's cricket. My thoughts were that at age 31, I should never be considered for a position on the JCA while being an active senior cup player. However, in responding to Roberts who was secretary of the Saint Catherine Cricket Club, I acknowledged the confidence of President Rae by agreeing to serve if elected. I also indicated to Roberts that I would not be able to attend the AGM as the Saints would be having a practice game on that Saturday and as captain it was imperative that I lead the team in the preparation process for that year's season. At the JCA annual general meeting, I was nominated by the former Kensington and Jamaica player Neville Hawkins, seconded by Locksley Comrie the former Boys Town player, and confirmed to the position as assistant treasurer. The position was never before occupied by anyone as young as I was. Neville Hawkins and I played Sugar Estate cricket for Bernard Lodge and for Saint Catherine at the senior cup level. Locksley Comrie opened the bowling for Boys Town with his above medium pace deliveries; his accuracy of length and line was consistent and difficult to score from. Both Comrie and Hawkins were privately asked by Allan Rae to have nominated and seconded my nomination.

At the first monthly Board meeting of the JCA new session, the President and the other eighteen elected members extended the customary courtesy of welcome to the governing body for the new term.

As explained by President Rae, "Len, as a member of the governing body of Jamaica's cricket, while being an active player would be advantageous to the players and that you were uniquely positioned to build trust and understanding between players and the administrative body." During the first of my twenty-three years as a JCA member, I was named to the committees of Grounds, Improvement, and the newly formed Players Welfare; additionally, I was appointed secretary of those committees.

The following year of the JCA Annual General meeting, I was elected as special assistant secretary with the title of "Additional Assistant Secretary." It was the consensus of the previous administration that my work load as secretary to the various committees was interrelated with that of the Secretariat portfolio, hence the rationalization for the change from that of Assistant Treasurer to Additional Assistant Secretary. The groundbreaking position as an elected Additional Assistant Secretary at the Annual General Meeting was the creation of President Allan Rae and had the full support of the members that increased the board membership from the constitutional eighteen to nineteen.

After the initial year as a board member, the ensuing years I was assigned to multiple committees that necessitated attendances at weekly meetings at Sabina Park for the greater part of each year. The administrative knowledge of the board members, most of whom played the game, was exceptional; as members of their Clubs and Parish Associations, they acquired the rudiments of cricket administrations that was fundamental and advantageous to the JCA.

The members of the Board during the early years at different periods while I served included from the Parishes, Rex Fennell, Pat Anderson, Keith Brown, Howard Bembridge, Dr. David Crawford, Hugh Perry, Bill Bennett and from the senior cup clubs Allan Rae, Sydney Abrahams, Esmond Kentish, Dr. Franz Alexander, Reggie Scarlett, Roy McLean, Jackie Hendricks, Professor Gladstone Mills, Maurice Foster, George Prescod, Keith Wedderburn, Roy Paul, Easton McMorris, Laker Levers, Dave Roberts, Gladstone Robinson, Michael HoShue, and Chester Watson.

Keith Reece, the former Melbourne Cricket Club cricketer, was coopted as an Assistant Secretary for as long as I serve. He was a very knowledgeable cricket administrator and served the administration admirably. The members from Kingston and the Rural Parishes were well known and very effective in their respective Senior Cup Clubs and Parish Associations.

In later years, the likes of Cecil Fletcher, Dr. Donavan Bennett, Colonel Leighton Graham, Basil Walker, Chris Dehring, Danny Keddo, Bobby Marsh, Osmond Erskine, Noel Jump, Carol Gordon, George Sterling, Verley Harrison, Newton Jacks, and Brian Breese, as Board members continued the good work of their predecessors.

 It was an imposing list of committed members, members all of whom from their experiences at club and parish levels were able as the governing body to garner intended sponsorship for the Board's programmes. The Chairpersons of the various committees were dynamic individuals cognizant of their ultimate roles for successes. The sharing of ideas for continued improvement of their respective Clubs and Parishes was admirable. The collective expertise and intimate relationship with corporate Jamaica was an asset to the viability of a well-structured Jamaica Cricket Association led at different periods by the remarkable President Allan Rae, Rex Fennell, and Jackie Hendricks. Rae, the Lawyer, understood parliamentary procedures to the core, the game, the players, the position of the Clubs and Parish Associations. He was a President who earned the respect of the administration. His love for the game and commitment was beyond reproach. Rae's successors Fennell and Hendricks were steadfast in continuing the legacy of the great Allan Rae, the former Jamaica and West Indies player and Cricket West Indies President. The JCA members were like a family; we enjoyed the weekly and monthly meetings. There was no animus. We respected the views of the members; we worked together for the improvement of the game.

Ins and Outs

After my debut season representing Saint Catherine Cricket Club and later the Jamaica Defense Force, a team I represented for two seasons, my consistency with bat and ball influenced my selection to the trials regularly, but for the year that I played just one game in the senior cup season. There were moments of disillusionment for me when named to the national squad of thirteen and not selected in the final eleven.

On one of my regional tours to Guyana, the West Indies and Guyanese batsman Basil Bucher at a cocktail party remarked, "Chambers, the last time you came to Guyana you were named a reserve. Will you be playing tomorrow?" I responded with a smile, "Yes. This time I will be playing." The feeling of frustration, especially when it was obvious to most that you would be in the final eleven, aggrieved me repeatedly. I recalled when as a member of the squad of thirteen against England at Sabina Park, I was extremely confident of being in the starting eleven that I procured tickets for my father, mother and sister Una for them to watch the game. To my disappointment, I was relegated to carrying the towels and there were other times as a member of the squad while on tours of the Eastern Caribbean I found myself subjected to similar situations .

After a two-year break not been named to the squad despite my continued good performances at the senior cup with the bat, JK Holt Jr. the former Lucas, Jamaica and West Indies opening batsman and at the time one of the four National Selectors was standing at the intersection of Harbour and Duke Streets; he saw me coming out of the Aguilar Sports Store on Harbour Street, and like so many of us who knew the former West Indies opener and as a theoretical thinker of the game who was always up front with his views on players, he enquiringly wanted to know why I rarely bowled in the senior cup since I became captain of the Saint Catherine team and if I had given up on representing the national team. He suggested that in order for me to be considered for selection, my bowling would enhance my position and he implored me to share the work load with the other two off spinners Colin

Hinds and Othniel Miles. He reminded me of my encouraging bowling in the first two games I played for Jamaica against Trinidad at the Queens Park Oval and Guyana at Sabina Park. Holt also mentioned that in the two matches I batted at number five and that I was a good enough player to regain a place in the team. I told the respectable Jamaica and West Indies opener, now a selector, that because I was one of the top order batsmen in the Saint Catherine team and with Miles and Hinds at the end of the batting order, it was for that reason I allowed them to have done the bulk of the bowling as spinners.

"Give yourself the opportunity for selection to the national team by bowling, Chimmy," responded the soft spoken JK Holt Jr.

The very next game, I bowled and had a five-wicket haul in a game restricted to first innings because of unabated rain on the second day's play. I continued my bowling contribution to the team in the next two games and a month after the encouragement from the former Jamaica and West Indies cricketer John Kenneth Holt Jr., I was in the 1974 Jamaica squad for matches, including one against the Leeward Islands at the Arnos Vale ground in St. Vincent. In that game of low scores, I batted well enough in scoring forty run out in one of the innings. Holt was coach of the team, managed by Major Abe Bailey, my teammate and skipper while I was a player with the Jamaica Defense Force.

The following year 1975, I was named player manager of the National senior team for two regional matches away from home, the last against Trinidad. At the conclusion of the Trinidad game, we went to Tobago for a two-day game against Tobago. Missing from the Tobago leg of the tour were Lawrence Rowe, Maurice Foster, and Arthur Barrett. The three were called up for West Indies test duties in Barbados and I was contacted by the JCA to be the skipper of the team in the absence of Foster.

I was honoured to have been the captain with the likes of Ron Headley, Desmond Lewis, Herbert Chang, Renford Pinnock, Michael Holding, Cecil Lawson, Uton Dowe, and Dr. Tim GoopeSingh, a Trinidadian who our players were familiar with, having represented UWI in the senior cup while been a student at the top Caribbean University. His inclusion to the team was acknowledged by the Jamaica Cricket Association. Having been an incumbent senior cup captain and the captain of several teams in Jamaica's local competitions from my earlier years starting at age twelve, prepared me adequately and positioned me in a comfort zone of leadership; the players responded to my captaincy with gusto.

In the game, Renford Pinnock kept the wicket and mentioned how hard Michael Holding's deliveries were hitting his gloves. It was an indication of how fast the deliveries were bowled by the young Holding. Holding, with his beautiful rhythm, generated pace of unusual velocity that left us as players in awe. Cecil Lawson and Uton Dowe were preferred to Holding for the opening overs because of a niggling discomfort he had. As captain, I had no intention of allowing him a spell and was surprised when he asked to have a bowl. I told him not more than two overs. He was motivated by the crowd reaction to the pace of Dowe and Lawson and wanted to show the large crowd what real pace was like and he certainly did.

The large crowd babbled with appreciation that a great future was imminent for young Michael Holding who had not yet played international cricket. His pace was unbelievably quick and menacing on that warm and sunny day at the picturesque Tobago ground. It was a wonderful period of three days spent in the beautiful island. The hospitality was exceptional and appreciated by every member of the Jamaica team.

Later that year, I was again appointed player manager of the senior team participation with the other five regional teams in a tournament that honoured the services of the legendary Guyanese quartet of Rohan Kanhai, Basil Butcher, Lance Gibbs, and Joe Solomon to Guyana and West Indies Cricket.

It was one of, if not the most bizarre flight arrangements experienced by a Jamaica cricket team on tour. The arrangement as I was briefed was for us to have left Jamaica on a KLM flight that day (Holy Thursday) to Curacao and be connected on a flight that night to Guyana with a rest day on "Good Friday" and that we were scheduled for our first game on the Saturday. On the first leg to Curacao, we anticipated no setback to the travelling plans as we arrived for the connecting flight to Guyana. Surprisingly, there was no flight time scheduled to Guyana before the next day and there was no assurance of the full squad being accommodated on that flight. I was told to check back with the Airlines the following day.

I explained the situation to the team members and then advised the Jamaica

Cricket Association through Rex Fennell, the JCA secretary of our predicament. He communicated with the Guyana Board and had our first game shifted to the Sunday instead of the scheduled Saturday. I was able to make the necessary hotel accommodation for the team at one of the hotels in the city. After booking in, we went by a fast-food restaurant. Shortly after, Sam Morgan was overheard shouting contemptuously at the cashier. His attitude was shameful and that prompted me to intervene and quell a volatile situation to normality. As a result of Morgan's insolent behavior, we all agreed that the following morning we would enter the dining area of our hotel together for breakfast at a specific time.

Unexpectedly the following morning before the agreed time for us to be at the dining area, I got a call from the co-manager's wife requesting me to be in the dining room as a matter of urgency. Entering the room, I was stunned to hear Morgan's inflammatory outburst at the co-manager. It was shocking; the lady was visibly shaken. It was not yet time for breakfast and Morgan was scolding the lady with words such as, "Cool your wheel and get back to the kitchen, you hear me!" I apologized for the insolent behavior that she was subjected to and observed that she was still traumatized by the incident. By this time, the other members had come together for breakfast. I let them know of the unsavoury incident and asked Desmond Lewis, the former Jamaica and West Indies player to stay close to Morgan in the event he loses his equanimity.

After breakfast, Linden Wright, a member of our squad, accompanied me to the Air Lines Office situated at the Airport. We were optimistic of obtaining a full flight for our members. Unfortunately, we were only able to finalize flights for the squad leaving in two groups, one that day Good Friday and the other the following day. When Linden Wright and I got back to the hotel, the players were seen outside with their luggage. They were evicted from the hotel because the lady was compelled to let her husband, who was her partner as owners of the hotel, aware of the incident and that led to the husband's eviction of the players. Needless to say, how stunned Linden Wright and I were seeing Jamaica's national cricketers sitting on the sidewalk in a foreign country because of one player's disorderly behavior.

I made sure that the first group of six on the first flight on that Friday out of

Curacao headed by the captain Foster did not include Morgan. It was incumbent on me to have had him on the next flight that I was a part of. After booking at a nearby hotel, the remainder of the touring party left for Guyana the following day. It was obvious to our players that Morgan was unstable and this was demonstrated shamefully on the Sunday, a day after the full team was together in the host country Guyana.

After breakfast and looking forward to our first game later that day, Lawrence Rowe who arrived in Guyana ahead of the team, Desmond Lewis, Anthony Campbell, and I were sitting at a table in the dining area of the hotel when David Holford and Derick Murray informed me that two of our players were at war with each other and sounded contemptable. The four of us rushed to the room and there was Sam Morgan standing on the middle of a bed shouting abusively at Chang. Desmond Lewis and I were able to quell their scorn for each other. I convened a team meeting before leaving for the ground and it was revealed that their contempt for each other had to do with a domestic matter back home. They apologized emphatically to me and other members of our team for their disorderly behavior.

Remorsefully, on behalf of the two, I expressed an apology to the legendary West Indies players Murray and Holford for the unpleasantness that occurred earlier and that the incident was dealt with at a team meeting of the Jamaican players. It was evident to a number of the players who were on the previous regional tour to Trinidad that Morgan should not have been selected for the Guyana tournament. In the game against Trinidad at the Queens Park Oval, there was an incident on the field of play that was of concern to the team led by Maurice Foster. Doctor Tim GoopeSingh a Trinidadian known to most of the Jamaican players, was at the ground. I asked him to check Morgan's condition. The diagnosis was for Morgan to have had a break from the game for a couple months and to be checked medically on his return to Jamaica. In my manager's report to the JCA, I mentioned the medical advice and was appalled that the information was not adhered to.

The sincere apologies from Chang and Morgan for their indiscreet outburst and the embarrassment to the team was followed with a handshake and then a hug. Like the other team members, I was confident that the two, Chang and Morgan, were genuinely distraught over the incident and for that reason and continued apologies from the two, I did not include the incident in my manager's report. At a team meeting before leaving Guyana, I asked that they, the players, refrain from talking about the episode when they got back home, to which they agreed.

I continued serving the JCA on several established and ad hoc committees along with my other duties at Saint Catherine Cricket Club as senior cup captain. For two years while being a senior cup player, I was secretary to the national selection committee, a committee with Gerry Alexander as chairman, Jackie Hendricks, JK Holt, and Roy McLean as the other members. I was humbled by the appointment that allowed me the opportunity to understand the selection process at the national level. I was allowed to make an input without voting credentials. The courtesy was extended to me by the chairman based on my intimate knowledge of the players.

While representing the Saints in a game against Boys Town at Collie Smith Drive, the selectors turned up just before the tea break. Unexpectedly at the break before entering the dressing room, Alexander, in company of the other selectors, signaled to me for a talk. I was told by Alexander that Basil Williams would be recommended to the JCA at the next board meeting to be the national captain for the regional tournament and on behalf of the selectors he would be recommending me to be the manager. Alexander further explained Williams's limited experience as a captain and that I would be of great help to him considering that I was, at the time, one of the better club captains in the island and that both of us were close friends.

The following Tuesday was the monthly JCA meeting; included on the Agenda was the Item "Appointment of Captain and Manager." On Alexander's recommendation, Basil Williams was confirmed to the captaincy, but unknown to most members of the Board that included the selectors Alexander, Hendricks, and McLean, the Executive Body of the Board had already agreed on Secretary Rex Fennell to be the manager. As the protocol dictated then, the manager was voted on by a process of the nomination principle; apparently the executive of the Board prior to the meeting decided on Fennell. Allan Rae enquired of Alexander who was the selector's choice as manager and was told that I was. The President was apologetic and went on to say, "I never knew the selectors were thinking of you, Len. You would have been a good choice."

Wherry Wharf - Kingston Wharves Competitions

During my first year as secretary of the senior selection committee headed by Chairman Gerry Alexander with Jackie Hendricks, Roy McLean, and JK Holt as the other members, I was baffled by the selection process of the national youth team; what needed to be known of the players left much to be desired. The reliance on hearsay from individuals who were mostly interested in players from particular schools was unacceptable. There was the need for a national competition, a competition that embraced eligible players, not only from the traditional cricketing schools of the Headley and Sunlight structures, but from those who were at other schools, clubs, and the workplaces.

The selection formula continued when I was first appointed a selector in 1983 under the chairmanship of Jackie Hendricks with Maurice Foster and Carlton Forbes as the other members. The committee had the responsibility for selection of the National Senior and Youth teams before the establishment of the Youth Selection Committee during the later months of 1983.

At a private discussion involving Hendricks, President Allan Rae, and I, Hendriks asked for the President's support related to the formation of the youth selection committee and got his approval. At a Board meeting, Hendricks in his capacity as chairman of the selection committee, explained in detail the importance of a youth selection committee and asked that the committee be chaired by Gladstone Robinson, a former All Schools and Jamaica National Colts team captain and later represented Jamaica's senior team before becoming an administrator of Boys Town and the Assistant Treasurer of the JCA. Hendriks, the brilliant former Kingston, Jamaica and West Indies wicketkeeper further recommended that I be a member of the new committee as well as the senior committee. The proposals were adopted.

After a couple of months in his new role as Chairman of the youth selection committee, Gladstone Robinson advised the Board that he could no longer serve the committee adequately because of the demanding duties of his job at Esso Standard Oil Company where he was the Financial Controller. Robinson recommended that I be his successor as Chairman, a suggestion that was agreed on by the Board. I was elevated to the chairmanship for the next thirteen years, corresponding with twelve years as a senior selector.

The first year 1983, as a senior selector before the formation of the youth selection committee, I was appointed manager of the National youth team. The intricacy of identifying youth players to the yearly youth camp was imperfect; at that time, the under-nineteens was the only age group regional tournament. I was aware of the complexity of the selection process that had the selectors befuddled in identifying the younger age group of players. Knowing what I knew then prompted me with a sense of urgency for the implementation of an island wide under-nineteen youth competition.

I discussed with a friend and neighbour the likelihood of Wherry Wharf sponsoring a competition that would include the city of Kingston and the Rural Parishes. The friend Ramsay was a Staff member of the company Wherry Wharf, a subsidiary of Kingston Wharves. He discussed the idea with his boss Mr. Thompson who was the general manager, and later informed me that his company would be happy to meet with a delegation from the Jamaica Cricket Association regarding the sponsorship.

The sponsorship was successfully negotiated by a committee headed by President Rae and Secretary Fennell. After a successful first year, the sponsorship was taken over by Kingston Wharves, the parent body of Wherry Wharf. The superbly structured competition was of immense value to the youth selectors during my tenure as a JCA member. After my departure for the USA, the unthinkable happened when the sponsorship by Kingston Wharves was shifted to the under-fifteen age group without a national competition for the age group fifteen to under nineteen. The JCA, from my perspective, should have negotiated sponsorship from another entity for the under fifteens and allowed the well thought of under-nineteen competition to continue its accredited effectiveness.

As chairman of the newly formed youth selection committee and manager of the National youth team, I experienced a phase of total and prolonged commitment to youth cricket; the development of youth cricket and the welfare of the players were foremost to me. Implementation of the Wherry

Wharf/Kingston Wharves competition unearthed the expected talent; the exposure of youngsters to the Zonal Competitions was expertly handled by the Rural Parish Associations and the JCA Youth Committee. As chairman of the youth selectors, I relied on a network of Rural and City Schoolboy Coaches that I initiated for their recommendation of qualified players to the selectors for perusal to the annual youth camp and trials. The four Zonal teams from Kingston and St, Andrew were managed by individuals who had a wide knowledge of the game and adequately guided the players; their service was admirable and deservingly appreciated by the JCA.

My position as chairman of the youth selection committee, manager of the national youth team, and as a national senior selector positioned me to interact regularly with the Players, Parents, School Principals and Parish Associations. As a member of the JCA, I was privileged to have delivered the main address at Parish Associations, Schools, and Youth events across the sphere of several parishes. The JCA, with a number of former club and Parish executives, including President Allan Rae, Esmond Kentish, Jackie Hendricks, Maurice Foster, Professor Gladstone Mills, Chester Watson, Rex Fennell, Gerry Alexander, Michael HoShue, Reggie Scarlett, Howard Bembridge, Hugh Perry, Carlton Forbes, Roy Paul, George Prescod, Sydney Abrahams, Pat Anderson, Bill Bennett, and Laker Levers showed utmost confidence in my ability as a selector at both the youth and senior levels and as manager of the youth team to perform efficiently.

It is of interest to know that all those board members played the game and served their clubs and Parish Associations administratively. They brought to the board the requisite cricket insight that was essential to the governance of the Wherry Wharf/ Kingston Wharves competitions in the early stages of its implementation to be the success it was before I migrated to the USA in 1996.

Corporate Goodwill and Mentorship

As manager of the national youth team and chairman of the national youth selection committee, I was actively involved with my club Saint Catherine as Club captain, Chairman of the Selection Committee, Manager of the Senior Cup team and at different times as Secretary and second VP, it was a challenge throughout the years. It was a period that called for enormous family and work sacrifices, sacrifices that I handled the best I could. I was fortunate to have been in the employment of the companies RS Gamble Shipping and J Wray & Nephew Group of Companies, their benevolence allowed me the time off as was required for regional tours and home tournaments with full remuneration and it was testament of goodwill beyond reproach. I am also grateful to the Port Authority of Jamaica secretary manager Ralph Taylor for the "Comprehensive Scholastic Benefits" provided to me and the time off with pay to represent the national team as a player while I was an employee of the company. Additionally, as the then sales representative for the parish of Clarendon, many thanks to my employers the sport loving J Wray & Nephew Group of Companies for the response to my request for sponsorship to the Clarendon Cricket Association with cricket gear and a cheque for the construction of an expansive cricket scoreboard at the old Sevens Estate cricket ground in May Pen. The gear was for the Youth Clubs of the Parish and was presented by the great Jamaica and West Indies fast bowler Michael Holding on behalf of the gargantuan Rum Company to Egbert Williams President of the Clarendon Cricket Association, the gear included bats, balls, batting pads, wicket keeping pads, gloves and stumps. President Williams was also presented with a cheque by Bibsy Millwood Marketing Manager of Edwin Charley an entity of J Wray & Nephew Group of Companies for building of the scoreboard. William McCormack the General Manager of the very popular Liquor producing company offered a stipend and the use of a company car for Holding's journey to May Pen for the presentation, Holding an active player on the English County circuit was in Jamaica for a while, when I told him of the offers, his response was "Uncle Vijay, you know where I am living, pick me up at the appropriate time and get me back before 6: PM, I am in training, not interested in stipend or any other offers". It was a wonderful gesture by the champion bowler, giving back to the youngsters who were delighted by his presence and the encouragement of his well measured speech to the gathering. The great Michael Holding on other occasions separate and apart from his duties a youth selector was very supportive of Jamaica's cricket. Holding was instrumental in obtaining monetary sponsorship from the Seprod group of companies in England, the funds as agreed by JCA was used specifically to help the 1990 Jamaica youth team preparation for the regional tournament in Trinidad .The period of coaching was headed by the great former world class champion cricketer and lauded by the players, management of the local Seprod Company and the Jamaica Cricket Association. Holding's early preparation of the players was pivotal to the team success as champions, as was alluded to by team coach Jerry Reid. Incidentally, Michael Holding was a member of the Jamaica youth selection committee that named the victorious 1990 squad. His service to Jamaica, West Indies and World cricket as a player, administrator and commentator places him at the pinnacle of those who played the game.

It was my absolute honour to have played on the same Jamaica team with Michael Holding one of the World's great fast bowlers, his beautiful rhythmic run up and delivery action was captivating to so many who were privileged to have watched him live and on television globally. As members of the Jamaica Cricket Association, we served on several committees including Youth, Players and Youth selection. The value of Holding's contribution to the three committees and the monthly meetings of the board was recognized as priceless by those of us who served with him.

Figure 19 Michael Holding

Figure 20 The President speaks: Mr. Allan Rae, President of the Jamaica Cricket Association addressing the gathering at the recent cricket match and presentation put on by the J. C. A. in honour of D&G contribution to Jamaica's cricket at Sabina Park

L-R: Leonard Chambers, Prince Francis, Sammy Haye, Owen Allison, J.K. Holt (Government Cricket Coach), Mr. Allan Rae (President J. C. A), C. Lloyd Allen (D&G's Advertising and Promotion Manager), Miss Kathleen Johnson (D&G's Public Relations Offer), H. Bent and Mike Dundas of D&G.

Initial Year as Jamaica's Youth Manager

The 1983 regional youth tournament divided in two zones was held in Jamaica beginning with our first game at Kensington Cricket Club. Playing at home should be considered advantageous to the players; their familiarity with the grounds they played at and local support augmented their confidence to do well. The fans wanted the team to do well and there were times when a player or two came under intense pressure for different reasons. There were times when team selection was acceptable by the fans, but for some there were expressions of dissatisfaction and abuses from partisan old boys of schools and clubs who wanted to see representation from their respective institution.

The absence of Robert Haynes from the tournament was a setback to the team. He was contracted as a professional to one of the English cricket leagues. The all-round ability of the gifted left-handed stroke player with his cunning right arm leg spin would have added stability to our batting and that as leader of our spin attack. Robert Haynes by his superlative performance for the West Indies youth team in England the year before would have enhanced our challenge for championship honours. Performances of players in the Headley and Sunlight schoolboy competitions got the concentrated focus of the selectors when compiling the names for camp and the trials; however, there were instances of players not in the school system who were selected. One such player was Rupert McKenzie who was employed by New Yarmouth Sugar Estate. The selected squad members were Patrick Harris captain, Paul Palmer, Nigel Kennedy, Dereck Francis, Jimmy Adams, Maurice Cole, Carl Brissett, Rupert McKenzie, Calvin Valentine, Kenneth McLeod, Patrick Richardson, Mark English, Derrick Worrell, and Malden Miller. Larry Cunningham joined the team as an emergency fieldsman.

In the opening match of the tournament against the Leeward Islands at Kensington Park, Jimmy Adams was shamefully jeered by a particular section of the crowd that included a prominent politician. The politician came face to face with me with his criticism of Jimmy as a white man's child and not good enough a player to be in the team. He was oblivious of Adams background and performances as a player at the Sunlight level and the trials. I corrected him on his assertion about the ethnicity of Adams father by letting him know that Jimmy's father was as black as he was and that Jimmy's wonderful performances with bat and ball in the Sunlight competition and the trials impacted his selection. I further I told him that someday he would see Jimmy playing at the test level and he laughed and remarked that would never happen. My prediction was vindicated. Jimmy not only represented the West Indies, but he also became captain and was considered the world's best batsman by his prolific batting prowess.

At the end of the three-day match at Kensington Cricket Club, Jimmy rode his green frame bicycle to Mico College where the home team was accommodated. As was the customary after each day's play, we had our team meeting and after the meeting Jimmy had a one-on-one talk with me. He was disturbed by the reaction of a group of spectators that made him feel unsettled. He asked to be left out of the team. I tried as best as I could for him to change his mind, but understandably, Jimmy stood by his conviction. Jimmy was a neighbour of the JCA President Allan Rae. I suggested to the young fifteen-year-old that I would brief the President on the issue and that I would appreciate if he was a part of the conversation.

I explained the situation to the President while Jimmy listened attentively without uttering a word. The experienced former champion West Indies opener Allan Rae and Cricket West Indies President had seen it all at every level of the game and advised me as only he could have. "Don't push him, Len," said Rae. Not having the talented Jimmy Adams for the remaining games was a setback to our chances of topping the table. His all-round ability as a batsman and left arm spin bowler together with his agility and brilliance in the field was greatly missed. Malden Miller, the left arm spinner, was the replacement for Adams. There were two other spinners in the squad: Carl Brisett left arm orthodox and Maurice Cole right arm off spin. Maurice Cole bowled cleverly with very good control, ending up as our top bowler and second to the Barbadian fast bowler Milton Small who was the tournament leading wicket taker. Jamaica, the home team, and Barbados won their respective zone of two matches each that led to the final.

The finals were played at Alpart Sports Ground in the food basket parish of Saint Elizabeth and was watched by a large gathering of cricket loving fans. We were up against an extremely powerful Barbados team. We were soundly and decisively defeated to the disappointment of the players and the local fans. The all-round depth and strength of the team was unquestionable; they were ahead of the other teams. They consistently played an attractive brand of cricket, a brand that demonstrated attacking stroke play. They had a balanced bowling attack spearheaded by fast bowlers Milton Small and Ricardo Elcock. Elcock was, at the time, a professional with English County Worcestershire, and along with Small, created uncertainties for the opposition batsmen. They were well supported by their spinners led by their left arm spinner and Captain Dave Cumberbatch. Their batting was formidable and had depth. They richly deserved the championship honours and were led by an astute captain.

The tournament produced several young talent that went on to represent their national senior teams and the West Indies. From Jamaica the likes of fast bowlers Kenneth McLeod and Rupert McKenzie, batsmen Nigel Kennedy and Jimmy Adams became national senior players with Adams attaining test status. I was impressed with batsmen Patrick Harris, Nigel Kennedy, Derrick Francis and Paul Palmer; but for Harris, it was their final year at the youth level. All four as batsmen were of interest to the senior selectors and so was Patrick Richardson aka Stylo, a member of the squad who did not play a game in the truncated format of two games to the finals. He was good enough to have been considered among the top seven to eight schoolboy batsmen in the island. The fast bowlers Calvin Valentine, Kenneth McLeod, and Rupert McKenzie, the off-spinning all-rounder Maurice Cole and left arm spinner Carl Brisett showed enormous ability. Calvin Valentine was exceptional; he bowled consistently fast with very good control and had a very good bouncer. His ability to bowl long spells without signs of tiring was admirable. Valentine was proportionately built and every inch an athlete. He was also a very good soccer player with the sport not far from his thoughts. Notwithstanding his prowess as a promising footballer, it was surprising to many when he decided to stop playing cricket to concentrate on the bigger ball. His preference for the big ball game earned him selection to the Jamaica national team. Kenneth McLeod as a left Arm fast bowler swung the ball at pace and was menacing with his steep bounce; he was selected to the national team and last appeared at age twenty-five. McLeod continued his cricket career in the Lancashire League and club cricket in Australia where he now resides. Maurice Cole was a very good off spinner; he varied his deliveries with excellent control and his impressive showing left an impression with the selectors headed by Chairman Jackie Hendricks as one to be followed with an eye for national senior selection. Cole's batting skills added credence to his all-round ability and so was Carl Brisett who was defined as a bowling all-rounder.

I was extremely disappointed with the JCA's inability to have provided the players with blazers and caps for the tournament. My late appointment as manager gave me little time to have procured sponsorship for those two significant items. The players were obviously disappointed, and I vowed as a member of the Board that the players would never again represent the nation without been presented with a cap and blazer to celebrate the occasion.

Figure 21 Jamaica Youth Team - St. Kitts, 1993. Standing L-R: Gareth Breese, Delroy Taylor, Richard Hoilett, Shemei Burton, Denville McKenzie, Mark Madan, Andrew Gayle, Mark Gray, Ray Stewart. Sitting L-R: André Coley, David Hoilett, Jerry Reid (coach), Alford Givance (captain), Leonard Chambers (manager), Valentino Ventura, Christopher Miller.

Figure 22 Jamaica Youth Team – Barbados 1994. Standing L-R: Kerron Baker, Karl McDonald, Mark Madan, Audley Sanson, Devon McKenzie, Wavell Hinds, Marlon Kennedy, Julian Royal, Merrick Causley. Sitting L-R: Delroy Taylor, Ray Stewart, Leonard Chambers (manager), Garett Breese, Junior Bennett (coach), Andre Coley, Andrew Gail.

Figure 23 Jamaica Youth Team v. England, Kirkvine Oval - Manchester, Jamaica 1985 Standing L-R: Deancourt Wright, Garfield Wildman, Delroy Morgan, Alton Turner, Kingsley Duncan, Nehemiah Perry, Kenrick Dennis. Sitting L-R: Michael Laing, Paul Beckett, Leonard Chambers (manager), Vernon Smith (captain), Perry Jennings, Patrick Gayle, Larry Cunningham.

Figure 24 Jamaica Youth Team -Trinidad 1986. Standing L-R: Roger Roy, Tedroy Broomfield, Garfield Wildman, Franz Soares, Donahue Trail, Kirk Watson, Hopeton Burke, Gary Neil, Ricardo Bramwell. Sitting L-R: Nehemiah Perry, Delroy Morgan, Leonard Chambers (manager), Derron Dixon (captain), Jimmy Adams, Rohan Kanhai (coach), Lucal White

Figure 25 Jamaica U-19 Regional Youth Champions – Barbados 1988. Standing L-R: Rohan Chambers, Larry Williams, Clive Banton, Raymond Ferguson, Valentino Ventura, Steve Gordon, Courtney Francis, Carlton Caster Jr., Darren Neita. Sitting L-R: Randy Nelson, Dixieth Palmer, Rohan Kanhai (Coach), Michael Millwood (Captain), Leonard Chambers (Manager), Vivian Sailsman, Robert Samuels.

Figure 26 Jamaica Youth Team - Guyana, 1989. Standing L-R: Errol Nolan, Rohan Chambers, Shane Ford, Courtney Francis, Valentino Ventura, Clifton Folkes, Donovan Clarke, Robert Manning, Kirk Hamilton. Sitting L-R: Steve Gordon, Vivian Sailsman Leonard Chambers (Manager), Richard Staples (captain), Renford Pinnock (coach), Robert Samuels, Carlton Carter Jr.

Figure 27 Jamaica Youth Team Champions – Trinidad, 1990 Standing L-R: Orville Pennant, Lloyd Black, Clive Legister, Alvin Bent, Franklin Rose, Larry Creighton, Marlon Gibbs, Tony Powell. Sitting L-R: Courtney Francis, Carlton Carter Jr., Leonard Chambers(manager), Rohan Chambers (captain), Jerry Reid (Coach), Valentino Ventura, Robert Samuels. Clifton Folkes.

Figure 28 Jamaica Youth Team 1990

Figure 29 Jamaica Youth Team – Jamaica, 1991. Standing L-R: Alford Givance, Kirk Forest, Mario Ventura, Maurice Pinnock, Edison Edwards, Rohan Alexander, Roger Neil, Ridley Hinds, Jerry Reid (assistant coach). Sitting L-R: Franklin Rose, Tony Powell, Rohan Kanhai, Rohan Chambers (captain), Leonard Chambers(manager), Valentino Ventura, Robert Manning, Alvin Bent.

Figure 30 Jamaica Youth Team - Guyana 1992. Standing L-R: Andre Coley, Alford Givance, Andrew Davis, Rohan Belight, Brian Murphy, David Hoilett, Mario Ventura, David Hoilett, Winston Heron, Christopher Miller. Sitting L-R: Roger Neil, Alvin Bent, Leonard Chambers (manager), Rohan Chambers (captain), Jerry Reid (coach), Tony Powell, Rohan Alexander.

Figure 31 Jamaica U-19 Regional Youth Champions – 1995. Returning home from the regional tournament in a jubilant mood with the Northern Telecom Trophy Manager Leonard Chambers (right), Gareth Breese -captain (center), Ray Stewart (left), Alf St. P. Grant (assistant secretary) met the team at the Norman Manley International Airport.

Figure 32 Jamaica Youth Team -Grenada, 1995. Standing L-R: Leon Garrick, Sheldon Gordon, Julian Royal, O'Neil Richards, Marlon Kennedy, Garsha Blair, Merrick Cousley, Kerron Baker, Carl Wright. Sitting L-R: Ray Stewart, Wavell Hinds, Leonard Chambers (manager), Gareth Breese (captain), Junior Bennet (Coach), Denville McKenzie, Andrew Gayle.

Figure 33 Jamaica Youth Team -1996. Standing L-R: Xavier Gilbert, Dwayne Cooper, Ryan Cunningham, Keith Wilby, Wayne Allen, Ricardo Powell, Llewelyn Meggs, Orlando Baker. Sitting L-R: Carl Wright, Christopher Gayle, Paul Tomlinson, Junior Bennett (coach), Wavell Hinds (captain), Derron Dixon, Leon Garrick, Julian Royal.

Figure 34 West Indies Youth Team 3-day Series against England in the Caribbean – 1995
Standing L-R: Marlon Black, Reon King, Adrian Murphy, Lincoln Roberts, Balty Watt, Rawl
Lewis, Ricky Christopher, Sylvester Joseph, Leonard Chambers (manager). Front Row L-R:
Dennis Rampersad, Rondelle Yearwood, Gareth Breese (captain), Dinanath Ramnarine,
Delroy Taylor

Figure 35 West Indies U-19 Youth Team Against England – ODI 50 Overs, St. Kitts 1995
Standing L-R: Delroy Taylor, Reon King, Marlon Black, Adrian Murphy, Lincoln Roberts, Balty
Watt, Gareth Breese, Dennis Rampersaud. Sitting L-R: Andre Coley, Rawl Lewis, Leonard
Chambers (manager), Andre Percival (captain) Vernon Springer (coach), Dinanath Ramnar-
ine, Ricky Christopher.

Figure 36 West Indies Youth Team to Pakistan 1995. Standing L-R: Vishal Nagamootoo, Raymond Casimir, Amarnath Basdeo, Shirley Clarke, Denville McKenzie, Wavell Hinds, O'Neil Richards, Tyrone Greenaway, Sylvester Joseph. Sitting L-R: Reon King, Nicholas de Groot, Leonard Chambers (manager), Gareth Breese (captain), Gus Logie (Coach), Mahendra Nagamootoo, Adrian Murphy, Ryan Hurley.

Regional Youth Tournament 1984

For the 1984 regional youth tournament, the national youth selection committee intensified the preparation and selection process leading up to the annual camp.

Having been re-elected a member of the JCA and the selection committee settled, I decided early before the manager was named to obtain sponsorship for the blazers, caps, and badges. Initially, I specifically solicited assistance from former national and club players including Lawrence Rowe, Basil Williams, Linden Wright, Maurice Chung, Maurice Foster, Steve Ashman, and a number of cricket enthusiasts of the game. I continued this method of sponsorship for a number of years from small business owners. In later years, I was able to influence my friend Roy Holness, Managing Director of Sherwin Williams, to have his company's sponsorship of the team blazers for the last four years of my tenure as a JCA member before migrating to the USA.

The support of my former Jamaica teammate and fellow board member Maurice Foster was influential in securing the caps from a British firm for two of the years. During the last several years of my fourteen years as manager, I procured the team track suits sponsored by Economic Maintenance Products based at Heroes Circle in Kingston. Mr. Samuels, the Managing Director of the company, was a former player at the club level of Jamaica's cricket and an ardent follower of the game.

Before my time and during my tenure as Chairman of the youth selection committee, the trial invitees accompanied by a camp father, spent three weeks at Up Park Camp, the headquarters of the Jamaica Defense Force. The Army provided an instructor for early morning calisthenics followed by daily net sessions supervised by coaches appointed by the JCA.

For the 1984 youth camp, the former great West Indies batting star Rohan Kanhai started his contractual arrangement with the JCA as head coach to the national youth and senior teams. Unfortunately for the regional youth tournament in Barbados 1984, Kanhai did not accompany the team. During that period of the regional youth tournament, only one official was allowed to travel with the teams. I was named Manager Coach of the team for that year's tournament. As of 1985, all the teams were allowed the option of having a manager and a coach. The great former West Indies cricket captain and world class stroke-player began his active assignment at the regional youth tournament to Guyana in 1985 and continued to Trinidad 1986, Jamaica 1987, Barbados 1988 and Jamaica 1991 when his contract with the JCA ended. For family reasons, he was unavailable in 1989 and 1990. There were other excellent coaches who served the team during my tenure as manager. The list included Carlton Forbes Jamaica 1983, Renford Pinnock Guyana 1989, Jerry Reid Trinidad 1990, Guyana 1992 and St. Kitts 1993, and Junior Bennett Guyana 1994 and Grenada 1995.

Throughout the years at Camp, the players were addressed at different times by former Jamaica, West Indies players, Jamaica Umpire's Association representative; the players were also addressed professionally on etiquettes.

Days before the naming of players to the 1984 camp, I watched a Sunlight game at Kingston College home ground at Elletson Road. During the game, Vernon Smith, who was then a student at Dunoon Technical High School, approached me with high praises of his talent as a batsman and that he was looking forward to being invited to the youth camp. Having seen his team Dunoon Technical play earlier in the season, there was no one with the type of performance to have convinced me worthy to have been named to the camp. I had never seen or heard of the youngster before and was struck by his self-belief; the confidence was riveting to my ears. I informed him of the protocol in advising each player of his selection to the camp by means of a letter to the school and parents listing what the players needed to take to the camp. I further advised him that the printed and electronic media would be given the names for publication.

At the selection meeting of the invitees, I asked of my fellow selectors if they knew of Vernon Smith from Dunoon Technical High School; the response was in the negative.

The players having been notified of their selection, assembled at the Army main ground Up Park Camp where they were welcomed and addressed by the JCA Secretary and Chairman of the senior and youth selection committees. The players were implored to follow the guidelines as handed out and to be comforted as one of the top 26 -28 under-nineteen cricketers selected from hundreds at the level of their age group. The camp father, physical trainer, and coaching staff were introduced before they departed to the selected area of the JDF complex where they spent as one big family under the same roof for the next three weeks.

On the opening day practice session, I was standing over the wicket observing from close up the bowlers and batsmen demonstrating their skills under the supervision of the masterful Rohan Kanhai when I was called to the pavilion by Darby, the ground's curator. He mentioned that there was a youngster sitting under one of the trees and was disappointed in not receiving an invitation to the camp and wanted to hear from me why. As I approached the youngster and recognized who he was, I greeted him with pleasantries. He expressed displeasure not to have been among the campers and argued emphatically his competence as a batsman and that he was as good and even a better batsman than some at the camp. I was impressed with his self-belief and decided to have him show me what his batting skills were like. I consulted with the coach Rohan Kanhai that it was worth giving him the opportunity to back his assertion. He brought along his batting gear and was very confident about himself when facing the fast men and spinners with an array of wonderful stroke play, stroke play that won the acclamation of head coach Kanhai and me. I told Smith that his batting was impressive and that I would seek approval for his inclusion to the group from the Board Secretary who I expected to be arriving soon.

When Secretary Fennell arrived, I told him how important it was for Smith to have been included to the group. He reminded me of the financial constraint that would not have allowed for an additional player. I told the secretary that I would cover the cost to which he agreed. In the end, I never had to pay. I confirmed to Smith that he was officially named to join the camp and that I would give him a letter for his parents outlining his stay at camp and the items he needed to take with him and that he should return the following day to join the group. Surprisingly, he told me he brought along all he needed and that he told his parents to expect him back home in the next three weeks after the camp. He showed remarkable confidence. He believed in his ability and that he had a case to be made. It was the beginning of the Vernon Smith saga.

After a couple days of training, the first of three trial matches was played and in that game Smith batted once and scored a magnificent century. His stroke play was sublime; the array of shot making on that afternoon won the approval of the great former West Indies captain and batting star Rohan Kanhai. So impressive was his knock that the selectors were convinced that he would be a certainty when the squad was to be selected. Smith was elated about his century and expressed gratitude for his belated entry to the camp. I reassured him of the strong belief he had in his ability that I could not have ignored and that influenced my decision for him to be at the camp. He asked for the opportunity to prove his worth and he delivered emphatically under the watchful eyes of the great Rohan Kanhai and me. We were very impressed with his wide array of strokes; it was the beginning of a remarkable journey for Vernon Smith. He was named to the team and played brilliantly throughout the tournament.

Before the beginning of the camp, at a monthly meeting of the board, I was appointed manager and coach of the touring squad. At the same meeting, I was informed that the squad number was increased by one from thirteen to fourteen as was agreed by Cricket West Indies. At the end of the trials, the selectors were very impressed with the performances of the players, some of whom were   marginally ahead, especially in the batting department. The experience acquired as a captain through the earlier years with the Saints and as a national senior selector guided my judgement in assessment of players for national duties, and as chairman to be mindful and respectful of my fellow selectors' views on their evaluation.

A squad of fourteen players was selected with the experienced Patrick Harris returning as captain, a position he admirably occupied the year before leading the team to the finals against Barbados. The other squad members were Derron Dixon, James Adams, Vernon Smith, Wayne Sutherland, Larry Cunningham, Patrick Gayle, Paul Beckett, Dwight Meikle, Clinton Lewis, Rupert McKenzie, David Jackson, and Rohan Britton. The players were overjoyed with their selection. They congratulated each other and vowed to do well as a team. I congratulated the squad members and offered consolation to the players who missed out. While all the players were still in camp waiting to depart the following day for their respective homes, I received a call from the JCA Secretary Rex Fennell later that night at 8: PM with the breaking news that Cricket West Indies rescinded its earlier decision of increasing the squad of thirteen to fourteen and that a player would have to be left out of the Jamaica fourteen as named. Fortunately for the other teams, they had not yet named their squad whereas the Jamaica squad was already selected and the players informed. I was very disappointed by the revelation of the Secretary and the turn of events that followed.

The selectors were confronted with the unavoidable situation of leaving out Perry Jennings, who a day before, shared the joyous feeling with others named to the squad. It was heart-wrenching for me to have informed Jennings of the situation that he was left out and equally distressing for him and his close family members.

The squad members, smartly attired showing off their beautiful blazers, left Jamaica for Barbados with great expectation of doing well. The team performed creditably and well placed in a couple of the matches to win outright, but fell short in pursuit of victory. A number of the Jamaican players had notable performances with Wayne Sutherland and Vernon Smith among the leading batsmen of the tournament. The two batted with sureness throughout the tournament. Jimmy Adams had a very good tournament with his left arm deliveries and batting skills; his bowling was pivotal to our attack that kept the opposition batsmen in check with his cleverly controlled deliveries. Deron Dixon with bat and ball was impressive; he had complete control with his medium to fast deliveries, and with the bat, played attractively. Larry Cunningham was not as impressive as was expected; there was no denying his enormous batting talent. The wicket-keeper Patrick Gayle was very good at his craft and considered the best of the tournament wicket keepers. Paul Beckett the off spinner had a number of good spells; his returns did not reflect how well he bowled. The quick bowlers Dwight Meikle, Rupert McKenzie along with Clinton Lewis a medium pacer bowled impressively that augmented their talent for senior selection. David Jackson as a batsman showed potential and could have become a national senior prospect by regularly playing at the parish or senior cup levels. Rohan Britton's all-round ability showed promise but the presence of Adams limited his chances for inclusion to the team. Patrick Harris, the captain, was not at his fluent best as a batsman; he lacked consistency with the bat and when seemed poised for a good score, he was dismissed.

At the end of the tournament, I was one of the three West Indies youth selectors appointed for the selection of the West Indies youth team that played against England's youth team in a home series during1985. The selectors were Ricky Skerritt as chairman from St. Kitts where the selection of the squad was done; the other selector was Kenny Hobson of Grenada. The squad included Jamaicans Deron Dixon as vice-captain, Jimmy Adams, Patrick Gayle, and Vernon Smith. The selection of Smith was a remarkable story to be told to aspiring sportsmen. His miraculous rise to prominence at the West Indies age group level was extraordinary. He was not among the players initially called to the national youth trials. He was an unknown quality, and yet, when the team entered the plane for Barbados, he was aboard. The consistency of his batting in the tournament led to his inclusion to the West Indies youth team, a truly amazing journey for the unassuming Vernon Smith. Wayne Sutherland, Jamaica's top run scorer, missed being selected but just; his marvelous century at the Kensington Oval was an innings that showed his class as a very good prospect for senior national representation. Apart from the marvelous century, his consistency with the bat was compelling. He would have been named to the West Indies squad but for his age going into 1995. He was months over the age limit that made him ineligible for selection.

Figure 37 (L-R) Derron Dixon, Len Chamber (Manager), Patrick Harris (Captain) - Barbados 1984

Figure 38 Jamaica National Youth Players – Barbados, 1984: David Jackson & Wayne Sutherland

Figure 39 Wayne Sutherland

National Youth Team Fixture 1985

The regional youth tournament of 1985 was preceded by a tour of England's youth team to the Caribbean, beginning with a series of matches against their Jamaican age group. There were three one-day games at the Kirkvine Oval in Manchester and a three-day game at the Alpart ground in Saint Elizabeth. It was heartening to see the response of the crowds, especially at the three-day game in St. Elizabeth; spectators appeared to have occupied every conceivable area from which the game could have been watched. The England team management was headed by Bob Willis, the former England fast bowler and captain. Among the English players were a number of individuals who later became first class and test players, including Phil DeFreitas, the Dominica-born fast bowler. The Jamaica team missed not having their two most experience players Deron Dixon and Jimmy Adams. They were both named to the national senior team for the regional four-day competition. The senior team's first game was against Barbados at Sabina Park coinciding with the youth opening game against young England at the Kirkvine ground. The Jamaican players were mindful of their performances that would have had a bearing on selection to the squad for the 1985 regional youth tournament in Guyana.

Members of the squad for the series of matches against their English counterparts were Vernon Smith captain, Michael Laing, Paul Beckett, Perry Jennings, Patrick Gayle, Larry Cunningham, Deancourt Wright, Garfield Wildman, Delroy Morgan, Alton Turner, Kingsley Duncan, Nehemiah Perry, and Kenrick Dennis with Leonard Chambers as Manager Coach.

The newcomers to the team were Perry Jennings, Delroy Morgan, Kenrick Dennis, Nehemiah Perry, Garfield Wildman, Michael Laing, Kingsley Duncan, Alton Turner, and Deancourt Wright.

The mode of transportation for the Jamaica squad during the ten-day series as was decided by the JCA never met my approval. I had reservations with the arrangement and successfully got Franz Botec who was the CEO at The

Carreras Cigarette Company of Jamaica to make available one of his company staff buses to the Jamaica Cricket Association. Franz Botec was a former UWI and Kingston Cricket Club senior cup cricketer; he was pretty good as a batsman and had enormous love for the game. I played senior cup cricket against Botec's team UWI, and from the environment of the cricket fields and beyond, we enjoyed wonderful respect for each other. This worked in my favour for his generous contribution of the bus. The offer did not include a driver which I communicated to the Board. I was taken aback by Secretary Rex Fennell's answer: "The Board could not afford the cost of a driver and what it entails." I was truly disappointed and let Fennell know that I would take responsibility to be the driver. He replied, "Be safe and good luck."

The following day was an exceptional day of fun. The players boarded the bus at Sabina Park not expecting the driver to be me. Vernon Smith the captain asked, "Manage, where is the driver?" I replied, "He is in the driver's seat." Paul Beckett then asked, "Manage, can you handle the wheel?"

"Yes for sure," was my response.

Not all the team members boarded the bus at Sabina Park. Arrangements were made for Larry Cunningham, Deancourt Wright, and Kingsley Duncan to proceed to the Mandeville Hotel where the team was accommodated for the duration of our stay. Patrick Gayle boarded the bus just outside of Spanish Town. He recognized that I was sitting behind the steering wheel and uttered the words, "Manage, you are in the wrong seat. Where is the driver?"

"He is at the right place," I responded.

It was fun operating the bus with the players teasers, such as, "Driver, turn straight," "Driver, the gas pedal too heavy for you," "Driver, do you know where you are going?" "Driver, you are sweating." I was amused by the witticism and gracefully responded, "Tighten your seat belt. I will get you there," to tumultuous applause from the youngsters. The games were well contested and the local players expressed themselves with encouraging performances. The form shown by newcomers Delroy Morgan, Perry Jennings, and Garfield Wildman as batsmen was encouraging. The pacers Kenrick Dennis and Michael Laing were very inspiring and so was the bowling of Nehemiah Perry, the off-spinning all-rounder.

The three-fifty over matches played at Kirkvine and the three-day fixture at

Alpart in St. Elizabeth were well contested. Skipper Vernon Smith was inspirational and made an impression as a good leader and would have been seriously considered for the leadership of the team to Guyana but for the experienced Deron Dixon and Jimmy Adams.

At the end of the tour, Bob Willis in a one-on-one conversation with me was unequivocal in his compliments of the Jamaican players. He identified Delroy Morgan, Perry Jennings, Larry Cunningham, Garfield Wildman, and Vernon Smith as very good batting material to work with and he was also impressed with the glove work of Patrick Gayle. The famous former England fast bowler and captain who finished his test career with 325 wickets from 90 matches lauded the Jamaican fast bowlers Michael Laing, Kenrick Dennis, and Deancourt Wright as young pacers who would get quicker and better with extended exposure as they moved into their early twenties. The former England skipper commented on Paul Beckett the Off Spinner, "He has such a beautiful off spinning action with a lovely loop reminiscent of Jim Laker, the great England Off spinner," remarked the former England captain.

At the end of the young England tour and a successful camp, Deron Dixon was named captain with Jimmy Adams as the vice-captain for the 1985 regional youth tournament held in Guyana; included in the squad was Perry Jennings who unfortunately, had to be left out of the squad the year before. The full squad was Deron Dixon captain, Jimmy Adams, Delroy Morgan, Larry Cunningham, Vernon Smith, Perry Jennings, Paul Beckett, Michael Laing, Patrick Gayle, Kenrick Dennis, Dalkeith Dempster, Kingsley Duncan and Lucal White with the West Indian stroke player Rohan Kanhai as coach and me as manager.

Our team performed admirably and just missed topping the points table ahead of Guyana the host country. The Jamaica team played consistently well and positioned themselves as the team likely to have won the tournament. Unfortunately, the field decisions in our game against the host country thwarted our victory effort that would have made us the champions. Our coach, the great former Guyana and West Indian batsman Rohan Kanhai, was outraged with the officiating bias of the two Guyanese umpires. The partiality was an experience that the young players of both teams should not have been subjected to at the level of the regional tournament. Brian Davis, the former West Indies test batsman who was the Trinidad manager, commended the Jamaican batsmen for their excellent batting prowess when the two teams met. The comments came after the Trinidadians set Jamaica a total in excess of 300 which we surpassed with superb batting from our batsmen.

"Len, I never expected your team was capable of surmounting the total we set you, not against our attack, I told my lads that the Jamaicans are gifted stroke players but the total was beyond their grasp," echoed Davis.

When Davis and I as West Indies youth selectors met to name two players from the Northern Telecom tournament for advanced coaching in Australia, he again expressed his impression of our batsmen Larry Cunningham, Perry Jennings, Delroy Morgan, Deron Dixon, and Jimmy Adams as fundamentally prepared for the next level of West Indies cricket. He predicted that Jimmy Adams would become a West Indian test player of eminence and that Morgan, Cunningham, and Jennings were special batting talent. Davis was also complimentary of the Jamaicans Paul Beckett the Off spinner and wicketkeeper Patrick Gayle. From a team perspective, Vernon Smith underperformed; his splendid showing the tournament before augured well for him to perform successfully on the batting wickets of Guyana; sadly, his performance could not match his 1984 superb runs scoring.

Northern Telecom as sponsors of the tournament, lasted for several years. The PR Personnel's interaction with team managers, coaches, and players, and the presentation of mementos were greatly appreciated. Northern Telecom, the gargantuan communications company, extended their interest in the development of Cricket West Indies by sponsorship of two players from the 1985 tournament to Australia for advanced coaching.

The richness of talent was in abundance; selection of the two Carl Hooper and Kenny Benjamin were exceptional choices. Carl Hooper, the elegant stroke player was exceptional; he played fluently on either side of the wicket with consummate ease and was likened to the classical Lawrence Rowe. He appeared destined for senior West Indies colours and so was Kenny Benjamin. Benjamin, a six-footer, was quick, accurate, and menacing; his rhythmic run up was impressive and was considered the best fast bowling prospect of the tournament. Hooper and Benjamin spent some time in Jamaica before being granted visas for the Australia visit.

There was no Australian consulate in Antigua nor Guyana, resulting in their stay in Jamaica while awaiting travel clearances. I was the Liaison to the two budding stars, both of whom were accommodated at the Sandhurst Hotel and they enjoyed the best Jamaican courtesies over a prolong stay in the island. As their Liaison, I was privileged and I valued the memorable experiences with the two talented youngsters and their teenage friends fellow youth players Deron Dixon and Jimmy Adams. The four regularly visited the Carib Cinema and for ice cream treats at Devon House; they also had a couple of visits to Sports Minister Edmond Bartlett's government home where Dixon resided. Dixon was the nephew of the Sports Minister. On a couple of Saturdays, Hooper and Benjamin accompanied me to our local senior cup matches while Adams and Dixon were representing their clubs Kingston and Melbourne, respectively.

The Remarkable Jimmy Adams

Through the years, there were players who while eligible for selection to the national youth were considered good enough to have represented the national senior team. Jimmy Adams and Deron Dixon were in that grouping. They both made their debut against Barbados at Sabina Park in 1985 with impressive performance. Surprisingly, both were unceremoniously dropped during the earlier   years of their career, a decision that infuriated me as a selector. I had no part in the selection process. The two young players were members of the Jamaica team in an ongoing four-day regional match at Sabina Park. As I entered the parking area of the Headley stand that Sunday morning before the commencement of the last day's play and having parked my car, I was met by an enraged Rohan Kanhai.

"Len, how could you be a party to the dropping of the two youngsters Deron and Jimmy?" yelled the fuming former West Indies champion batsman.

"What are you talking about Rohan?"

Chester Watson, the chairman of the selection committee told me that the team would be selected sometime between lunch and tea time today. Kanhai, still exasperated, concluded that the team was selected the night before. I was disturbed by the selection process of deception that left me dumbfounded. Kanhai was always impressed with the talent of Adams and Dixon. He worked with both at four and three youth camps respectively, and at regional youth tournaments.

"They are young, talented players that needed the exposure. They need to play," reiterated an upset Kanhai.

I shared Kanhai's assessment of the two young players, both of whom I was privileged to have seen while I was manager of the national youth team from their earlier years. It was wrong to have changed the time of the selection without me been notified. Following the conversation with Kanhai, I immediately lodged a complaint to President Allan Rae.

The President expressed surprise seeing that the night before the other selectors with the captain Michael Holding having a meeting in the Secretary's box without me been present. The President assured me that he would address the issue with Watson and that he was extremely disappointed with the omission of the two youngsters and made the comment: "Adams and Dixon dropped? Really?" Adams was not discouraged by the early setback and with admirable resolve, went on to be a permanent fixture in the Jamaica team, a team he later became captain of. Adams' consistency as a batsman added to his ability as a left arm spinner and a brilliant fieldsman in any position and was rewarded with test match status later on. The talented batting all-rounder from his youth years was seen and acknowledged by many across the region, starting with his home country Jamaica to Barbados, Guyana, and Trinidad as an emerging star. His batting and bowling skills were attributes that contributed to his progression to national and international representation. At the international level, Adams amassed a run glut of amazing consistency that separated his valued performances from other leading batsmen. Adams' remarkable batting talent was blessed with an uncomplicated basic mindset to achieve; his disciplined training habits were a factor to his successes. The ability and impetus for his runs scoring accomplishment was highlighted by the recognition conferred on him as the top international test batsman at a time when there were so many top-class batsmen in the game.

Of his 54 test matches, the first 12 were very special, with an aggregate of 1,132 runs; only the great Sir Donald Bradman had a better record in his first 12 test matches.

Adams became captain of the West Indies team, replacing his great mate Brian Lara who he first met in the 1986 Northern Telecom West Indies youth tournament played in Trinidad. Adams, with a test career of 54 matches aggregating 3,012 runs at an average of 41.26 with a top score of 208 not out with 6 hundreds and 14 fifty's placed him in the comfort zone as a very good test batsman. Adams was relieved of the West Indies captaincy and at the same time dropped from the team. The decision created disquiet by followers of Jamaica's cricket; losing the captaincy was not as concerning as being dropped from the team. The dropping of the much-admired Adams was a talking point amongst the Jamaican cricket fraternity, a fraternity that held their attention from his adolescent years. Adams' test debut in 1992 against

South Africa in Barbados was met with acclamation by the sporting fraternity of his homeland Jamaica. Having played nine years at the international level, he was no longer a test player after the last test of the West Indies 2001 Australian tour played at Sydney. His performance at the test level was good; the termination of his test career at age thirty-three was baffling when there was so much international cricket left in the gifted allrounder.

Adams' cricketing career included playing league cricket in Durham, representing the English County Nottinghamshire, South Africa's Orange Free State Berkshire, Secretary of the West Indies Players Association, President of the Federation of International Cricket Association (FICA)head coach at Kent after serving as "Technical Director of Cricket to the Jamaica Cricket Association." Adams is currently, in the year 2024, the Director of Cricket for Cricket West Indies.

Jimmy Adams' road to success as a cricketer had setbacks dating back to when he first represented the national youth team at age fifteen. He withstood adversities during his illustrious career to the successes he achieved along his admirable journey, a journey of respect and goodwill to fellow cricketers and officialdom. A remarkable and revered Jamaica and West Indies sports personality is James Adams. There are experiences with the gifted Adams that linger. I was enthralled by a letter of congratulation from Adams to me on the 1990 championship victory of the national youth team while he was away from Jamaica. The Jamaica team was winning the coveted trophy for the first time in the last ten years. "So many years as the Brides Maid, we are now the Bride," quoted Adams in the letter. Adams was a member of the youth team for five years 1983 to 1987; during that time, we were runners-up on three to four occasions in close finishes that characterized our standing until our glorious triumph in 1990. There was an example of extraordinary love and commitment for the game of cricket shown by the esteemed Jamaica College, Kingston Cricket Club, Jamaica and West Indies sports Icon, when in 1985 before leaving for the regional youth tournament in Guyana, there was a game with the youth team and a JCA eleven at Kensington Park. Among the officials from the JCA was Professor Gladstone Mills who had attended Jamaica College, just like Jimmy who at the time was a student of the famous boys high School. He asked of me for an introduction to the young Adams. Professor Mills expressed pleasantries to Jimmy and then, "I take it that after high school you will be attending a University to further your studies?" asked the Professor.

"To the University of Cricket," replied Jimmy Adams.

In 1995 while in the departure lounge at the Norman Manley International Airport, Gareth Breese, Andre Coley as players, and I as manager of the young West Indies team were preparing to depart on a flight to Trinidad where the first of a series of matches was played against England's Youth team, other matches were played in Barbados, Guyana, St. Kitts and St. Vincent, when Adams unexpectedly entered the departure lounge to see us off. He expressed congratulations to us and his well-measured words of encouragement to the two youngsters were inspirational. As I listened to Adams' and his articulation of what it meant as a Jamaican to represent the West Indies team carried responsibility of significance.

Adams implored the two young Jamaicans to represent the team embodied with self-esteem and unmatched togetherness as a team. Adams, at the time of his encouraging talk with the two young cricketers was a current and successful West Indies player. It was comforting to both Breese and Coley who were cognizant of Adams' prowess as a player having represented Jamaica and the West Indies youth teams during his teenage years. Adams' excellent encouragement to the two youngsters was reassuring and characteristic of the individual he was and continues to be, always inspiring others to do well. His achievements through the years have not changed his demeanor; his humbleness personified his remarkable character. On the flight to Trinidad, the players were thrilled that Adams took time out to have had that talk with them.

That is who Jimmy Adams was and still is, always there for others.

Adams' contribution to the game on the field and administratively is well-documented. To have met him during the formative years of his cricketing journey starting at the Sunlight schoolboy competition and regional youth cricket, a period that I was the manager of the Jamaica under-nineteens to his current top position as Director of Cricket for Cricket West Indies in 2023 is a privilege, and his accomplishments characterize him as exceptional for his diverse services to the sport of cricket. It was most fitting for the Jamaica Government to have bestowed on Jimmy Adams the Order of Distinction in acknowledgement of his tremendous value and contribution to the game nationally and internationally. The recognition was richly deserving of a true son of his beloved country and was welcome unreservedly by the wider Caribbean region that he aptly represented as a player and administrator.

I was privileged to have shared the same platform with the International Cricket Icon Jimmy Clive Adams, when on that night in New York October 6, 2018, we were both inducted to the USA Cricket Hall of Fame in the International Category. The setting at the ballroom of the Hilton Hotel nearby the Kennedy Airport was a night of glitter attended by USA Congress woman Yvette Clarke, State Representatives, Diplomats, and dignitaries from the cricket fraternity headed by the then Cricket West Indies President Dave Cameron.

Figure 40 Jimmy Adams

Leonard Chambers

The Gifted Marlon Tucker

Through the years at the leadership level, Jamaica has had exceptional cricket captains, most of whom were recognized starting at the schoolboy competitions (Headley and Sunlight). There were others who were identified at the senior cup and parish competitions. At the schoolboy level was the beginning for the talented Marlon Tucker; he was gifted with incomparable astuteness as a cricket captain. His shrewdness at the helm was remarkable and won praises and acknowledgement from the leaders of Jamaica's cricket and followers of the game. Tucker's meteoric rise to Jamaica's senior regional captaincy was predictable; he replaced the great Jamaica and West Indies wicketkeeper batsman Jeffrey Dujon who ascended to the leadership role when Lawrence Rowe lost the captaincy for the contentious tour of South Africa. As a captain, Tucker was very special; the respect of the players he led at the different levels responded with admiration. He was well-prepared for the job, having been the captain at Kingston College, Jamaica youths, West Indies youths and JCA Under 25 in the Islands local Red Stripe competition, a competition where I was the manager for a couple of years. Tucker's shrewd captaincy won the approval, not only of the players he led, but also the fans and administrations around the region. Many from Jamaica's cricket fraternity thought that Tucker would have been the preferred choice of the Jamaica Cricket Association to have succeeded Lawrence Rowe and not Jeffrey Dujon as the national senior captain. When the JCA convened at a special meeting and decided Rowe's successor, both Dujon and Tucker were nominated with Dujon overwhelmingly supported for the position.

Before Tucker's captaincy, there were several who had the distinction of the leadership of Jamaica's team, including Jackie Hendricks, Easton Morris, Maurice Foster, Basil Williams, Lawrence Rowe, Jeffrey Dujon, and Michael Holding, all of whom were former West Indies players. Surprisingly, there were complaints from players about the indifferent attitude of certain captains that caused uneasiness; some players were disgruntled and lacked the confidence to perform as was reported to the selectors.

The emergence of Marlon Tucker at the helm was refreshing; the team members were imbued with confidence. Having watched like most fans, the progression of Tucker's cricket from that day when the great Sir Garfield Sobers predicted that the preteen prodigy was one with a bright future, the measured views of the great Sir Garfield Sobers on young Tucker was followed with keen interest.

The former West Indies captain, Sobers, was conducting a coaching session at Boys Town, the institution where his late friend and former West Indies teammate Collie Smith started his cricket journey. Sobers' visit to the celebrated club in a community that gave birth to the legendary Colie Smith was the respect he had for a teammate and a friend, a friend who was revered as a paradigm for the young and grownups of the Boys Town community. The awareness as to the early journey of the gifted Marlon Tucker's progression was followed with profound interest, an interest injected by the prediction of cricket immortal the great former West Indies captain Sir Garfield Sobers. Having served as manager of Jamaica's under twenty-five team in the local Red Stripe competition captained by Marlon Tucker, I was privy to his perceptiveness in the leadership role, a position he relished and was most comfortable in. On the field, Tucker's captaincy was positive, his game awareness was admirable, and the players responded effectively.

It was the dream of most, if not all, young sportsmen to have the satisfaction of having represented their country at their specific sport of choice. So many cricketers with cherished intent for success failed in their pursuit, unsuccessful not because of talent; they possessed inherent ability, but the competitiveness created challenges for selection in a team. So often it was settled with just one or two places to be filled, particularly at the senior level of Jamaica's cricket. There were aspirants by discipline and purposeful training habits who achieved their revered goals. In a team sport such as cricket, the Jamaican players were expected to be led in an atmosphere of respectability by a captain whose responsibility it was to be inspirational. The captain must show leadership with respect to all players and most importantly, the newcomers for a sense of belonging. There were so many young talented players who had the confidence of the selectors to perform and established in the ideal framework of the team. The lack of player management was a most important factor to the player's mindset; it was incumbent on our captains to ease any form of trepidation by lifting the confidence level among the players. Most, if not all, of Jamaica senior captains before Tucker were all test players and it was the expectation of successive selection committees that the players in their charge would be in a conducive team environment.

The captaincy appointment of the gifted Marlon Tucker was well received by the players and fans alike; his appointment to the top post was long-awaited.

The all-round quality of his game at all levels was very impressive and once he settled in the Jamaica team, his ascendancy to the captaincy was predicted. As a JCA member and close to the selection policy in the capacity as secretary to the selectors and then as a selector, it was my personal belief that Marlon was well prepared for the leadership role. As captain, the atmosphere in the dressing room demonstrated a sense of togetherness within the team structure; every player understood their role and that was the situation with Tucker at the helm.

During the period of the eighties before and after Marlon's captaincy to the mid-nineties, there was a preponderance of young talented players parading their skills at the local level with the likes of Mark Neita, Wayne Lewis, Odelmo Peters Nigel Kennedy, Dereck Francis, Robert Haynes, Kenneth McLeod, Delroy Morgan, Nemiah Perry, Laurie Cunningham, Franz Cunningham, Aaron Daley, Cleveland Davidson, Paul Ellis, Courtney O'Connor, George Herron, Alexander Morgan, Patrick Patterson, Jimmy Adams, Everton Coach, Patrick Gayle, Robert Samuels, Deron Dixon, Richard Staple, Paul Palmer, Joseph Grant the fast bowler, Hopeton Barrett, and there were Michael Holding, Courtney Walsh, Patrick Patterson, and Jeffrey Dujon; by then the four were well established at the international level.

It was from this group of talented players that the selectors were able to assemble the teams of 1988, 1989, and 1990 led by the amazing Marlon Tucker to Jamaica's back-to-back championship honours in 1988 and 1989, and denied a three-peat in 1990 by the inclement weather that prevented a ball being bowled in the third and fourth matches after wonderful results in the first two games.

Tucker's gift as a captain was known to most and when leadership was entrusted on him, the true value of his captaincy acumen was exemplified. He created an atmosphere of trust among the players and won their confidence as a leader. His method of one-on-one and collectively with team members built that respect and trust.

After three years as captain of the Jamaica senior team, Marlon Tucker's favourability was elevated to immeasurable heights; the successes he had as captain of the national senior team superseded that of captains before him. He was recognized as one of the most revered sportsmen in the country when surprisingly, he stepped away from the game after India's tour game against Jamaica in 1991. Tucker, who toured Zimbabwe with the West Indies A team in the eighties just wanted a break from the game. Marlon, admired by so many, found that the once enthusiastic and heartening feeling as a first-class player was waning. He advised the JCA of his retirement and expressed thanks for the opportunity afforded him to have captained the national youth and senior teams. The JCA acknowledged his remarkable service to the game and wished for him the very best. Tucker's absence from the glamour and stardom of the regional game was self-imposed before his departure for the USA.

Figure 41 Jamaica Local U-25 Red Stripe Team. Standing L-R: Hopeton Barrett, Everton Coach, Leroy Gordon, Cleveland Davidson, Milton Taylor, Glen Atkins, Leonard Chambers (manager). Sitting L-R: Patrick Patterson, Odelmo Peters, Wayne Lewis, Marlon Tucker (captain), Mark Neita, Alexander Morgan.

Figure 42 Sir Garfield Sobers with Marlon Tucker - Boys Town, Summer of 1972

Figure 43 Jamaica Regional Red Stripe Cup Champions – 1989. Standing L-R: David Bernard, Patrick Gayle, Delroy Morgan, Aaron Daley, Nehemiah Perry, Courtney Walsh, Patrick Patterson, Jimmy Adams, Wayne Lewis, and Cleveland Davidson. Sitting L-R: Michael Holding, Robert Haynes, Marlon Tucker (Captain), George Sterling (Manager), Jeffrey Dujon, and Mark Neita.

Contentious Tour to South Africa

T he absence of Lawrence Rowe, Richard Austin, Everton Mattis, and Herbert Chang from Jamaica's national team in the 1980's created vulnerability in our batting strength. The quartet were all West Indian players with years of quality cricket left in them and so it was with the fiery fast bowler Ray Wynter. Wynter, although uncapped at the test level, was about the fastest of our bowlers in the region and had a lot to have offered Jamaica's cricket. The unauthorized tour by the five enraged the region for different reasons. Some showed preference to the government in castigating the players, whereas others displayed magnanimity to their cause. The benevolence of some towards the players plying their trade as they advocated as a concept to attract people of colour, the opportunity of seeing the games and to help in the healing of racial discrimination, somewhat gave them hope that there was support for their cause.

The composition of the West Indies squad was former test cricketers and others without test appearances. It was apparent at the time that the only player in the entire group who might have had a chance for selection to the first choice West Indies team was Colin Croft; the others were out of favour with the selectors. There was apprehension amongst members of the Jamaica Cricket Association; they had no confirmation of the tour and tried to obtain from the players supposed to have been selected but to no avail. About that time, there was a tour by Bermuda to Jamaica for a number of matches, including a three-day game at Sabina Park against a Jamaica eleven captained by Lawrence Rowe beginning on a Friday and ending two days later. At the end of the match on that Sunday evening, Lawrence Rowe asked Linden Wright and I to have a walk with him to his car. Our walk was from the players' enclosure situated at ground level of the George Headley stand to the back of the Kingston club pavilion where Rowe's eye-catching maroon colour Volvo was parked. It was known to most at the time that Rowe, Wright, and Basil Williams were very good friends. Some fans dubbed them "The Three Musketeers." The three considered me a big brother and a friend.

The friendship continued through the years to this day but for the sad passing of Basil Williams October 2015.

It came as no surprise that Rowe wanted to share with Linden and I what was on his mind. I was, however, surprised and unprepared for what he revealed to us. He started out by saying:

"What I am about to say is extremely confidential and should not be told to anyone. There is a tour to South Africa by a West Indian team that is in the final stages with all the players confirming their availability and I was named captain of the team."

Rowe further explained that there was a clause in the contract that the players should remain silent about the tour before departure. Knowing that for any West Indian as an individual or as a team was forbidden to tour the Apartheid country of South Africa, a decision agreed on by the ICC and must be adhered to by all affiliates, left me momentarily flabbergasted.

Rowe explained that he had given serious thought to the tour and he felt by the team going would help towards the healing of the South African people, especially the ones of colour, and that sports could be an integral component of that process. Wright and I gave Rowe the assurance that we respected his views and as friends would not divulge to anyone, regardless.

Surprisingly, the following day Monday at 6:25 am, I received a call from Hugh Crosskill, Sports commentator at the Jamaica Broadcasting Corporation. Crosskill enquired if I knew of an intended tour of West Indian players to be led by Rowe to South Africa and that both Wright and I were seen in the company of Rowe walking to the back of the Kingston Cricket Club members pavilion the evening before. Crosskill alleged that Rowe discussed the tour of South Africa with us. Crosskill, a leading Jamaican sports commentator, wanted me to confirm that the tour was on. It was inconceivable that I would break the confidentiality of my agreement with Rowe. I simply told Crosskill that as friends, we were talking generally about our lives. A couple days after (Tuesday) was the monthly meeting of the Jamaica Cricket Associations. A glance at the Agenda was the item "South Africa tour." When we got to that item, I was asked by the President Allan Rae if I knew about the tour and that it was being rumored that Rowe had a conversation with Wright and I related to the intended tour. At that time, Wright was not yet a member of the Jamaica Cricket Association. I replied that the conversation we had was about our lives as friends. The President then said, "Next item, please." There were members who wanted to have had their say and felt that I should have revealed to the Board what I knew about the rumored tour but President Rae the wisely lawyer, never allowed the discussion to be prolonged. After an adherence to a pledge that lasted for 36 years, I got permission from Rowe on February 6, 2019, that I could break my silence about what I knew then, if ever I was asked about the tour that branded the players as Rebels.

Evaluating the absence of the five, especially the batsmen Rowe, Austin, Chang, and Mattis created a vacuum in the stability of Jamaica's batting. They were, along with the masterful stroke player Jeffrey Dujon, the mainstay of the Jamaican batting line-up. There was no doubt that the absence of the gifted four from the playing fields of Jamaica was felt; they had so much cricket left in them. The decision of the five Jamaicans to disregard nonparticipation by cricketing nations to the Apartheid country of South Africa, a ruling that was established by the International Cricket Council (ICC) the world governing body of cricket continued to be a mixed-reaction amongst the Jamaican public. Other countries were more lenient to their players, including England's Graham Gooch and the Barbadian Ezra Moseley, whilst the Jamaican were banned from participation at the club and national levels. A poll conducted by the esteemed Pollster Carl Stone identified 70% of the Jamaican public had no consternation at the players going to the country where apartheid was prevalent.

The prospect for a number of our talented batsmen who were in and out of the team and others on the fringe to address the selectors was incumbent on them now that Rowe, Austin, Mattis, and Chang were no longer eligible for selection. The succeeding years proved the reliability of the batting pool. A number of younger players coming through the regional youth tournaments and our local competitions dealt with the transition admirably. There were obvious challenges within the group, challenges to impress the selectors for inclusion and be a mainstay in the team.

There were a number of players who were subjected to one or two appearances at the national level. To me, it was a system that required introspection of the selection policy. Once a player performed impressively at the Senior cup and Parish competitions and followed with convincing performances at the trials and selected to the national team, such a player should be valued and given a run of at least three to four games instead of the in and out system after one or two games.

Thanks to the Jamaica captain Easton McMorris, his belief in Lawrence Rowe's enormous ability had an influence on the selectors to have overlooked the eventual cricket immortal substandard early performances. The purest of stroke players, the gifted Rowe was a failure in his first three games that were all played away from home. Rowe was selected for his fourth game against Guyana played at Sabina Park, a game in which he displayed his wide range of beautiful shots from backward point to long leg, bisecting the fielders who would frustratingly retrieve the ball after crossing the boundary to the delight of the adoring Jamaican fans. The champion batsman went on to become the stroke making darling of the Jamaican cricket fraternity; his mastery and crease management was a treat to the region and beyond.

Figure 44 Lawrence Rowe. Test cricket immortal on his debut, Sabina Park, Kingston, Jamaica 1972.

A Plethora of Talent

In the earlier years of the '50s to the end of the '80s, the standard of the senior cup and cricket in the parishes was remarkable; the games were highly competitive with a galaxy of talented batsmen showcasing their amazing skills against well-balanced bowling attacks. The teams had in their ranks batsmen one to six known for their exciting and attractive stroke-play and well-balanced bowling attacks. The opening bowlers, most of whom were very quick on pitches that were properly rolled, offered encouragement to bowlers and batsmen.

The matches attracted sizeable crowds; some grounds, especially at the senior cup, the fans paid at the gate with no regrets. They got value for the excellent performances provided. The entertainment exceeded the cost of admission, as many alluded to. It was a period in Jamaica's cricket when the sport was well-organized at the different levels; the senior cup and the parish competitions were feature attractions; the admirably structured Rural Sugar Estates competitions played on midweek attracted large attendances. A significant number of the Sugar Estates players were representatives of Parish teams with a minute number journeying to play in the Kingston-based senior cup.

The regular tours by visiting teams of past and current International and first-class cricketers participating in matches against the West Indies, Jamaica's Senior and Jamaica's Colts, Combined Parishes etc. across the sphere of the island helped significantly in bolstering the popularity of the sport. So many local players performed admirably in our domestic competitions and were deservingly rewarded for places against the multitalented overseas teams. There were others with matching local performances and were never selected, not even to the national trials, such was the magnitude of truly very good players causing intense competitiveness for places.

The plethora of excellent players that existed in the island was of established value to the respectable standard of the game and was profoundly idolized by the fans. The players identified below were excellent performers for their respective senior cup teams and had strong support for recognition by the selectors. The bowling of pacers Lester King, Harold Price, Tom Dewdney, Esmond Kentish, Chester Watson, Henry Sewell, Louis Teape, Stanley Goodridge, Percy Tomlinson, Junior Williams, Uton Dowe, Kenneth Barnett, Junior Hall, Patrick Patterson, Neville Brown, Edwin Calneck, Alvin Rose, Roy McCatty, Glen Aikman, Ray Wynter, Ivan Richards, Wesley Taylor, Frank Brown, Lloyd Seivright, Hopeton Barrett, Cecil Lawson, Vincent McKayle, Castel Folkes, Eric Hentley, Michael Archer, Clem Thompson, Carlton Gordon, Bob Allen, John Earle, Michael Mitchell, Michael Holding, Gregory Brown, Barrington Saunders, Glen Atkins, and Glen Aikman stood out.

There were a number of fast bowling allrounders who stood out consistently with the ball. The names include Calbert Minott, Everett Whittingham, Aaron Daley, William Haye, Lloyd Ross, Earle Daley, Livern Wellington, and John Mercurios. The spinners Left Arm, Right Arm, Leg and Off were aplenty, the left arm spinners included Alfred Valentine, George Mudie, Bob Maragh, Miguel Walker, George Prescod, Ronald Tomlinson, Roy Deleon, Charlton Barrett, David Henry, Bruce Wellington, Lloyd Morgan, Carlton Forbes, Ferdie McDonald, Basil McLean, Donavan Malcolm, Carl Henry, Oscar Hamilton, Robert Scarlett, Courtney Daley, and Hylton Gordon.

The Right Arm leg spinners were Vivian Archer, Vinnie Binns, Leonard Mullings, Colin Gordon, Canute Kelly, Linden Wright, Lawson Matthews, Robert Haynes, Harold Phillips, Leroy Gordon, Bobby Hall, Darnell Buckles, Arthur Barrett, Harold Richardson and the Off Spinners, Leonard Levy, Robert Berry, Reggie Scarlett, Bobby Young, Walford Williams, VG Rose, Laker Levers, Basil Brown, Edward Cox Ralph, Frankie Lewis, Ronnie Savariau, Clive Campbell, George Herdsman, Colin Hinds, Othneil Miles, Neville Hawkins, and Errol Wilson. It is noteworthy that a number of the spinners were considered bowling all-rounders.

The wealth of our batsmen was in abundance including the likes of Allan Rae, Easton McMorris, Neville Bonitto, Maurice Foster, Owen Mitchell, Teddy Griffiths, Renford Pinnock, Herman Bennett, Keith Pryce, Gerald Charlton, Buddy Josephs, Dixie Adams, Peter Taylor, Horace Reid, Ferdie

Harvey, Dennis Thorbourne, Herbert Bailey, JK Holt Jr. Joe Carter, Ken Rickards, EB King, Franklyn Dennis, Winston Davis, Gerald Wollaston, Colin Fletcher, Donald Morgan, Mark Neita, Delroy Morgan, John Gordon, Wayne Lewis, Vin Lumsden, Jimmy Cameron, Donald Edwards, John Prescod Snr., John Prescod Jr, Joe Henry, Johnny McLeod, Sola Binns, Boris Smith, Neville Glanville, Lloyd Dyer, Alexander Charvis, Lloyd Dunbar, Abe Bailey, Allan Alberga, Fitz Nangle, Canute Bartley, Lawrence Rowe, Elroy Campbell, Milton Wisdom, George Pullum Smith, Arthur McKenzie Jr., Bunny Goodison, Donavan Ferguson, Neville Walker, Arthur Brown, Clinton Johnson, Bunny Shaw, George Chambers, Trevor Henry, Sam Morgan, Desmond Lewis, Neville McKoy, Robert Clarke, Medroy Williams, Terrence Corke, Herbert Gordon aka Dago, Herbert Chang, Richard Austin, Jeffrey Dujon, Lincoln Sterling, and Basil Williams.

The categories of Bowlers and batsmen were of genuine quality. To have watched the crème of our batsmen facing up to the excellence of our bowlers weekend after weekend was enthralling. The categories of player's specialty as mentioned, some were considered all-rounders, I elected to place them in the category that they were most effective in. The wicketkeepers were brilliant against pace and spin. It was great watching them in action; their efficiency to the spinners and pacers was absolutely amazing. Most of the keepers were very capable batsmen including Allie Binns, Jackie Hendricks, Gerry Alexander, George Clarke, Freddie Brown, Anthony Campbell, Fitz Nangle, Desmond Lewis, Prince Francis, Roy Paul, Hume Parris, Junior Powell, Jeffrey Dujon, Leroy Dago Gordon, Victor Hunter, George Richards aka Bula John, Patrick Gayle, Renford Pinnock, Aston Sherwood, Ruddy Marzouca, Delroy Bembridge, and Junior Powell. All the players mentioned were seen by me. I played with most and some I would have seen while scoring the board and book for Saint Catherine Cricket Club before becoming a senior cup player.

The matches were given extensive coverage before and after each round by the printed and electronic media; radio commentaries were provided on games considered the feature game of the round. The score sheets of the latest round of matches were published in the Daily Gleaner Sport page on Wednesdays /Thursdays of each week, "It was cricket, lovely cricket" at the grounds Saturdays and Sundays. Cricket was played and enjoyed by the populace of the country from the villages to the main clubs and grounds; as a player, you were very special.

It was disappointing that cricket in the rural parishes never had the coverage enjoyed by the city clubs. There were several outstanding players who performed exceptionally at the parish competitions and were never seen by the national selectors. There was the occasional breakthrough by a minute number called to the national trials. Their wonderful bowling performances could not be overlooked. It would have been a travesty of justice were they not selected to the national senior team. The spinners were Wilbert Plummer, Errol Rattigan, Neil HoSang, Lloyd Williams, and Samuel Francis who was born in St .Vincent and moved to Jamaica where he represented Manchester. The wicketkeeper Hume Paris and batsman Trevor Henry from Trelawny and St Ann, respectively, were also selected to the national senior team.

Figure 45 Roy McCatty. Lucas Cricket Club and Jamaica fast bowler – Queen's Park Oval, Trinidad – 1969

Figure 46 Mark Neita

Figure 47 Wayne Lewis – Jamaica National Batsman
A Sensational stroke player

A Son's Passion

During my years of service as a member of the Jamaica Cricket Association, serving on multiple committees did not distract from my responsibility with the Saint Catherine Cricket Club. From the first of the 23 three consecutive years I served the governing body of Jamaica's cricket. I was the captain and assistant secretary of Saint Catherine Cricket Club. After my retirement from the game, I had designated responsibility as First VP, Chairman of the Senior Selection Committee, Team Manager, and Club Captain.

The years as a national Senior and Youth selector for twelve and thirteen years respectively, and as Manager of the Youth team for thirteen years, allowed me to interact with the parents of youth players and frequently invited as a special speaking guest at schools, Parish Associations and club events. My tenure as manager of the Jamaica's Youth team and that as Chairman of the youth selection committee was a period of understanding the lives of the young aspiring cricketers.

There were the parents who would call and talk about the life of their sons balancing the game with school curriculum; it was a situation that I was familiar with as a father. My son Rohan, from preteen years through high school, demonstrated an absolute passion for the game. He had his own bat at a very early age and used every opportunity to play with neighboring youngsters without neglecting his school curriculum. Additionally, he accompanied me to matches where he was able to see players at the city and rural grounds, his presence at senior cup matches created the opportunity for him to have scored the book for Saint Catherine Cricket Club at the tender age of nine.

Rohan, still at age nine, was privileged to have scored the book at a JCA senior trial match at Melbourne Park. During the early stages of the game, the umpires had difficulty recognizing his responses to their signals. Gifford Anderson, one of the umpires, suggested that because of his height, he should sit in an area where he would be more discernable. Conforming to the Umpire's suggestion, it was comical to hear the screeching of the chair on the concrete each time he got up to acknowledge the umpire's signals. Another aspect of Rohan's love for the game was that he expanded his knowledge by reading cricket books from my wide collection. At a JCA match at Chedwin Park, there was an interruption of play because of rain. During the delay, there was a chit chat amongst a group of approximately eight veterans of the game, including Maurice Foster, Len Levy, and I. We were uncertain as to Sir Garfield Sobers test aggregate at the end of his remarkable career when Rohan said, "8032." We were taken aback. Foster asked, "How do you know for sure, young Chambers?"

"From one of my father's cricket books," replied Rohan.

"Well done, Rohan," said Len Levy.

On my first regional tour as manager of the youth team to Barbados 1984, I was granted permission from the JCA for Rohan to join me in Barbados a day after the team arrived. Rohan was to have been the guest of my cousin Kenneth Chambers who was a school teacher at one of Barbados schools. Two days after Rohan's arrival, I introduced him to the Barbados Cricket Board secretary Cammie Smith. Mr. Smith offered the choice of Rohan staying at the same venue (Cave Hill Campus) where the six participating teams were accommodated with no financial cost to me. I gratefully accepted the very generous proposal. The affable Cammie Smith was a member of the very popular Sir Frank Worrell led West Indies team to Australia 1960-61.

Rohan was known by most of the Jamaican players from back home when he accompanied me to the various grounds in the city and rural parishes. Jimmy Adams named him the team mascot. Rohan later became captain of his school Wolmer's under 14, Colts and Sunlight teams the same year. His next visit to Barbados was as a member of the National youth squad in 1988 and he went on to represent the team for five consecutive years, the last three as captain. The first year as captain at the national youth level in 1990, the team won the coveted trophy after ten years of close finishes as runners up including a playoff with Barbados in 1983.

Throughout the years, from Alpha Prep school where he was the captain of the school's football team, to Wolmers Boys High and the University of the

West Indies, Rohan's seminary work was excellent and he got the acclamation of his Teachers/Lecturers.

He spent six years at the University gaining his Bachelors and master's degrees in accounting. During the first two years at UWI, he continued as captain of the National Youth team at the regional tournaments and matches against Australia and South Africa youth teams. Rohan was also captain of St. Catherine Parish youth team in the JCA Kingston Wharves competition. He represented Melbourne Cricket club minor cup team before becoming a member of Kingston Cricket Club minor and senior cup teams. I was more than happy to see his interest in the game, which was a natural obsession derived from my love for the game.

Rohan was always keen on reading books on cricket, books that he had easy access to from my collection. One of my regrets was not to have seen enough of his cricket at the Sunlight and Senior cup level because of Club and JCA duties. His centuries at the Colts final, Sunlight and senior cup were not seen by me. I was present at other cricket grounds as part of my responsibility as a national selector. As manager of the Jamaica Youth team, I was present when he scored a century in the regional youth tournament against Trinidad at Bourda in Guyana 1989. At the school boy level, there were many with the natural skills and a passion for the game, that many expected would have done well at the national senior level; instead they opted for the pathway to a higher education. No one could argue their decision, not with a field of so many before them who were naturally gifted and who failed to make it chasing that goal of selection nationally and internationally.

I remember the great West Indian players Desmond Haynes and Malcolm Marshall who were in training for a test match at Sabina Park and watched Rohan as a teenager batting in the nets during a Kingston Cricket Club net session. They were so impressed with his batting that they asked me if he were under consideration for the Jamaica senior team. Easton McMorris, chairman of the Jamaica senior selection committee, once suggested I encourage Rohan who completed his Bachelors at age 22 to stay with the game before doing his Masters. Rohan was unwavering about being at the University for another two years in pursuing his Masters. I did not mention to Rohan McMorris's idea; he would have had a laugh at the notion of putting a hold on his educational pursuits for the uncertainty of excelling at the game, notwithstanding his profound love for the sport.

Figure 48 Northern Telecom Trophy Presented to Rohan Chambers (Captain) by President Emile Gratton, Trinidad 1990

Flagship Competition and Development of Under-23 Players

During the '80's to 1996, as a national administrator at different levels of Jamaica's cricket, (schoolboy, senior cup, parish competitions, regional youth and senior tournaments) I experienced instances of disappointments in the way the game was administered. I advocated early in my tenure as a member of the JCA for changes, including the establishment of a national senior competition inclusive of the senior cup teams along with UWI and the rural parishes.

The importance of a competition comprising the then existing senior cup teams Kingston, Boys Town, Lucas, Kensington, Melbourne, Jamaica Defense Force, Police, Saint Catherine along with UWI and the rural parishes divided into four Zones would have provided Jamaica's cricket with a competition enriched with the best talent across the sphere of the island, a competition that would have been recognized as the Flag Ship of Jamaica's Cricket. The inclusion of UWI was justified based on their earlier participation as a senior cup team in the '60's, a period that as a team was very good with talented players, some of whom were from other Caribbean Islands and selected to Jamaica's Colts teams, including Louis Yearwood from Barbados. He was like most batsmen from that area of the Caribbean, very attacking with charming stroke play on either side of the wicket and Harewood from Trinidad, an off spinner who was the captain when he represented the colts team.

There were others who performed superbly for the UWI team, including Dominica's Irving Shillingford, the former West Indies test batsman. I was a member of the Saint Catherine team when he scored a magnificent double century representing UWI against our formidable bowling attack at the Lime Tree Oval. There was also the Trinidadian fast bowler Doctor Gopal Singh. He had pace and swung the ball appreciably. He was among the leading fast bowlers at the senior cup. The rural teams, divided into four Zones would have had the better players competing with the top City players. The competition would be self-motivated by the players and created nationwide interest within the cricket fraternity, especially the rural fans who were steadfast in their belief of the enormous talent from their communities.

The idea of a national competition encompassing the better players from the parishes and the senior cup clubs should have been a priority of the Jamaica Cricket Association, I regret the failure to have effectively ratified the proposal, a proposal that would have embraced the nation's best talent. The awareness of such a competition was inculcated in me from my playing years at the Parish (Nethersole), Sugar Estates (Wray & Nephew, Crum Ewing, Bustamante) and the Senior Cup competitions, it was an idea that won favour with the players from the senior cup and the rural competitions. As a selector travelling across the island watching players in competitions at different levels, I observed a steady decline in the standard of the game attributed to the rapid closure of a number of the Sugar Estates. The Estates provided in a big way the participation of more players within the rural parishes and by extension for continued development of the players.

The downward trend of Sugar Estates financial viability was devastated to the sport by the continued closure of all but for a few. The once strong and powerful cricket entity demise was a severe blow to the aspirations of so many to be employed and play the sport, a sport that had the overwhelming support of the Estates management and workers from the factories to the farms and communities in and around the Estates. The many who have played in the Estates competitions and the fans would all agree, there was never a more competitive and wonderfully organized competition. The JCA headed by Alan Rae mourned the loss of the once flourishing garden of hope for cricketers in the island parishes, a garden that was once an integral pillar of Jamaica's cricket popularity.

An important aspect of our cricket was the development of our under 25 players, the Jamaica Cricket Association was concerned at the progress and growth of the younger players especially after leaving school. It was for that reason that the JCA with the sponsorship of D&G introduced the local Red Stripe competition that included an Under 19, Under 25, All Senior and four Zonal teams. The format was changed after one season as the under 19 was scrapped from the competition for reasons that was incomprehensible to me.

The board continued its interest for the development of our younger players by having Rohan Kanhai and Andy Roberts to conduct a three a week coaching programme for a selected group of our under 23 players. Roy Paul was assigned as liaison to Kanhai while I was to Roberts. It was a monumental achievement to have had the two great West Indian super stars supervising our youngsters, the sessions were of immense value to the selected group of batsmen, bowlers and wicketkeepers, they responded enthusiastically to the valued coaching performed by the two giants from the earlier years of West Indies Cricket. As an observer in a privilege position, I was able to have watched and listened to the brilliance of their work, the professionalism was of the highest quality. At the end of a successful programme, the players expressed appreciation for the opportunity that allowed them to be coached by the two West Indian Legends. The success of the programme was influential in the JCA securing the sponsorship for Rohan Kanhai's contract as Jamaica's National Cricket Coach for the period 1984 to 1991 with a two-year break 1989 and 1990.

Talent Pool and Administrative Leadership

T he youth team's failure at regional championship honours during the 80s was not a reflection of how well the teams performed. They played good cricket and challenged the eventual winners for championship honours by finishing runners-up on several occasions. After ten years without championship honours, we became champions in 1990, captained by Rohan Chambers, and in successive years, 1994 and 1995 led by Gareth Breese, we were champions. At the senior level, the drought dated back to 1969 when Jamaica won the Shell Shield captained by Easton McMorris, before the all-conquering Marlon Tucker led 1988 and 1989 teams won the coveted regional Red Stripe Trophy.

Over the years at both youth and senior levels, we were very fortunate to have had a strong cadre of talented players, players capable of national selection drawn from the Schools, Parishes and Clubs. Unfortunately, there were some who missed out and were never selected to any of the national teams for different reasons. At the youth level, there were several good enough but who failed selection for that year because of others who were considered marginally ahead of them; in a different year those players would have made it to the team. At the senior level for those considered on the fringe, there were more opportunities for them to be included later. They were good at their specialty, but oftentimes could not have found a place in the team where the established individual players were performing consistently.

In the meantime, our local cricket at the senior cup level was dominated by championship holders Kensington, Kingston, Melbourne, and Saint Catherine. The declining performance of the once powerful Boys Town Cricket Club reached a low ebb which was of great concern, not only to the Jamaica Cricket Association, but by the fraternity of our local fans. The concern was a built-up narrative of neglect that was apparent to the city clubs and the adoring followers of the game. The JCA was periodically deluged with letters from fans, printed and the electronic media to restore and maintain the longstanding and admired image of Boys Town contribution to our sport. Boys Town, at the time, was experiencing difficulty and needed significant assistance to sustain the viability of the famous institution.

The JCA members were deeply troubled at the precarious position the glorious and revered club was undergoing. "The history of the admired Boys Town Club was of monumental value and must be preserved for the talent it has given to Jamaica and must be continued to provide a garden of hope for the young sportsmen to fill the basket of Jamaica's cricket, football and civic duties," was my expression at a board meeting.

A way had to be found to honour the documented and well recognized deeds of the Rev. Hugh Sherlock. Father Sherlock was the known pioneer of the remarkable establishment of Boys Town, an institution that gave the talented Colie Smith to the world of cricket, and so many others who have represented the country nationally at both cricket and football, and there were our cultural and excellent entertainers who have given recognition to our country.

It was incumbent and justifiable in the eyes of the sports-loving fraternity that the JCA address with urgency the problem for survival of one of Jamaica's most revered sports institutions.

The members, but for one member George Sterling, were supportive of the Board intervention to help in the sustainability of the very popular institution. "Kick them out," said Sterling the former Melbourne Cricket Club President. I was stunned just like other members sitting around the huge oblong Board room meeting table. The expression emanating from an official of the Board was unbecoming. How anyone with Sterling's experience could be so contemptuous to an institution that provided for so many a lifestyle of prosperity by exposure of hope to the pathway of sports, education, and job opportunities? Boys Town provided our national Cricket and Football teams with players through the years, players of exceptional talent and a role model for succeeding generations.

The legendary Collie Smith was one of the finest cricketers to have represented Jamaica and the West Indies. His beginning was at Boys Town and extended across the Caribbean and global continents. Collie Smith's contribution to the game inspired his contemporaries and generations that followed. The names of Bob Maragh, George Pullum Smith, Gladstone Robinson, Len Levy, Linden Wright. Marlon Tucker, Mark Neita, Kenneth Barnett, Hopeton Barrett, Ray Wynter, Victor Fray, Donald Miller, Leroy Morgan, Alexander Morgan, and Courtney O'Conner were national players and had their beginning and recognition at the garden of sportsmen that bloomed so many. There was Winston Davis, the former Jamaica stroke player who became a member of the club after Railway Sports Club's withdrawal from the senior cup.

The magnificent Jamaica and West Indies wicketkeeper batsman Jeffrey Dujon also represented Boys Town towards the ending of his career. There were others of known quality who were considered in many quarters as aspirants to national senior selection, the list included Cleveland Richards, Victor Hunter, Neville Larger Reid, Canute Kelly, Leroy Shaw, Franklyn Dennis, Paul Ellis, Leroy Gordon, Joe Carter, Archie Reid, Harold Richardson, and the champion batsman Bunny Shaw who was as good as any Jamaican batsman during his senior cup years. The achievements of the gifted super star Collie Smith was inspirational to succeeding generations of the revered club.

The monumental status of the club was a beacon of hope for the many in and around a community that was inspired by the civic consciousness of the club founder, the beloved Reverend Hugh Sherlock, and there were other administrators such as R.O.C King, Conrad Ball, John Maxwell, and Carl Goodison, all of whom gave valued service to the growth and respectability of the club.

To have the club subjected to exclusion from the senior cup would have been an affront to so many youngsters' aspiration to belong.

Thanks to President Alan Rae the former Jamaica and West Indies opener, his civic insight put expulsion out of the question. The area where Boys Town is situated was having a prolonged political unrest by rival gang warfare; players were unable to practice and to have played home matches in an atmosphere conducive to the norms of the great game. President Rae was able to accentuate the importance and gains for Boys Town continued participation.

"The aspiration of the young ones from the community would be dashed and severely derailed and be starved of hope," reiterated the greatest Jamaica Cricket Association President.

So many of us as players established long lasting friendships with players from Boys Town, an institution that continues to inspire hope to a community that produced not only famous cricketers and footballers, but also a galaxy of top Jamaican entertainers. I revered the excellent leadership of the magnificent JCA president Alan Rae who guided the members with unquestionable leadership qualities, leadership that inspired confidence to the membership of the city and Rural Board representatives. As one who came through a system emblematic to Boys Town, I was enthralled by the oratory outlined by President Rae that must have clearly changed the mind of that member who without remorse said, "Kick them out."

Figure 49 St. Catherine Senior Cup Champions -1966. **Standing L-R:** Samuel McFarlane, Ruddy Brown, George Chambers, Frank Farquharson, John Prescod (Manager), Clifton Folkes, Oswald Doswell, and Ronald "Crody" Williams. **Sitting L-R:** Collin Hinds, Leonard Chambers, Micky Murdoch, Renford Pinnock, Herbert Bailey, and Clive Ogilvie.

Figure 50 St. Catherine Cricket Club Joint Senior Cup Champions with Melbourne 1973 Leonard Chambers (St. Catherine Cricket Club Captain) receiving Senior Cup from Sir Florizel Augustus Glasspole, Governor- General of Jamaica, Rudy Williams (Melbourne Cricket Club Captain) at right.

Figure 51 St. Catherine Cricket Club Senior Cup Champions – 1993 **Standing L-R:** Leonard Ramdial (Club Executive), Delroy Barron, Steve Nelson, Clifton Folkes, Maurice Pinnock, Colin Bucchanan, Dwight Williams, Lloyd Rattray, and Mark Nelson. **Sitting L-R:** Randy Nelson, Ephraim McLeod, Leonard Chambers (Manager), Milton Thomas (captain), Dolly Bacchus (President), Ransford Evans, Tony Powell, Melbourne Austin, and Courtney Francis.

Figure 52 St. Catherine Senior Cup Champions -1995. Standing L-R: Mark Nelson, Clinton Clarke (Manger), Micky Murdoch, Shawn Lodge, Glenroy Edwards, O'Neil Richards, Maurice Pinnock, Michael Bacchus, Osmond Dann (Treasurer), Sidney Gapour (VP), **Sitting L-R:** Randy Nelson, Delroy Barron, Milton Thomas, Tony Powell, Dolli Bacchus (President), Ransford Evans (Captain), Courtney Francis, Michael Martin, and Andrew Greenwood.

Figure 53 Boys Town Senior Cup Champions -1960. **Standing L-R:** Baldwin Muir (scorer), Kenneth Kelly, Locksley Comrie, Mike Bardowell, Littie Cargill, John Maxwell (Director), Boyd Morrant, Donald Miller, and Bob Maragh. **Sitting L-R:** Septie "Bunny" Shaw, Cleveland Richards, Sir Frank Worrell (Captain), Keats Hall, and Lewelyn Brown.

Figure 54 Boys Town Championship Team – 1970. **Standing L-R**: Locksley Comrie, Michael Mitchell, Linden Wright, Winston Davis, Neville "Larger" Reid, Leroy "Respic" Morgan, Clive Campbell, Baldwin Muir (Scorer). **Sitting L-R**: Anthony Wright, Franklyn Dennis, Conrod Ball (Director), Victor Hunter, (Captain), Leroy "Gabby" Shaw, and Leonard Levy.

Figure 55 Boys Town Senior Cup Team – 1973. **Standing L-R**: Locksley Comrie (Manager), Mikey Phillips, Winston Davis, Carl Brown, Ken Rose, Herbert "Dago" Gordon, Vincent Hartley, Linden Wright, Baldwin Muir (Scorer). **Front Row L-R:** Michael Mitchell, Leroy "Respic" Morgan, Leonard Levy, Les Brown, and Neville "Lager" Reid.

Figure 56 Jamaica Regional Championship Team -1969. **Standing L-R:** Livern Wellington, Sam Morgan, Othneil Myles, Roy McCatty, Anthony Campbell, Castel Folkes, Herman Bennett, Lawrence Rowe, and Linden Wright. **Sitting L-R:** Arthur Barrett, Renford Pinnock, Easton McMorris, Jackie Hendricks (Manager), and Maurice Foster.

Figure 57 Kensington Cricket Club Senior Cup Champions 1962. **In Front L-R**: Selbourne Mitchell, Milton Wisdom, Eric Austin, Neville Hawkins, and J. K. Holt (Captain) **Standing L-R**: Brandis Johnstone, Oscar Hamilton, Owen Mitchell, Alfred Valentine, Fitz Nangle, Lester King, and Llyod Dunbar.

Figure 58 Kingston Cricket Club Senior Cup Championship Team – 1976. **Standing L-R:** Bruce Lyn, Hilton Gordon, Bobby Mignott, Michael Provost, Alty Sasso (manager), John Gordon, Terrance Corke, Ronnie Savariau. **Sitting L-R:** Jeffrey Dujon, Carlton Gordon, Anthony Campbell, Maurice Foster (captain), Cortney Daley, Carrol Gordon, Reggie Scarlett.

Figure 59 Kensington Senior Cup Championship Team 1984. **Sitting L-R:** Wayne Lewis, Lincoln Sterling, Maurice Chung, Basil Williams (Captain), Junior Williams, Everett Whittingham, Prince Francis, **Standing L-R:** Christopher Daniel (Scorer), Harcourt Grant, Errol Wilson, Brenton McKenzie, Winston Morgan, David Bernard, Linval Crawford, Michael Wright, Dennis Lewis and Chester Watson (Manager)

Figure 60 1987: Members of Kensington team which retained the Sealy Senior Cup Cricket title on July 6. **Standing L-R:** Pete Plunket, Dave Bulli, George Heron, Dwight Meikle, Leary Williams, Vernon Smith, and Chester Watson (manager). Sitting L-R: Linval Crawford, Wayne Lewis, Errol Wilson, Basil Williams (captain), Maurice Chung, and Prince Francis.

Figure 61 Kensington Senior Cup Championship Team 1989, **Standing L-R:** Sellie Mitchell (Manager), Brian Blair, Mario Ventura, Clifford Windith, Rober Turner, Ezra Hewitt, Dave Cameron, Laurie Williams, Pete Plunkett, Wayne Malcolm (Scorer)
Sitting L-R: Wayne Lewis, Maurice Ching, Noel Silvera (Club President), George Heron (Captain), Eroll Wilson, Cleveland Davidson.

Figure 62 Kingston Cricket Club Senior Cup Championship Team – 1983. **Standing L-R:** Peter Jones, Michael McIntosh, John Gordon, Owen Chung (manager), Terrance Corke, Ray Wynter, Irvine Hamilton. **Sitting L-R:** Carrol Gordon, Ronnie Savariau, Carlton Gordon, Maurice Foster (captain), Anthony Campbell, Jeffrey Dujon, and Hilton Gordon.

Figure 63 Kingston Cricket Club Senior Cup Team – 1994. **Standing L-R:** Alfred Savariau (manager), Dayne Buddo, Merrick Cousley, Ryan Cunningham, Roneo Palmer, Matthew Fender, Mario Ventura, Garfield Smith(scorer). **Sitting L-R:** Raymond Ferguson, Nehemiah Perry, Wayne Lewis, Wayne Sutherland (captain), Michael Howell, and Michael Millwood.

Figure 64 Lucas Senior Cup Champions 1954. **Standing L-R:** Seymour Melbourne, Everton McCulloch, Horace Reid, John McLeod, Lloyd Ross, Joe Prescod. **Sitting L-R**: Lewin Stewart, Graydon Sealy, Calbert Minott, George Prescod (captain), Easton McMorris, E. B. King, and Lascelles Collesso.

Figure 65 Lucas Senior Cup Champions- 1971. **Standing L-R:** Romey Morris, Elroy Campbell, Michael Provost, Percival Rhoden, L. McGibbon, George Herdsman, Ferdinand McDonald. **Sitting L-R: Kenneth Barnett, Roy Paul, Easton McMorris (captain), Donald Morgan,** Uton Dowe.

Figure 66 Melbourne Cricket Club Senior Cup Champions 1974. **In Front L-R:** John Tucker, Wally Baugh, Gerald Wollaston, Rudy Williams (Captain), Arthur Barrett, Ruddy Marzouca, and Rudolph Findlay. **Standing L-R:** Sam Morgan, Clive Campbell, Michael Holding, Cecil Lawson, Colin Fletcher, Sam Allen, Oswald Haughton, and Carlton Carter.

Figure 67 Melbourne Cricket Club Senior Cup Champions 1978. Standing L-R: Delroy Bembridge, Mark Neita, Michael Leslie, Barrington Saunders, Oswald Haughton, Percival Tomlinson, Earle Daley. In Front L-R: Errol Peart, Colin Fletcher, Carlton Carter (Captain), Arthur Barrett, and Michael Holding.

Figure 68 Melbourne Cricket Club Senior Cup Champions -1980. **Standing L-R**: Clinton Johnson, Mark Neita, Donny Spencer, Courtney Walsh, Earl Daley, And William Cole. **Sitting L-R:** Earl Melbourne, Carlton Cater Sr., Authur Barrett, Carlton "Wally" Baugh, and Collin Fletcher

Figure 69 Melbourne Cricket Club Senior Cup Champions 1988. **Standing L-R:** Aubrey Wollaston, Carlton Carter Jr., Alton Turner, Errol Nolan, Vivian Sailsman, Larry Crichton, Kirk Watson, Robert Samuels, Kirk Ebanks, Gregory Sailsman. **Sitting L-R:** Junior Hall, Dennis Gordon, William Cole, Ruddy Williams (Manager) Mark Neita (captain), Odelmo Peters, Derron Dixon, and Paul Palmer.

Figure 70 Police Senior Team 1988. **Standing L-R:** Dean Taylor, Patrick Gayle, Patrick Hanson, Kipling Chin, Sir Arthur Brown, Leonard Coley
Sitting L-R: Winsor Fyffe, Michael Grant, Carlton Moore, Arthur Brown, Tan Mattis (manager), and Samuel Anderson (scorer).

Coaches and Mentors

During the years as chairman of Jamaica's youth selection committee, I was fortunate to have been associated with dedicated schoolboy leaders of the Headley Cup, Sunlight Cup, and Youth Clubs. They demonstrated unending commitment to a cause that inspired so many to stardom. The admirable transition of their tutoring to the youngsters during the formative years to adulthood in a world of challenges, challenges that the youngsters encountered in team sports, at the workplace and life in general, was commendable.

The uniquely placed leaders continued on a pathway as if it were a blueprint manifesto of their predecessors. The Sunlight competition got started in 1906 and the Headley cup 1958. It is of interest knowing that the Headley Cup during the inaugural year was contested by boarding schools only. The system was made very convenient for the players to be assembled on match days (Saturdays). The historical background on the beginning of the two competitions was provided to me by the remarkable schoolteacher and cricket journalist Wilbert Parkes.

Parkes was a cricket coach at Campion College, one of the top schoolboy teams during the 80s into the 90s. Parkes' amazing knowledge on Sunlight Cup cricketers was of immense value to me as Chairman of the youth selectors. I recall one night about 11:30 PM when he called and provided me with information on a young cricketer from the remote district of Crofts Hill in Clarendon. He was impressed with the natural ability of the youngster and made the recommendation that I have a look at. The well-respected knowledge on schoolboy cricket by the admirable Wilbert Parkes was good enough for me and the youngster was invited to the trials.

Wilbert Parkes was born in the agricultural district of Croftshill that I was familiar with. As a sales representative of the Wray Nephew Group of Companies, the Crofts Hill district was a constituency that I served for ten years. He was recognized for his remarkable years of service in tutoring Campion

College young cricketers. The youngsters were characterized, not only by their batting and bowling talent, but also by their remarkable self-esteem. Wilbert Parkes inculcated the rudiments of sportsmanship in the youngsters on and off the field of play that drew commendation from those connected to school boy cricket. Through the years, there were others that I relied on for their insight, including Pat Anderson of Manchester, Robert Lewis of Holmwood, Derek Azan of Garvey Maceo, Jerry Reid St. James, Cleon Smith of York Castle, Noel Cousins at Titchfield High, Dr. Donavan Bennett, Junior Bennett and Horton Dolphin St. Elizabeth and Westmoreland, Winston Brown from Clarendon, Vincent Dixon St. Mary, Joe Spencer St. Jago, Canute Reid and Leonard Levy, Henry Williams, Carl Goodison, Gladstone Neil and Roy McLean from Kingston. Their contribution was immeasurable to the national objectives.

The growth of schools' participation in the Headley and Sunlight competitions was a positive development for the aspiring young cricketers. The exceptional quality of players from the rural schools was reflected in the steady numerical growth called to the national youth trials through the years 1983 to 1996. The talent and performances of those young players never went unnoticed by the national selectors, a testament to the wonderful preparation of their school coaches and mentors/ managers.

Interestingly, a number of rural schoolboy players after leaving school went on to play for Saint Catherine and Kingston Clubs in the senior and junior cup competitions instead of their parish teams. In most cases the players were driven by the overwhelming coverage given by the printed and electronic media and very little to the rural parish competitions.

The selection process of the national youth team was always a monumental challenge to the selectors year after year. The Kingston Wharves competition identified the very best available talent from which the selectors utilized the compilation of players to the camp. Regrettably, there were many who were considered almost equal to those selected for both the trials and squad and missed out. The ones overlooked included Dunstan Barclay, Kevin Murray, Julian Robinson, Milton Thomas, Paul Brown, Wayne Cuff, Krishana Edwards, Garry Pink, Buxton Mitchell, Alrick Lawson, Dave Blair, Pete Plunkett, Dillon Ebanks, Aubrey Wollaston, Alton Williams, and Christopher Cheddar, and there were others. At the end of each Camp, it was always mixed feelings for the unselected. They came with extreme confidence of doing well and very optimistic of selection; to be left out was disappointment that brought uncontrolled tears to most of them. I understood their disappointment and reminded them of players Cleveland Davidson and Odelmo Peters who were at earlier camps and missed selection, and with exceptional resoluteness improved their game significantly to national senior selection in relatively quick time. I implored the unselected who were eligible for the following year to be unwavering in their pursuit of selection.

Figure 71 Black River High School Headley Cup Finalist. **Back L-R:** Victor Stewart, O'Neil Forester, Ashley Parchment, Jason Parchment, Troy Forrest, Ricardo Gayle (Principal) Michael Lawson (Coach). **Middle L-R:** Christopher Parchment, Teddy Johnson, Dennis Barnes, Patrick Smith, Andy Wynter, Cephas Reynolds, Clive Colquhoun. **Front L-R:** Christopher Miller, Phillip Brooks, Kirk Powell.

Figure 72 St. Mary Parish Team – 1991. **Standing L-R:** Bull "Gear" Samuel, Clive Garrison, Michael Mignot, Andy Morant, Wenworth Pendley, Heinsley Wilshaw, Simon Bell, Christopher Gayle, Oscar Hinds, Ossie Champagne (Manager). **Front Row L-R:** Garfield Silvera, Tousaint Hassan, Vincent Dixon, Keith McCrae, Winston Benain, Ralston Samuels, Raymond Lue (Assistant Manager).

Figure 73 Monroe College Headley Cup Winners – 1974. **Standing L-R:** R. Roper (Headmaster), K. Senior, E. Benjamin, K. Ledgister, C. Hamilton, J. Williams, H. Dolphin (coach). **Front Row L-R:** M. Hewitt, C. Chang, M. Clarke (captain), B. Nelson, P. Lue, R. Chin, J. Palmer.

Figure 74 Meadowbrook High School Sunlight Cup Champions - 1982. **Standing L-R:** Graham Rhoden, Lloyd Williams, Dane Miller, Christopher Cheddar, Timon Waugh, Michael Hall, Glaister Prince, Captain, Hopeton Burke, Stanford Brown, Michael Hare (Coach)
Front L-R: Gary Simms, Noel Curtis, Leon Johnson, Kevin Reece, Byron Nunes, Devon McDonald, Hugh Green, Garfield Marston, and Clive Edwards.

Figure 75 Campion Sunlight Champions – 1987. **Standing L-R:** Wilbert Parkes (coach), Steven Botek, Joseph Levy, Jamie Douglas, Carlton Carter Jr., Paul East, Ruford Davis, Robert Chung, and Ian McNally. **Sitting L-R:** Julian Robinson, Larry Crichton, Vivian Sailsman (captain), Sean Cadogan, Gregory Sailsman.

Figure 76 Campion Sunlight Champions – 1988. **Standing L-R:** Wilbert Parkes (coach), Jamie Douglas, Joseph Levy, Ryan Knott, Paul East, Michael Dawson, Andrew Simmonds. **Sitting L-R:** Sean Cadogan, Steven Botek, Julian Robinson, Gregory Sailsman (captain), Larry Crichton, Carlton Carter Jr., Ruford Davis.

Figure 77 Campion College Tappin Cup Champions – 1989. **Standing L-R**: Wilbert Parkes (Coach), Lawrence Barrett, Kurt Anderson, Jamie Douglas, Ryan Knott, Paul East, Michael Dawson, Andrew Simmonds, Duane Forrester, Daniel Abbott. **Sitting L-R:** Julian Robinson, Carlton Carter Jnr, Joseph Levy, Gregory Sailsman (captain), Larry Crichton, Sean Cadogan

Figure 78 Gareth Breese & Ray Stewart. Record breaking partnership of 558 runs for the 3rd wicket. Breese, 299 run out & Stewart, 284, in a team total of 644 for 4 declared in the Colts Semi-finals against Campion College 217 for 4.

Figure 79 Wolmer's Sunlight Champion Team – 1971. **Standing L-R:** J. Dujon, M. Kirlew, F. Lawrence, S. Newman, Lloyd Chambers, W. McLean, D. Oliver, M. Jacobs, L. Tyndall. **Sitting L-R:** P. Rae, Mr. D. L. Bogle (Headmaster), J. Mordecai (Captain), Mr. Ron Jones (Sport Master), N. Mattis.

Figure 80 Wolmer's Sunlight Champions - 1975. **Standing L-R:** Collin Williams, Lance Hibbert, Donovan Summers, Rudyard Morgan, Anthony Sewell, Peter Williams, Nigel Pennycooke, Glen Campbell. **Front Row L- R:** Wayne Fullwood, Fitzgerald Lee, Carl Johnson, Jeffrey Dujon (captain), Mark Lawrence, Cecil Sutherland.

Figure 81 Wolmer's Sunlight Cricket Champions - 1992. **Standing L-R:** C. Sterling (assistant coach), Ray Stewart, Paul Buchanan Jr., Simon Ormsby, Owen Fairclough, Craig Perch, Damion Lyon, Joel March, Carrington Clarke, George Walters (coach). **Front Row: L-R:** Gareth Breese, Dwayne Buddo, Alford Givans (captain), Stefan Steer, Donald Hillocks

Figure 82 Wolmers Sunlight Squad – 1984. **Back Row L - R:** Howard Copeland, Rohan McFarlane, Gary Paisley, Bert Smith, Brian Lewis, Adrian Laidlaw, Martin Sutherland (captain). **Middle Row L - R:** Kevin Gooden, Robert Dillon, Francis Wade, Lloyd Blackwood, Terrence Robinson, Llewelyn McPherson. **Front Row:** Rohan Chambers.

Figure 83 St. George's Sunlight Team – 1962. **Standing L-R:** Major Binns (Coach), Clovis Metcalfe, Keith Mitchell, Roy McCatty, Wes Taylor, Rogelio Chin, Bruce Lyn, Damion Thomas. **Front Row L-R:** Arthur Dixon, Eric Carty, Gladston Bardowell, Michael Witter, Michael Bell, Lascelve Talbot, Errol "Dixie" Hall.

Figure 84 St. George's Sunlight Champions - 1996. **Standing L-R:** Kurt Blair, Kevin Guy, Sha-courie Wilson, Maurice Silvera, Dalian Salmon, Ramon Hutchinson, Jotham Watson, John Martin (wicket keeper), Cheswick Chambers, Carlington Ebanks, Anthony Meyers, Hugh "Goosey" Edwards. **Sitting L-R:** Michael Lee (asst. coach), Brian Mitchell, Oral McDonald, Ryan Cunningham, Winston Wilson (coach), Gerard Christian, Maurice Rhoden (manager), Kavon Gillespie, Xavier Gilbert, Christopher Matthews.

Figure 85 STETHS Headley Cup Champions – 1985. **Standing L-R:** Junior Bennett (Coach), Deancourt Wright, Trevor Samuels, Roger Roye, Paul Murray, Dixeth Palmer, Tedroy Broomfield, Paul Patrick, Donovan Bennett (Manager).
Sitting L-R: Delroy Morgan, Mark Simpson, Larry Cunningham (captain), Michael Millwood, Lindley Coach, Wayne Billings.

Figure 86 STETHS Headley Cup Champions - 1987. **Standing L-R:** Dixeth Palmer, George Nelson, Shane Ford, Paul Patrick, Steven Allcott, Milton Thomas. **Sitting L-R:** Lyndon Johnson, Lindley Coach, Wayne Billings, Michael Millwood (captain), Steve Gordon, Trevor Samuels.

Figure 87 St. Jago High School Sunlight Team- 1963. **Standing L-R:** PE Teacher, Chester Dacres (scorer), George Mudie Jr., Norman "Dickie" Brown, Dennis Keane-Dawes, Raymond Anglin, Melmoth Rhoden, George Mudie Sr.(coach). **Sitting L-R:** Ewart Brown, Trevor Lyons, Abe Bailey (captain), O. R. Bell (headmaster), Paul Tai, Anthony Mah-Lee, Clive Goldson

Figure 88 St. Elizabeth Technical Headley Cup Championship Team - 1986. **Standing L-R:** Junior Bennett (coach), Deancourt Wright, Trevor Samuel, Roger Roye, Paul Murray, Dixeth Palmer, Tedroy Broomfield, Paul Patrick, Dr. Donovan Bennett (manger). **Sitting L-R:** Delroy Morgan, Mark Simpson, Laurie Cunningham(captain), Michael Millwood, Lindley Coach, Wayne Billings

Back Row: C.E. Buchanan; F.A. Dyer; D.A. Clarke; J.P. Harris; Mr. L.D. Neil (Master in charge of Cricket).
Second Row: T.A. Campbell; P.W. Brandon; J.E. Morrisson; R.A. Paul; M.A. Vernon; C.A.DeCarish; T.L. Harris.
Front Row: W.A. Rhoden; Mr. D. Forrest (Headmaster); G.I.Neill (Captain); Mr. T.D. Davis (Sportsmaster); A.P. Strachan(Vice-Captain)

Figure 89 Kingston College Sunlight Team - 1962

Figure 90 Kingston College Sunlight Team - 1985. **Standing L-R:** Gary Neil, Philip Ringrose, Derron Dixon, Kirk Watson, Donald Bennett, Antarrio Clarke, Dwight Mowatt. **Front Row L-R:** Peter Thomas, Delroy Sloweley, P. Brown, Dalkeith Dempster, Robert Samuels, Alton Turner, Errol Nolan.

Figure 91 Garvey Maceo Headley and Spaulding Cup Champions – 1991. **Standing L-R:** Clayton Malcolm, Derrick Azan (Coach), Marlon Carty, Garth Davis, Rohan Belight, Audley Sanson, Glenroy Nelson, Junior Sibblis. **Sitting L-R:** Kevin Hibbert, Darren Dyer, Junior Forbes, Alton Williams, Andrew Davis, Hamlet Stewart.

Figure 92 Vere Technical High School Cricket Team Headley Cup Champions – 1975. **Standing L-R:** Crenton Boxhill (coach), Danny Smith, Denis Hamilton, Vincent Wint, Neville Solomon, Wayne Jordon, Raymond Clarke, Michael Newman.
Sitting L-R: Donovan Lazarus, George Richards, Delbert Lewis, Donald Clarke (captain), Carlton Johnson, Alexander Morgan.

Figure 93 St. Jago Cricket Team – 1977. **Winner of Sunlight, Tapin, and Spaulding Cups. Standing L-R**: Headley Lawson, Carlton Cooke, Ludlow Rowe, Garnett Walker, Ransford Evans, Norman Radcliffe, David Chuck, Patrick Reece, Errol Eccles. **Sitting (L-R):** Everton Blair, Joe Spencer(coach), Gregory Brown(captain), Victor Edwards (Headmaster), Robert Harley, Keith Gowie.

Period of Reflection

From 1983 to 1996, there was a preponderance of exceptional talented players at the local senior club level. The consistency and overall performances propelled a number of them to the national and international platforms, an achievement that they should be extremely proud of. The majority of those who represented the national senior team would have played at the national youth level, a level that had hundreds of contenders which in itself was a tremendous landmark achievement. The journey for some, by their dedication and self-belief to succeed, took them to the zenith of a sport that was their choice and aspiration to be identified with. There were others with superb talent and they performed consistently with the expectation of many to have been selected to the national and international level and disappointingly, they were overlooked by the selectors.

The players who achieved stardom nationally and internationally were Patrick Patterson, Michael Holding, Courtney Walsh, Delroy Morgan, Robert Samuels, Kenneth McLeod, Wayne Lewis, Laurie Williams, Nehemiah Perry, Robert Haynes, Leon Garrick, Mark Neita, Marlon Tucker, Larry Cunningham Cleveland Davidson, Richard Staple, Odelmo Peters, Basil Williams, George Heron, Everett Whittingham, Kirk Ebanks, Richard Austin, Terence Corke, O'Neil Cruickshank, Steve Gordon (fast bowler), Brenton McKenzie, John Gordon, Prince Francis, Patrick Gayle, Jeffrey Dujon, Raymond Ferguson, Clem Thompson, Tony Powell, Wavell Hinds, Clifton Folkes, Courtney O'Conner, Gareth Breese, Dixieth Palmer, Steve Gordon (batsman), Marlon Gibbs, Mario Ventura, Franz Cunningham, Ray Wynter, Errol Wilson, Nigel Kennedy, Dwight Meikle, Orville Pennant, and Joseph Grant (fast bowler). My apology for anyone that I have left out from this group. The named players formed the nucleus from which their performances were followed closely by succeeding selection panels of which I was a member. At the trials, occasionally a batsman impressed with good scores was overlooked for national selection because of the consistency of settled players in the team; injuries also affected players selection when they were enjoying superb form.

At the youth level, a fit Rohan Belight from Garvey Maceo School in Clarendon was a fast bowler with very good control. He was able to move the ball off the wicket appreciatively at pace and was considered a certainty for the 1991 youth tournament in Jamaica. He was injured during the trials and missed selection for the entire 1991 home tournament. A fit Rohan Belight in 1992 restored his fitness and was selected for the 1992 tournament in Guyana. Before Belight's misfortune, there was Kirk Hamilton, the genuinely quick bowler from Titchfield High in Portland. He bowled menacingly to opposing batsmen in the 1987 tournament at home in Jamaica and was ruled unfit for the 1988 tournament in Barbados. Hamilton regained full fitness bowling at top pace reminiscent of his speed shown in 1987 and returned to the team for the 1989 tournament in Guyana.

At the senior level, the fast-bowling all-rounder Gregory Brown and fast bowler O'Neill Richards were on the fringe for national selection and were both ruled unfit; however, Richards's regained full fitness and was selected a year or two after. Brown's injury was more serious; he was incapable of bowling fast again and converted his bowling style to that of an off spinner. Gregory Brown, the former Jamaica youth cricket captain fast bowling all-rounder, showed early signs of becoming a senior national player before the injury. Gregory Brown was my teammate at Saint Catherine Cricket Club. As a teenager, his early promise was recognized by the senior members of the team that included Renford Pinnock, Colin Hinds, George Chambers, Carl Henry, Errol Chambers, and Herman Bennet. Brown's talent as a fast bowler was also recognized by others, including former West Indies players Lawrence Rowe who was the incumbent Jamaica captain and Basil William; they were in support of the selectors Chester Watson, Roy Paul, and I for Brown's inclusion to the Jamaica team after a special bowling spell for the under 25's vs the All Senior's at Melbourne Park when he dismissed the top half of the All-Senior's batting. Gregory Brown was certainly one for the future; sadly, a future that promised so much was no longer possible.

There were others who were considered by the selectors on their showing at the local schoolboy and club competitions and at the regional youth level as aspirants to the national senior team as their game progressed. Unfortunately, they were not able to achieve the distinction of representing the national senior team at the four-day level. Players like Wayne Sutherland, Wayne Billings, Paul Palmer, Dereck Francis, Courtney Francis, Rohan Chambers, Perry Jennings, Sheldon Gordon, Larry Creighton, Michael Millwood, Randy Nelson, Valentino Ventura, Ray Stewart, Delroy Taylor, Calvin Valentine, Raymond Ferguson, Maurice Cole, and Vivian Sailsman as former national youth representatives were on that list of truly talented individuals. There were others including Milton Thomas, Aubrey Wollaston, Dillon Ebanks, and Pete Plunket, all of whom missed selection to the national youth team, showed exceptional improvement to their game while performing convincingly at the senior cup. Their performances had an impact on the selectors to have considered them as contenders to the national senior team.

There were exceptional situations of players gaining national selection by unusual circumstances such was the unexpected inclusion of the teenager Alford Givance. He was taken from the classroom at Wolmers as a late replacement for Nehemiah Perry who was a mainstay of the Jamaica team. Perry having picked up an injury minutes before the start of play in a regional game at Sabina Park made him a nonstarter for the game. Givance was similar to Perry; he bowled off spin, very competent with the bat and was a very good fieldsman anywhere in the field.

At the youth level, he was the Jamaica captain in 1993 and vice-captain of the West Indies youth team to England that same year. His natural all-round ability was an indication to most local Jamaican fans that he would be at the national senior level for some time. He was not yet at the level of Perry, but his all-round talent was very special and would have been strengthened by regular exposure which he was denied. His early promise as an all -rounder was good enough for him to have been in the same Jamaica team with the champion off spinning all-rounder Nehemiah Perry. In my capacity as manager of the youth team, I had seen enough of his talent in the three years he played. His performances were impressive with both bat and ball and that was taken into consideration when the West Indies youth team was selected for the 1993 youth tour to England. The selectors, chaired by the great West Indies fast bowler Sir Andy Roberts, William Bourne the former West Indies Youth, Barbados and Warwickshire fast bowler, and I named Givance as the vice-captain to Ian Bradshaw the Barbados captain. Bradshaw was a very gifted left arm pacer and dependable middle order batsman; he later represented the Barbados senior team before gaining selection to the West Indies senior team.

Givance migrated to the USA at age twenty-four where he excelled educationally, majoring with an MBA. He was President of the Tropical Cricket Club in Atlanta, Georgia for a number of years.

For some of our young cricketers, educational pursuits and work locations were extenuating factors that mitigated their efforts for sustained and purposeful training habits. Significantly, the ones who made it nationally and internationally were rewarded by their unswerving perseverance, notwithstanding setbacks.

My elevation to the role of a national selector at both levels of the senior and youth placed me in a position of preparedness for the role, according to President Allan Rae. At a Board meeting, the President stated, "Having before represented the national team and as an established captain at the senior cup level and served as secretary to the selection committee, Len, you are ideally placed for both positions." Before the creation of the youth selection committee, there was only one selection committee that named teams on behalf of the JCA. When I was secretary to the committee, the chairman was former West Indies skipper Franz Gerry Alexander, the other members included the former West Indies opener JK Holt Jr., Jackie Hendricks the former West Indies top class wicketkeeper, considered by many to have been the best ever to have worn the big gloves for the West Indies, and Roy McLean the former Melbourne Cricket Club all-rounder and Jamaica Cols captain. It was on Hendricks' recommendation that I served on both committees when the new youth selection committee was formed.

During the 80's, the Jamaica's Youth Cricket teams championship honours were denied on several occasions after being well positioned to have won the coveted title. As manager of the teams and chairman of the selection committee, it was incumbent on me to have offered solace to the players, some of whom were tearful. There were outstanding individual performances that stood out that never went unnoticed. The 1984 tournament held in Barbados was a very good one for Jimmy Adams, Patrick Gayle, Wayne Sutherland, Vernon Smith and Deron Dixon, the five but for Wayne Sutherland, were rewarded with selection to the West Indies youth team against England during the early months of 1985. Unfortunately for Sutherland who topped the aggregate for the Jamaicans and one of the tournament leading batsmen, he just missed out on selection because of the age benchmark.

I was one of the three selectors including Kenny Hobson of Grenada with Rickey Skerritt of St. Kitts as chairman. The players selected were based on their participation in the 1984 regional Barbados tournament. It was a formidable squad including the likes of Rohan Holder, Kenny Benjamin, Carl Hooper, and Wendell Coppin. The selection process went smoothly but for who should have led the team. Carl Hooper was strongly identified as the leading contender for the job; as captain of the Guyana team, he showed astuteness in handling his bowling changes and field placings and looked the part as a competent captain. An incident of his making ruined his chances to the captaincy. During the Jamaica Guyana game, he lost his composure by showing resentment at one of the umpire's decision. His reaction was seen as indiscreet and left much to be desired.

At the end of the game, with the urging of his coach Singh, he made an apology to the umpires. The incident quickly permeated within the other competing teams which made it untenable for us to have appointed him to the important captaincy role. We consider the nature of the offence was unbecoming of any player and more so the captain. We nevertheless included him in the squad. He was a delight to watch when batting and stood out as the most complete batsman of the tournament. Zoral Bartley, captain of the Leeward Island team, was named to lead the team. His credentials were impressive, which made him the obvious choice after Hooper. The four Jamaicans' contribution to the West Indies team effort was praiseworthy with wicketkeeper Patrick Gayle exceptional behind the stumps.

In 1982, the year before I became the full-time youth manager, I was secretary to the selection committee headed by Gerry Alexander ,and along with the other selectors, we were pleased with the performances of the team in the 1982 regional tournament. By their tournament performances Patrick Harris, Courtney Walsh, and Robert Haynes were selected to the West Indies youth team for the tour of England 1982. Walsh's appearance in the matches was limited because of back strains; Harris was consistent with the bat in the tour matches and was selected for one of the international games. The all-rounder

Haynes had a very successful tournament; his exquisite stroke play was exceptional; his bowling ability as a cunning leg spinner made him a key player in the West Indies team. In one of the games, his performances was spectacular with a brilliant 80 plus and a five-wicket haul that gave the West Indies victory over their English opponents.

The manager of the West Indies team, Rhodil Clarke of Tobago, was manager of the 1983 Trinidad and Tobago team that participated in the regional youth tournament in Jamaica. As manager, he briefed me on the performances of Jamaica's three on the England tour. He was very complimentary of the trio and singled out Robert Haynes as the most valuable player of the three-match series.

The next West Indies youth team selected was for the 1988 Youth World Cup in Australia. Included in the team were the Jamaicans Jimmy Adams, Nehemiah Perry, Robert Samuels, and Trevor Samuels. The experience of that tour was significant to their development as Jimmy Adams, Nemiah Perry, and Robert Samuels with consistent performances for the Jamaica senior team became International players. Trevor Samuels, after one game for Jamaica's senior team, was earlier selected by the JCA for an ongoing cricket programme of two players each year playing cricket over a three-month period in England. Later in his early twenties, Trevor Samuels migrated to England where he played in the Bristol Cricket League before injuries brought an early retirement for the talented all-rounder. Amazingly, I was the chairman of a one-man selection committee for the years of the Victoria Mutal Building Society sponsorship programme. Others who benefited from the programme included the brothers Laurie and Alton Williams, Edison Edwards, Michael Millwood, Clifton Folkes, Delroy Morgan, Brian Murphy, Buxton Mitchell, Asonu Spencer, Brenton Beckford, Krishana Edwards, Delroy Taylor, O'Neil Richards, and Ray Stewart.

For the preparation of the regional youth squad of 1988, there was, like years before, a preponderance of quality players coming to the trials. Unfortunately, all 28 could not have been selected to the squad of 14. The gifted stroke players Richard Staple and Milton Thomas were in that non-selection group of 14. It was very challenging for the selectors to have finalized the fourteen-member squad; for both Staple and Thomas it was disappointing not to have been selected. Staple, at eighteen, had another year; whereas

Thomas at nineteen had his last opportunity for selection. As chairman, I have over the years experienced the situations of player's non-selection and their disappointment. After the naming of the squad, it was incumbent on me to offer congratulations to the selected ones and express reassurances to the ones left out that other opportunities would come for them later at the youth or the senior level.

As I continued my reflection of the 1980s cricket calendar, it was an experience of full engagement; the presence at rural and city venues of school boy, parish and club cricket was part of my weekly scheduled. The matches at the school boy level were played on week days and Saturdays, the parish on Saturdays ,and the senior cup of two days duration on Saturdays to Sundays.

In preparation for the yearly regional youth tournament, it was imperative for the selectors to have as much as possible information on the players. It was impractical for four selectors to be visible at all the school boy matches across the island. During my chairmanship, I created a system to augment the coverage. It was a system of support from school coaches, managers, and known city and parish administrators to advise me of players to look at. They were excellent with unquestionable knowledge of the game; their impartiality impressed me, and their contribution was immeasurable. Geographically, they were strategically placed to see the players, not just from their school, but also of other schools. I would often times visit as many matches as I could.

Figure 94 Gregory Brown with Sunlight Cup –St. Jago Champions, 1977

Figure 95 Raymond Ferguson – Kingston Cricket Club and Jamaica national player

Regional Youth Tournament Jamaica 1987

After a gap of four years, the regional youth tournament of 1987 was held in Jamaica with the local fans prepared to see the region's best young players displaying their natural talent. There were high hopes of championship honours for the Jamaica team led by the experienced Jimmy Adams who was in his fifth and last season at the youth level. Also included was the vastly improved Nehemiah Perry, the talented spin bowling all-rounder, as vice-captain. The squad was Jimmy Adams captain, Nehemiah Perry, Robert Samuels, Randy Nelson, Dixieth Palmer, Steve Gordon, Wayne Billings, Michael Millwood, O'Neil Cruickshank, Kirk Ebanks, Lyndon Johnson, Trevor Samuels, and Carlton Carter Jr. The team included several talented batsmen that were expected to do well, they were outshone by the 16-year-old Robert Samuels who scored two centuries and batted splendidly throughout the tournament, and with the Trinidadian Brian Lara were the batting stars of the tournament. It was again a year of misfortunes for the Jamaican lads finishing runners-up to winners Trinidad. In the match with Trinidad, the Jamaica team was looking for significant batting and bowling performances from Adams and Perry; that never materialized. The failure of the two in the match against Trinidad and the early injury to Steve Gordon, who was in tremendous batting form, was a mitigating factor that affected the team in their quest for championship honours.

The Trinidadians, led by their two top players, Brian Lara and Rajindra Dhanrag, played. Lara batted majestically as he always does when playing against Jamaica. He flayed the attack with a big century, and the excellent bowling of the leg spinner Rajindra Dhanrag derailed our progress with a defeat that ended our chances of winning the trophy. From a Jamaican perspective, batsmen Michael Millwood, Dixieth Palmer, and Randy Nelson had important innings that were significant to the team totals. Nelson got high praises from Jamaica's cricket boss Allan Rae, as one who was organized in his stroke play, particularly in front of the wicket. President Rae further commented that the St. Jago High School opener possessed the quality for progress to the national senior level.

The bowling of Kirk Hamilton was inspiring. He generated exceptional pace with steep bounce that unsettled most of the opposing batsmen. In the game against Barbados played at Chedwin Park, he had the batsmen fearful of his pace and awkward bounce. The fans were buzzing. The sight of Hamilton running in at a speed similar to Usain Bolt over 100 meters was exhilarating; it was a spectacle that was great watching. He was spurred on by a spirited home crowd fans with encouraging wordplay; the continuous banter allowed him to sustain the pronounced hostility of his deliveries throughout his bowling spells. It was great watching. Captain Adams, who had an uncomfortable first year at this level demonstrated during the next four years his enormous talent with the bat and ball with several outstanding performances. His understanding of the game was invaluable to me in my capacity as manager. As captain during his last year, he was given the responsibility to do duties behind the wicket in the first match at Desnoes and Geddes Oval. The decision by the selection panel at the recommendation of Rohan Kanhai was short lived, as during the early stages of the first day's play he was replaced behind the stumps by Wayne Billings, a more accomplished wicket keeper and one of the top batsmen in the team. Adams, who was a regular national senior player, having represented the senior team in 1985 as a batsman and left arm spinner was considered by coach Rohan Kanhai as a potential wicket keeper batsman at the regional senior level and beyond. Kanhai's assessment of the gifted Adams had merit and for that reason the selectors with me as chairman complied by having the Jamaica College, Kingston Cricket Club, and Jamaica national senior player the eighteen-year-old Jimmy Adams starting behind the stumps.

Figure 96 Wayne Billings, Jamaica National Youth Player

Figure 97 Victoria Mutual Building Society selectees to England. Edison Edwards and Alton Williams with Bristol Club executive member.

Figure 98 Laurie Williams, Jamaica & West Indies all-rounder

Figure 99 Robert Samuels

Jamaica's 1988 Youth Tournament & Senior Champions

For the regional youth tournament played in Barbados 1988, eight newcomers were included. There was no Jimmy Adams, a mainstay having played for five years; he was no longer eligible.

The selection committee's job was challenging in the finalization of the squad as there were compelling performances to influence the selection process. The squad included six players from the previous year's tournament, namely Michael Millwood as captain, Robert Samuels, Randy Nelson, Dixieth Palmer, Vivian Sailsman and Carlton Carter; the remaining members were Courtney Francis, Raymond Ferguson, Rohan Chambers, Valentino Ventura, Laurie Williams, Clive Banton, and Darren Neita, with Rohan Kanhai as coach and me as manager.

Robert Samuels and the captain Michael Millwood batted with authority and relished the easy pace wickets of Barbados; each had a century during the tournament. Samuels's century against Trinidad at the Empire Cricket Club was dominant and thrilling; it was an innings laced with several boundaries and beyond. His dominance over the Trinidad attack led by Scott Rodriquez. the left arm pacer and Ragindra Dhanrag, the wily right arm leg spinner was captivating. Samuels' knock on that day at a ground that produced the great West Indian batsman Sir Everton Weeks was entertainment of truly greatness for the sizeable crowd. It was an amazing innings that stamped the class of a truly exceptional youth player that separated him from most batsmen at the age group level for the four years he played. His repertoire of stroke play was masterful with exhilarating shots that thrilled the sparsely gathering of spectators. It was a knock that Samuels promised the players, coach, and I as manager that he would have played; it was breathtaking and will long be remembered by his teammates, Coach Kanhai, and I as manager.

In the same game, the great Brian Lara had one of the most brilliant centuries at this level. His timing was unquestionably glimpses of a genius in the infancy of greatness. For those present, the impact of his batting will always be remembered for the execution of majestic stroke-play on either side of wicket; it was artistry fully on display and acknowledged by our coach, the immortal West Indian batsman and captain the magnificent Rohan Kanhai.

Apart from Samuels and Millwood, a number of players on this their last participation at the regional youth level performed below expectation. Laurie Williams was the exception. Initially, he was not in the group preparing for the trials. On the recommendation of Winston Brown, President of the Clarendon Cricket Association--who used his green painted Ford Lazer motor car to block the pathway of my brown painted Ford Lazer car on the main street of May Pen in front of a Supermarket parking area to get his attention-- Brown asked, most graciously, for me to have a look at Laurie Williams, the all-rounder who was practicing with his schoolmates at his school ground Garvey Maceo just outside of the capital town of May Pen, Clarendon.

Having had a look at the young batting all-rounder who bowled at a lively pace and was easy on the eye with his batting talents, I was convinced that he would be on the plane to Barbados. He never had a passport and I arranged with Brown to have him meet with me at a photography center in May Pen the following day to have his picture taken and to sign a passport form with the photographs. I then took the necessary steps to procure his passport (During my tenure as a JCA member, I was assigned the responsibility of procuring birth Certificates and Passports for selected national players).

President Winston Brown's optimism was vindicated. Laurie Williams proved himself with bat and ball in the trial games and was selected for the tour. Soon after, Laurie Williams ,by consistency with bat and ball playing for Kensington Cricket club was rewarded with his national senior cap and continued to perform impressively with the bat and his lively medium to fast bowling at the regional senior level that led to his selection to the West Indies ODI team. Sadly, the talented Laurie Williams, at age thirty-three, was killed in a car crash on the Portmore Causeway in his native country Jamaica. Laurie Williams' untimely death sent shockwaves across the cricket fraternity of the Caribbean nations. His passing was painful to his family, the many of his beloved home parish Clarendon, including his Alma mater Garvey Maceo, Clarendon Cricket Association, Kensington Cricket Club, and the wider cricket communities of Jamaica.

Michael Millwood's century was well organized with beautifully controlled strokes on either side of the wicket.

"That innings showed exceptional class," echoed coach Kanhai.

I concurred with the former champion West Indies batting star. It was a lovely, compiled century. Millwood's leadership showed imagination. His bowling changes and field placing, especially when the opposition batsmen were well entrenched, demonstrated shrewdness. So impressed I was with his captaincy, I recommended to the Saint Catherine Club that he be supported for the captaincy of the Senior Cup Team for the 1989 season. At the Club's Annual General meeting, Michael Millwood was nominated and confirmed unanimously as the senior cup captain. For the regional senior team, Jamaica was the 1988 champions. It was time for celebration by the players, a celebration embraced by the fans who have seen years of continued hope for championship honours that ended a nineteen-year drought. The team was one of the better-balanced teams to have represented the country and was well led by the first-time captain Marlon Tucker. Tucker's captaincy was inspirational. The players were high spirited and they knew that they were being led by a captain who was full of confidence, proactive, and made remarkable bowling changes, changes that brought intended results. The batting led by Wayne Lewis was consistent at the top of the order with wonderful stroke-play including a century, two 50's and other scores in the 40's. Delroy Morgan and Jeffrey Dujon scored a century each and other significant scores. There were other important innings played by Mark Neita, Cleveland Davidson, and Robert Haynes, innings that bolstered the batting at crucial periods of the game.

The bowling of spinners Robert Haynes and captain Marlon Tucker bowling in tandem had rewarding success; they applied a lot of pressure on the opposing batsmen. Tucker the off spinner, was very economical with his variation and controlled spin and overspun deliveries. Robert Haynes was just as effective with his leg spin bowling that played havoc with most of the opposing batsmen. It was a dream tournament for the two highly respected

Jamaican cricketers.

The experience of the great Michael Holding, Courtney Walsh, and Patrick Patterson when they were available was a major component of the bowling resources and played their role as was expected. The all-rounder Aaron Daley bowled well within himself and lend support to the varying attack. It was, by all accounts, a very wonderful year for Jamaica's regional senior cricketers.

The fans were always backing the players through the lean years and the rewards of 1988 were received with overwhelming joy and satisfaction.

Jeffrey Dujon

Delroy Morgan

Nehemiah Perry

Patrick Patterson

Motivation and Successes

At the local level, there was an upsurge of fan support at venues in the city and most rural grounds. The Red Stripe winning performance of the national senior team was the principal factor for the increased interest. The senior team defense of their 1988 title was bubbling with confidence. The Marlon Tucker led team was very confident of a 1989 performance similar to the previous year's championship achievement. The preparation leading into the competition went well as was customary of our national teams over recent years. As one of the selectors who chose the group, I was pleased at the team members' form in the trials. The sign was evident to us that the squad was settled and very confident of their respective roles as a team.

The inspirational captain Marlon Tucker was upbeat at the team's 1988 performance and made it clear that the team was in a better position to win the championship than they were the year before. The bowling was again formidable with the vastly improved Perry with his off spin leading the way with wonderful match figures, and with Robert Haynes, they were always a penetrative combination that created concern for the opposing batsmen. Having the services of the experienced Holding, Walsh, and Patterson made the attack more formidable. They might not have picked up a lot of wickets, but the pressure they created up front with masterful control of swing, movement, and pace set the platform for Perry and Haynes to cast a web of indecisiveness on the opposition batsmen. Support from Tucker with his off spin and Aaron Daley with his medium pace deliveries were invaluable to the attack.

Again, Tucker handled his bowlers without blemish. His changes were well calculated and made with the intended effectiveness. The out cricket was outstanding, led by the skills of Dujon behind the stumps and the efficiency of Jimmy Adams, Aaron Daley, Nehemiah Perry, Cleveland Davidson, and Delroy Morgan in the field, tightened the grip for the bowlers to have contained and created pressure on the opposition batsmen. Our batsmen delivered efficiently as a well-organized batting order with remarkable consistency; the depth and reliability of the batting was consequential to our team totals.

Delroy Morgan consistently exhibited a batting treat with his wide array of magnificent stroke play that won the acclamation of his teammates. The brilliant batting of the unassuming Delroy Morgan was reminiscent of his tremendous batting skills as a youth player at the regional level in Guyana 1985 and Trinidad 1986, two tournaments that won praises from the fans of both countries. Morgan's batting in the 1989 senior regional tournament was superlative; reports from team members and Captain Tucker were overwhelmed with compliments of his batting talent. Cleveland Davidson's undefeated double century against the Leeward Islands, and other important innings, positioned him as an integral link of the team batting strength. Captain Tucker played a couple of sterling knocks, innings that were significant in the context of the game. Jimmy Adams batted pretty well with significant runs to help shore up the batting.

Wayne Lewis' delightful century was one of complete dominance that unsettled the Windward Island bowlers. Mark Neita's contribution with the bat was also useful with a half century and an innings of 49. Jeffrey Dujon's 64 against Barbados was an innings of pure beauty, a style of batting that he was recognized for throughout his career.

The solid all-round strength of the team with batting, bowling, and fielding, and the expertise of the astute leadership quality of captain Marlon Tucker were the hallmarks that piloted the Jamaicans to championship honours. The success of the senior team in capturing the regional tournament for a second successive year was inspiring to the 1989 youth team, a team that had among their ranks eight players with previous tournament experience. Among the newcomers was the explosive batsman Donavan Clarke. Clarke showed tremendous form in the trials with impressive scores, including a double century. He was well-organized in compiling his runs at a very good pace and looked prepared for a successful tournament with the bat.

The batting on paper was imposing with the likes of Robert Samuels, who was in his third year and was one of the better batsmen coming out of the two earlier tournaments with three centuries to his name. There were Court-ney Francis, Rohan Chambers, and Valentino Ventura, all of whom were in their second season, and the batting stylish captain Richard Staple as the other main batsman. Shane Ford the wicket keeper and a batsman in his own rights, Vivian Sailsman the off spinner, and Carlton Carter the left arm spin-ner were considered bowling all-rounders. Robert Manning the lanky left arm spinner who was in the original 1987 squad and replaced by Carter be-fore the tour got underway was also included after missing two tourna-ments. For the record, Carter although a member of the 1987 squad, did not play a game with Jimmy Adams and Nehemiah Perry being the two pre-ferred spinners who played in all the matches. The fast-bowling quartet of Clifton Folkes, Errol Nolan, Kirk Hamilton, and the Left Arm Steve Gordon was expected to cause concern for the opposing batsmen with their pace, bounce, and swing. The team coach was the former outstanding Jamaica batsman Renford Pinnock in the absence of the master batsman Rohan Kanhai who was unavailable. Pinnock was my teammate for many years at Saint Catherine Cricket Club and was a popular choice replacing Kanhai.

The team performance fell well below expectation; a batting line up that was expected to build winning team totals failed to deliver. Courtney Francis and Rohan Chambers scored centuries when Chambers, well set for another with an innings of 70 plus against a very strong Leeward Islands bowling attack dominated by their vaunted fast bowlers spearheaded by Hamish Anthony. Captain Richard Staple was consistent with the bat and looked ready for the senior Jamaica level.

The past two seasons, Jamaica batting star Robert Samuels did not have the type of returns with the bat as was anticipated. He had promising starts with-out going on to his usual imposing scores. The fast bowlers, headed by the awesome and sustained pace of Errol Nolan, was most impressive. Kirk Hamilton was least effective when compared with his threatening pace and bounce of 1987. The spinners Sailsman and Carter, bowled with control and were rewarded with useful wickets. Robert Manning's, the other spinner, appearances were limited; Sailsman and Carter were preferred ahead of him.

In our game against the eventual tournament winners Leeward Islands a well-balanced team with a very strong fast bowling attack, it was an attack that created discomfort to our batsmen. Hamish Anthony's pace and swing was consistent; most of the batsmen found it disconcerting coping with the pace of his deliveries. The other pacers were also effective and presented problems for the batsmen with the exception of Captain Richard Staple and Rohan Chambers. Both batsmen were able to withstand the barrage of very fast bouncers and threatening wicket taking deliveries with a strong defense and selective shot making in an excellent partnership. Chambers' top score with a splendid 70 plus and Staple with a lovely half century. The effort of the two Jamaicans on a pitch that was tailor-made for the fast bowlers was commendable. The Leeward Islands' team were worthy champions and deserving of the accolades showered upon them at the presentation ceremony.

During the presentation of trophies, a West Indies youth team was announced for a short tour to Canada. Richard Staple, Robert Samuels, and Errol Nolan were in the squad, and surprisingly for Rohan Chambers, who had a century against Trinidad at Bourda plus that magnificent 70 against the champions Leeward Islands, these were not convincing enough for his inclusion to the squad. I recalled as manager of the West Indies team that Stanley Franks, who was the Leeward Islands manager, was impressed with Rohan Chambers' innings against the vaunted Leeward' bowling attack. He was disappointed that Rohan was not selected for the tour.

The Glory of Championship Honor

From the first meeting I attended as secretary of Jamaica's selection committee, a committee chaired by Gerry Alexander the former West Indies wicketkeeper batsman and captain, I was given the responsibility of procuring the birth certificates and passport for players selected to the Jamaica senior and youth teams who never had a passport. This practice continued throughout the years to my last assignment obtaining Chris Gayle's Passport in 1996 when he was selected to the West Indies under 19 team to play against the touring Pakistan under 19's in Guyana.

So many were beneficiaries of the service provided by expressing their gratefulness and so it was with Marlon Gibbs, a member of the 1990 youth champion team. In 2020 from his home in the UK with me in New York, he reminded me of his reaction when I handed him his first Passport and the original copy of his Birth Certificate while we were at the Norman Manley Airport in Kingston before going through Immigration on our way to Trinidad for the 1990 regional youth tournament. He gleefully uttered the words, "Manage, for this you will be rewarded with the 1990 Trophy." As so often happened, the air of nostalgia prevailed when reminiscing with past players, players who I have had the opportunity of interacting with during the formative years of their development as cricketers and life beyond the cricket fields.

The conversation I had with Marlon was thirty years after that memorable 1990 tournament. He expressed how emotional it was for him and the other members of the team when the final game ended with the result the Jamaica team needed, a result that clinched the 1990 title in their favor. Marlon Gibbs currently lives in Wolverhampton, England.

Before crowning themselves as champion, the Jamaicans hold on championship honors was a ten-year gap. As the manager of the team from 1983 to 1989, I was a witness to their disappointment. I saw the tears of sadness, especially during the years when the team lamented their near misses of championship honours. Jimmy Adams, a member of the squad for five of the ten years, was quick to congratulate the 1990 team's resounding success. In a letter to me while plying his cricket in the UK:

"Years of team disappointment, years of being the brides maid, years of just missing out been champions, my congratulations to the team, Manage," quoted the very popular former Jamaica youth captain and a senior regional player at the time.

Winning meant so much to the players. The scene of happiness in the player's enclosure with tears of joy was understandable; the scene of happiness was shared by the coach Jerry Reid and me as manager. Jerry was on his first assignment as a national coach. His success as the coach was a vindication of the rural parishes long held belief that there were individuals in that part of Jamaica who played the game with valued knowledge to do the job efficiently. As manager, I shared the happiness of the players; so many before them during the last decade were denied the wonderful feeling of championship honours. The heartbreak of coming so close to be runners up on several occasions was excruciating to be a part of. The achievement of the 1990 champions was shared by many past players including past youth captains Gregory Brown, Marlon Tucker, Patrick Harris, Deron Dixon, Jimmy Adams, Michael Millwood, and Richard Staple, all of whom were exemplary with laudatory comments.

The team performances were remarkable with outstanding individual bowling performances led by fast bowler Clifton Folkes who mesmerized the batsmen with two-way swing and movement off the pitch with well disguised change of pace. He was absolutely skillful. The effectiveness of his bowling was a nightmare to the opposing batsmen who found him a serious threat in negotiating his deliveries. It was one of the better bowling performances by any quick bowler during the 1980's to the mid 1990's regional tournaments. His splendid bowling figures stood out among all bowlers and was recognized as the player of the tournament with 31 wickets to complete a great bowling achievement. A truly great performance by the son of Castel Folkes the former Jamaica fast bowler and my teammate with the Saint Catherine Cricket Club during our playing years. Castel, like any father would, was ecstatic with Clifton's exceptional performance, a performance that was pivotal to the team championship success. When we arrived at the Piarco Airport for the beginning of the tournament, the young Folkes, whose hair was prematurely grey, was approached by a reporter who mistakenly believed that he was the team manager. Folkes indicated to the reporter who the manager was and smilingly said, "At the end of the tournament, I will be interviewed and no apology would be required." At the presentation ceremony, Folkes was lauded for his excellent tournament accomplishment and was justly bestowed with the celebrated honour as Player of the Tournament and was indeed interviewed by a reporter.

Carlton Carter Jr. had a good tournament with the ball; his left arm leg spinning deliveries and a well disguised arm ball presented difficulty for the batsmen. He was always a threat to the batsmen who were never able to master his spin and guile. His tournament haul of 22 wickets was testament to how well he bowled. He was also a very reliable batsman in the middle of the batting order. His brilliant knock for an innings of 63 against Trinidad helped to bolster the Jamaica first innings total in that decisive tournament final fixture. The batting and bowling of Carter was enhanced by his superb fielding ability close to the wicket and in the outfield.

Clifton Folkes' schoolmate at St. Elizabeth Technical High School the long-limbed Alvin Bent was a good foil to the brilliant top wicket taker. Bent's contribution was significant to the champion team's success; his highly intelligent controlled fast bowling was the model of accuracy that kept batsmen from scoring freely while picking up crucial wickets in his tournament tally of 16. Captain Rohan Chambers knew Bent's role and used him judiciously to be the success he was after missing the first game against Guyana. His first innings spell of 6 for 45 against Trinidad set the stage for Folkes' demolition of the Trinidadian batsmen with figures of 7 for 47 in their second innings. Franklyn Rose about the quickest of the tournament fast bowlers, Clive Ledgister the lanky fast bowler with his controlled, Valentino Ventura with his steady off spin, Marlon Gibbs the off spinner and skipper Rohan Chambers together lend useful support to the top wicket takers Folkes, Carter, and Bent.

The tournament matches involving the Jamaicans were low scoring; our batsmen were required to occupy the batting crease for unusual long periods in accumulating their runs, runs that were not substantial in numbers but valuable in worth to the team totals. Tony Powell and Carlton Carter were the only Jamaicans with individual innings over fifty.

Tony Powell the attacking left-handed shot making batsman got 97, which was the highest individual score by a Jamaican. Tony is the son of George Powell the former Jamaica left-handed opener who scored 95 in his second game for Jamaica; he was caught on the long leg boundary by Eldine Baptise off the bowling of Noel Guishard just before lunch on the opening day of a regional four-day game against the Leeward Islands at Sabina Park. Tony and his dad were similarly built and were both left-handed batsmen with a penchant for attacking stroke play. Carlton Carter Jr., son of Carlton Carter Snr. the former Melbourne Cricket Club captain top score of 63 vs Trinidad, was an innings very crucial to the team total. He offered so much to the championship success of the team.

On our return home, we were met by officials of the JCA at plane side with adulation that was most fitting for the young champions, followed with exceptional praises by Immigration and Custom Officers for their praiseworthy accomplishment. Fans outside joined in with their compliments. In my capacity as manager of previous national youth teams returning home, this time it was different. It was a victorious and jubilant group of youngsters basking in the glory of a title well earned.

Figure 100 Castel Folkes

Figure 101 Valentino Ventura, Larry Creighton, and Rohan Chambers - Former teammates of Jamaica's 1990 youth championship team

The Young Australians Visit

After a successful 1990 regional youth tournament, Jamaica the regional Under-19 champions were host later that year to the touring Australian youth team in a two-day game at Kaiser Sports Club St. Anns Bay on August 1 and 2 and a three-day game at Sabina Park, August 4, 5 and 6.

The Australian players, some of whom exceeded age 19, including Shane Warne and Damion Martin, were age 20 and not far from being 21 and others at 20, whereas the Jamaicans were between the ages of seventeen and nineteen.

There were a number of players on the Australian team who were exceptionally talented and very active in Australian club cricket and later became first class and test cricketers. The ones who made it to test level were Shane Warne, Damion Martin Jamie Cox, Cameron White, Michael Bevan, and Damion Fleming. The Jamaican selectors retained all of the 1990 championship team members with Corey Phillips from Holmwood Technical High School added to the squad.

Phillips' inclusion was for his remarkable century in the final of the Spaulding Cup between his school Holmwood Technical, winners of the Rural Headley Cup competition, and Kingston College winners of the Sunlight competition. His brilliant knock was one of dominance against a varied opposition bowling attack. He dictated the passage of his innings with lovely attacking shots and in defense, he was superb. A century in a final and the manner in which the innings was compiled said a lot about the youngster's mindset and with the selectors looking on, he certainly made a statement for his selection. In a final to crown Jamaica's schoolboy supremacy watched by a crowd in the hundreds, they were enthralled with the batting of the Holmwood student who had a wonderful Headley Cup season with the bat leading to the matchup with the city schoolboy champion Kingston College.

On the final day to decide the champion schoolboy team, the game was abandoned because of continuous rain to the disappointment of the fans. They were denied seeing the strong batting lineup of the Kingston College team led by Robert Samuels, one of the most dominant local schoolboy and regional youth batters, and the very accomplished Valentino Ventura against the varied attack of the rural champions led by the giant fast bowler Franklyn Rose, Sheldon Broomfield similarly built like Rose and much quicker, and the very effective medium pace of captain David Campbell.

The first match against the Australians played at the picturesque Kaiser Sports Ground was buzzing with excitement, which was to be expected. The Kaiser ground was known for large spectator attendance when the national senior team was involved and so it was for the youth team against the visiting Australians. The fans were engrossed with the well contested game. Among the fans were my daughter Roxanne Chambers and her high school friend Shelly Glasgow, both of whom were at the time students at Immaculate Conception High School.

My daughter Roxanne, who never saw me play or accompanied me to watch local club matches, was always keen to watch Jamaica and West Indies test matches at Sabina Park and so was Shelly. Jamaica having won the toss, inserted the Australians to take first strike, their openers had a quiet and comfortable start for an opening partnership of 41. After losing the first wicket of Craig White to Alvin Bent, Skipper Rohan Chambers and Carlton Carter then had a stranglehold on the Aussie batsmen. Captain Chambers, with figures of 5 for 26 from 12 overs, had the batsmen guessing to his medium pace off cutters and cleverly disguised straight deliveries; he often times lured the batsmen in false strokes, resulting in their dismissals. The wicketkeeper Lloyd Black was superb with the gloves in stumping two batsmen off the medium pace of Chambers. Carlton Carter again demonstrated his exceptional value to the team with 3 for 54 off 18.4 overs and got the key wicket of Damian Martin bowled for 91 when he was well entrenched and comfortably moving towards a century. Carter's fielding was again admirable with his swiftness and assured hands. After both teams batted in the first innings, not much time was left in the two-day game to have a clear winner.

The Australians had a second knock reaching 104 for 4 with Jamie Cox leading the way for an attractive 41 and Michael Bevan 31 before the declaration setting Jamaica the daunting task of getting 165 to win the match with very little time to do so. In the end, it was too much to ask of for the home team with Jamaica 40 for 3 when the game was called off.

The first of the two days was riveting with both teams trying to have the ascendancy, and at the close of play, the writing was on the wall that the game was heading for a predictable draw. The match was well contested and played in an atmosphere of excellent sportsmanship. Many thanks to the giant bauxite company, Kaiser for hosting the game and our stay in that Jamaican area of splendor. The hospitality extended to both teams before and after the game was deserving of commendations as was expressed by both the Australian and Jamaican managers at the closing ceremony.

For the three-day encounter at Sabina Park, the selectors brought back to the starting eleven Larry Creighton and Valentino Ventura, both of whom were members of the regional championship team. The two changes were made at the expense of Rose and the new comer Corey Phillips.

The full complement of the team was Rohan Chambers Captain, Valentino Ventura as Vice-Captain, Larry Creighton, Robert Samuels, Courtney Francis, Tony Powell, Orville Pennant, Carlton Carter, Lloyd Black, Clifton Folkes, and Alvin Bent.

Having won the toss, the Jamaica team took first strike on a pitch that appeared ideal for batting. It was obvious from the early overs that the balls were not coming on to the bat as expected. After losing the early wicket of Creighton, Ventura was joined at the wicket by his Kingston College teammate Robert Samuels; they stabled the innings with a productive partnership of 59. It was a partnership of watchfulness by the two with purposeful intent in defense and scoring freely before the dismissal of Samuels the team top batsman for 36 and the score 61. After the dismissal, Jamaica then lost the wickets of Courtney Francis and captain Rohan Chambers to make it 102 for 4.

Tony Powell, playing his first game for the national youth team, joined Ventura who was batting confidently and holding the innings together. Powell, known for his attacking style of batting, was subdued at the beginning before unleashing his wide range of runs scoring strokes, while Ventura was unruffled and batted assuredly in scoring his runs. Against the run of play with the two batting beautifully in a partnership worth 112, the well secured Ventura was dismissed for a brilliant 71. The Ventura-Powell century partnership was magnificent; it was a partnership of great understanding between the two. They batted with the mindset of rebuilding the innings after been precariously placed at 102 for 4 to 214 before the partnership was broken.

Valentino Ventura, popularly called Tino, was a model of exceptional confidence in defense. His shot selection was precise in execution; he was an excellent partner for the more attacking intent of the dynamic   Powell. The partnership was excellent; it was a partnership of great understanding between the two. Their frequent talks between overs meant that they needed each other's support to amass a respectable team total. The running between the wickets was remarkable. Powell went on to register a wonderful century laced with exciting shots on both sides of the wicket. Powell's century was an innings that signaled the inherent talent of his prowess as a batter for future senior national selection. His attacking shots against the wily Warne were amazing and had the fans cheering.

The Jamaica innings closed at 306, which was a good showing against a very talented attack led by Shane Warne who went on to be one of the greatest test wicket takers with 708. The Australians replied with 338 for a first innings lead of 32 runs; it was a total built around two solid innings by opener Craig White 93 and wicketkeeper D.S Berry with a brilliant 102. Damion Martin had a supporting knock of 45.

Both White and Berry played beautifully against a Jamaican attack that never allowed the Aussies' innings to extend beyond their eventual total. The bowling of Folkes, Bent, and Carter was impressive with Folkes leading the way with a 5-wicket haul. His spells were steady and kept the batsmen watchful of his swinging deliveries and movement off the pitch. In his spell of 25.5 overs, he was used strategically by captain Chambers to pick up wickets and restrained the free flow of runs scoring.

Folke's opening bowling partner Alvin Bent with 2 for 64 was accurate and never allowed the batsmen to get on top of his probing deliveries. Carlton Carter figures of 34 overs for three wickets took a lot of watching from the Aussies' batters. He never allowed any form of dominance by the batsmen with his tantalizing and penetrative deliveries. The Jamaicans in their second innings scored 136 for 4 wickets, thanks to a solid undefeated knockoff 45 by Robert Samuels who was playing his last game after four seasons at the youth level. Larry Creighton and Valentino Ventura contributed 26 each.

The young Jamaicans should be comforted by their performances during the two-match series, a series that confirmed their talent against an Australian team that was a quality one. The Australians were much older and showed the maturity of their exposure at club level and Shefield state level. Their team was well-balanced and exciting with the richness of talent.

As Chairman of the youth selection committee and manager of the Jamaica team, I commended the players for their resoluteness as a team. It was a successful journey for them in a year when they crowned themselves as regional youth champions, and to perform the way they did against the star-studded Australian team was admirable. Captain Rohan Chambers led a team of players that displayed confidence and belief in themselves as one for all and all for one; the unity was pronounced in the manner in which they played. They did what was expected of them as national representatives. The respect and appreciation to coach Jerry Reid for his significant contribution was shown by all the players. They loved him and saw him as a caring father figure. Their high level of sportsmanship was exemplary and was a testament to their parents, schools, and coaches for preparing them to that level of truly wonderful representatives of their country.

Figure 102 Tony Powell

Going for Triple Championship

The very successful Jamaica senior team under the inspiring leadership of Marlon Tucker, who led the regional team to championship honours in 1988 and 1989, prepared intently with great expectation of a successful tournament in 1990.

The team again had early training under the methodical guidance of the very competent physical trainer David Bernard. Bernard played cricket and soccer for the Jamaica Defense Force. At cricket, he was a lively medium pacer and dependable with the bat. We played on the same Jamaica Defense Force senior cup team during the two years I represented the Army. Playing soccer for the Army and Cavaliers, a team that provided Jamaica with several outstanding players with the big ball, Bernard was a stalwart in defense and was considered one of the better players in that key position to have represented the country. His strong showing in the position of defense gained him selection to the Jamaica National team over a long period.

David Bernard's prowess as a soccer player, a sport that he demonstrated proficiency and reliability at the back line demanded his presence most time and limited his involvement in cricket. After his playing years with the bigger ball ended, he offered his services as a physical trainer to the Jamaica squad and was accepted by the JCA. Previously, the players controlled their fitness programme individually, a format not good enough for a season of five four day matches with one day matches a part of the season's itinerary. Bernard's exceptional work ethics with the players during the years was commendable. The discipline and method of his training was deeply respected and appreciated by the players, coaches, managers, and selectors.

Monetarily, there was no gain for David Bernard during the period I served as a member of the Jamaica Cricket Association. He diligently prepared the players for home games without a stipend and never travelled for the away games. Thanks to Dickie Coke and Kingsley Goodison, two employees of the

Desnoes & Geddes, who with undying love for cricket and football were influential in presenting the case to their company bosses for Bernard to accompany the team on tour. Goodison, the tall and well-built fast bowler, represented Lucas Club at Cricket and Football (Soccer) as a sturdy centre half. Dickie Cooke, who also played at centre half, represented Melbourne and Jamaica at Football (Soccer). The two sports stalwarts' effectiveness in having secured the sponsorship for Bernard's travel arrangement with the team was lauded by the players, team management, and the selectors.

The Jamaica Cricket Association acknowledged its gratefulness to both Dickie Coke and Kingsley Goodison, as well as their employers Desnoes & Geddes Limited, brewers of one of the world's finest beers "Red Stripe Larger."

The defending champions started the defense of their title away from home against Trinidad at the Queens Park Oval during the first week of January with a victory after been dismissed for 203. It was a low scoring first innings score by the Jamaican batsmen, Delroy Morgan, top scorer with a lovely 52 followed by Robert Haynes with 38. Ian Bishop 5 for 43 led the way for the Trinidadian bowlers. In reply, it was a tense battle for first innings lead. Eventually, Trinidad edged pass the Jamaica score with 205 a lead of 2 runs; batting for Trinidad R. J. Bishop got 42 followed by Gus Logie with 41.

Patrick Patterson bowled remarkably at top speed. He was at his best with good rhythm and wicket taking deliveries. His effort restricted the opponents to make it a second innings game; a magnificent century of 108 by the left-handed Jimmy Adams followed by another left hander Robert Haynes with a very attractive 55. Ian Bishop again bowled at top pace with wicket taking deliveries to finish with 6 for 81 and match figures of 11 for 124, a truly remarkable feat by the broad-shouldered Ian Bishop.

Trinidad was asked to get 279 for an outright victory and were bowled out for 221 giving Jamaica victory by 58 runs. This was a very good start by the defending champions in pursuit of a three-peat.

The second game against Barbados at home was high-scoring in the first innings by both teams. Batting first Barbados amassed a score of 423 with Carlisle Best getting a lovely and imposing 175, Thelson Payne 59 and Stanton Proverbs 58 with Patrick Patterson bagging 5 for 59 and Courtney Walsh 2 for 79.

The strength of the Jamaican batting was on show with a total of 485, Delroy Morgan getting a stroke filled 94. Davidson in his customary unruffled style with 91, Dujon with a classic 76, and the left-handed all-rounder Robert Haynes a solid 72 packed with blistering drives.

It was comforting to the home fans to see the batsmen on show displaying their repertoire of delightful strokes; Morgan and Dujon delighted the fans with exquisite drives on either side of the wicket and Haynes with Davidson in their contrasting styles were brilliant.

Barbados, in their second turn at the wicket replied with 168 for 9 with the match ending in a draw. Top scores for Barbados was Desmond Haynes with 39 and Proverbs 34, Robert Haynes 5 for 28 and Nehemiah Perry 3 for 55.

The Jamaica team was growing in confidence. After a good showing in the first two games, the batsmen were now showing their wonderful talent and were ready to give their team imposing totals as a cushion for the fast bowlers and spinners. Having won the first game away from home against Trinidad and having the better of Barbados with first innings honours, they were playing at a level of high expectation going into the next two away games against the Windward Islands and Guyana. Led by the inspirational captain Marlon Tucker, the passion for success was felt, not only by the talented players, but was also in evidence by the overwhelming support of the Jamaican fans.

Championship honours to the Jamaicans for 1990 was shattered by unending rain fall that prevented a ball being bowled in both the Windward Islands and Guyana games.

In the final game at Sabina Park against the Leeward Islands, the Jamaica team was able to lead on first innings but crumbled in the second. Jamaica batting first through lovely knocks by the majestic Jeffrey Dujon 92 and the compact and durable Cleveland Davidson 65 and Courtney Walsh with an entertaining 34 were able to finish with 337. The Leeward Islands were bowled out for 281, with two half centuries, one by Livingston Harris 81 and the other by the experienced Keith Atherton 53. Noel Guishard also batted well for a pleasing innings of 48, Walsh 3 for 74, Perry 2 for 52, and Patterson

2 for 68 secured a first innings lead by the home team.

In their turn at the wicket a second time, the formidable Jamaican batting could not withstand the penetrative bowling by the promising twenty-year-old pacer Hamish Anthony 5 for 40 and the consistent wicket taker Eldine Baptise 4 for 47 to end with a disappointing and paltry total of 130. Hamish Anthony, a year earlier in 1989 representing the Leeward Islands in the regional youth tournament, his pace was electrifying and created uncertainly in the minds of our youth batsmen with Rohan Chambers and captain Richard Staple as the only two who were able to negotiate and who played with any semblance of comfort as they both got half centuries. Hamish Anthony, in the youth tournament, was a threat to the batsmen of all the competing teams with his pace and awkward bounce; such was his effectiveness against the senior Jamaican batsmen.

The Leeward Islands set to get 187 for an outright victory were hard pressed to get up to 190 for 7 with Skipper Marlon Tucker 4 for 43 and Robert Haynes 2 for 43 applying pressure on their batsmen. Thanks to the resolute batting of Baptise 44, Guishard 40 and Luther Kelly 38 saw their team home to victory and championship honours for the 1990 tournament.

It was a satisfying and remarkable period towards the ending of the 1980's by the Jamaicans. The successive titles by the seniors in 1988 and 1989 and the solid start to the 1990 season was so much to be celebrated, only to be thwarted for a three-peat by inclement weather causing the abandonment without a ball being bowled in two of the five matches. The Jamaica team before Marlon Tucker's remarkable run as captain was always a team with players good enough to win titles but were unable in closing out games.

Fundamental Improvement of Jamaica's Cricket

The 1980's to the mid nineteen 90's was a period of greater participation for players at different levels of Jamaica's cricket. The implementation and significance of the local Red Stripe competition played on weekends and the Kingston Wharves for players up to age 19 were competitions that created an avenue for the better players in the country. The Red Stripe competition initially was contested by seven teams that included a Youth team, an Under twenty-five, All Seniors and the Zonal teams of East, West, Central, and Northern. After the first season, the youth team participation was discontinued. It was a decision that was perplexing to a majority of the fans. The competition was intended to have embraced the best talent in the country of which the youth players development was of paramount importance. Participation would have enhanced their growth in a timely fashion. There were adequate number of matches played that allowed the senior selectors a wide perception of the players, especially from the Zones (Rural Parishes).The competition was perceived by most as the Flag Ship of Jamaica's local competitions.

The three-week coaching programme for our considered best under twenty-three players included a number of players in their teens supervised by the famous West Indies giants of the game, Rohan Kanha and Andy Roberts, and was very helpful to their development. The programme was coordinated by Roy Paul and me on behalf of the Jamaica Cricket Association. The under nineteen age group WherryWharf/Kingston Wharves competition ongoing from its inception in 1983 to 1996 when I migrated to the USA was sponsored initially by Wherry Wharf, and after the first year was sponsored by the parent body Kingston Wharves. The cross-country competition helped significantly in the selection process of youth players called to camp in preparation for trial matches that led to the naming of our national youth teams for Cricket West Indies regional tournaments. As secretary of the Senior Selection Committee chaired by the former West Indies captain Gerry Alexander with JK Holt, Roy McLean and Jackie Hendricks as the other members, I experienced the ineptness of the selectors identifying both city and rural schoolboy players for the national youth camp. The system needed a robust transformation in place, a system that would be comprehensive and offered encouragement to the many aspiring schoolboy players, particularly those who were at a disadvantage of not being seen because of their geographical location. The belief that their performance at this level enhanced the opportunity of playing at the zonal level and be called to national trials for possible selection to the Jamaica Youth team was a motivating factor for the youngsters.

It was of tremendous value to Jamaica's cricket when the Wherry Wharf competition got started. It was a competition of my inherent feeling for the many youngsters who were previously denied recognition. I was driven to have discussion with the President Allan Rae on the possibility of a competition that embraced the under nineteen group of players. The then President of the JCA, the former left-handed West Indies opening batsman, a strong backer of schoolboy cricket was receptive of my concern and listened attentively to my verbal blue print advocacy for this important competition.

Allan Rae, considered by most as the most influential JCA President, encouraged me to make representation on any area of our cricket by talking to him first. On this principle, I mentioned to the president a discussion I had with a friend and neighbour Ramsay aka Sugar, a staff member of the city-based company Wherry Wharf, a subsidiary of the giant Wharf operators Kingston Wharves of an island wide competition for the under-nineteens. I recapped Ramsay's endorsement of the proposal and that after discussion with his boss, it was arranged for a delegation from the Jamaica Cricket Association and Wherry Wharf led by Mr. Thompson convene a meeting. The talks were successful and the competition got underway for one year and subsequently taken over by the parent body Kingston Wharves.

The competition, as structured then, was central to the growth of the game at the age group level and was of immense value to the selection of players to the national youth camp. The domestic Red Stripe competition served the purpose similar to the Kingston Wharves; it brought the best group of players under the microscope of the selectors. The competition as was structured, improved the standard of the younger players of the competing teams. The games were followed with keen interest by the cricketing public and significantly by the selectors. The appearances of national and international players on both the under twenty-five and the all-senior teams add credence to the quality to a competition that fulfilled the expectations of the Jamaica Cricket Association. My position as manager of the under twenty-five team allowed me to have seen the many remarkable local players in action. The performances were encouraging and improved their standing as players under the microscope of the selectors, I was also privy to the shrewdness of Marlon Tucker's captaincy.

Flashback

My experience during twenty-three years as a member of the JCA was exceptional and gratifying.

I served with several dedicated administrators, administrator's very knowledgeable with a cricket background. The administrations were led by three excellent Presidents beginning with Allan Rae the former Jamaica captain and West Indies opener, Rex Fennell and Jackie Hendricks the former Jamaica captain and West Indies wicketkeeper. Rex Fennell's knowledge of cricket was enhanced by his managerial involvement in the game as manager of the Monymusk Sugar Estate teams for many years and for his active role with the Clarendon Cricket Association.

Allan Rae was indeed the President of Presidents. His leadership was inspirational. He was a good listener and encouraged members to express their views on any cricket issues relevant to the development of the game. Allan Rae's presidency was acknowledged with confidence by succeeding administrations. At the beginning of my first term as an executive member (Assistant Treasurer) with Rae as President, I was helped immensely to settle in my elevated role by Rex Fennell, the secretary. I got to know Fennell from my earlier years as a Sugar Estate cricketer representing Bernard Lodge while he was manager and mentor of the Monymusk Sugar Estate cricket team.

The members of the administration, but for Dave Roberts a member of Saint Catherine Cricket Club, were in their late fifties and sixties and were not individuals that I knew well. It was natural for Roberts, Fennell, and I to have socialized over drinks away from Sabina Park at the end of our regular monthly board and committee meetings. Members of the then administration included President Allan Rae, Esmond Kentish first Vice President, Keith Brown Second Vice President, Laker Levers secretary, Dave Roberts Assistant Secretary, Keith Wedderburn Treasurer, Leonard Chambers Assistant Treasurer, Professor Gladstone Mills, Gerry Alexander, Jackie Hendricks, Sydney Abrahams, Easton McMorris, Reggie Scarlett, Rex Fennell, Howard Bembridge, Carlton Forbes, Bill Bennett, George Prescod, and Hugh Perry. They were enormously respected as Clubs and Parish Associations representatives; their contribution at committee and monthly meetings was very productive.

Rex Fennell having succeeded Allan Rae as President was acknowledge by the Rural Parishes as a significant elevation to the top position of Jamaica's cricket. He was the first President who came to prominence while he was a member of a rural Parish Association; he was a very effective President. Jackie Hendricks as President was adept at cricket issues and chaired our monthly meetings productively. Hendricks got exceptional support from the Board members and playing members at both the senior and youth levels. He was always available to interact with the players.

There were periodic changes through the years with new members replacing outgoing members who, for personal reasons, choose not to contest reelection. The new members included Roy Paul, Chester Watson, Gladstone Robinson, Dr. Donavan Bennett, Patrick Anderson, Dr. David Crawford, Maurice Foster, Keith Reece, Cecil Fletcher, Carol Gordon, Michael HoShue, Noel Jump, Chris Dehring, Basil Walker, George Sterling, Noel Jump, Newton Jacks, Verley Harrison. Danny Keddo ,and Basil Williams.

Keith Reece was co-opted to the Board year after year for as long as I was a member; my tenure was for twenty-three years, such was the quality of his administrative ability.

The members of the JCA were active administrators at the senior cup Clubs and Parish Associations, a prerequisite that worked admirably in their favour at the highest administrative level of Jamaica's cricket. They came with known values of their established administrative ability and love for the game that prepared them adequately for transition to the governing body of Jamaica's cricket. At the senior cup level, the decade of the eighties was a dominant championship period for Melbourne Cricket Club and Kensington Cricket Club with each winning four titles, Melbourne won 1980, 1981, 1988 and 1989.Kensington 1984, 1985, 1986, and 1987. Both teams were represented by a cadre of talented players, some of whom were national and international. The Kensington team was led by the experienced campaigner and former Jamaica captain and West Indies player Basil Williams in all four years that they were champions. Williams was an attacking and astute captain, a captain who analyzed expertly the vulnerability of batsmen against certain bowlers. As a team, they showed consistency in winning matches. Not many changes were made to their starting eleven during their championship achievements. There was the occasional unavailability of players through illness, national, and international representation. The success of Kensington was evident in the undeniable coordination of team spirit. The players were blessed with the presence of the remarkable fitness trainer David Bernard, the Jamaica physical trainer. Bernard kept the players superbly fit with his routine calisthenics and was embraced by all the players, players who were fully cognizant of the importance of an attribute that was integral to quality performances.

The Kensington Club of the 80's and the earlier decade of the 70's produced players of exceptional ability with the likes of Lawrence Rowe, Basil Williams, Uton Dowe, Everett Whittingham, Errol Wilson, Prince Francis, Oscar Hamilton, Neville Hawkins, Desmond Lewis, Herbert Chang, Donavon Malcolm, Richard Austin, Wayne Lewis, Junior Williams, Robert Haynes, Linval Crawford, George Heron, Kenneth McLeod, Dwight Meikle, Cleveland Davidson and Colin Gordon; but for Oscar Hamilton, all the players named represented Jamaica, with a number of them becoming international players. Additionally, there was the well-built frame of Lincoln Sterling, a talented batsman and indeed a fine player but lacked consistency in his runs scoring ability and Maurice Chong a batsman with the biblical patience of Job, lacked flashy drives was matched by a sound defense and selective runs scoring opportunities at his own pace to the benefit of the team. The Kensington Cricket club at different periods going back to the ending of the nineteen fifties to the mid-sixties led by JK Holt was served by some very talented players including Ferdie Harvey, Neville Hawkins, Lloyd Dunbar, Donald Edwards, Oscar Hamilton, Milton Wisdom, Alfred Valentine, Owen Mitchell, Silbourne Mitchell, Lloyd Seivright, Fitzroy Nangle, Linval Stockhausen and others of known quality.

The successes of the illustrious Kensington Cricket Club was built on years of service by two ardent, skilled and unswerving Presidents, Noel Silvera and Vincent Wong. They were Presidents *extraordinaire*; their love for the game and exceptional leadership was a model befitting of greatness. Melbourne Cricket Club continued to enjoy and embrace social activities at their new location comparable to when they occupied the Elliston Road facility in the earlier years. The fraternization of club life epitomizes a continuation of a family reunion evening after evening. So many young players were attracted to the famous club, a club of earlier players with remarkable batting and bowling skills, skills that were comparable with the best of any generation of club cricketers. The names of Neville Bonitto, Dennis Thorbourne, Buddy Josephs, Gerald Wollaston, Teddy Griffiths, Sam Morgan, Carlton Carter Snr., Colin Fletcher, Mark Neita, Arthur Barrett, Cecil Lawson, Bruce Wellington, Michael Holding, Courtney Walsh and the very competent wicketkeeper batsman Rudy Marzouca, were players of undeniable excellent talent.

There were and it continued to be so for a very long time the presence of former players who became administrators and mentors to the young ones. The names of Gerald Wollaston, Ruddy Williams, Ruddy Marzocco, George Sterling, Keith Reece, Bruce Wellington, Gladstone Robinson, and the renowned Sports writer Tony Becca, epitomized their goodwill.

The club administration included the resolute effectiveness of the very pleasant and wonderful Monica Williams, now Mrs. HoShue. Her contribution to the club was immeasurable and her beloved husband Michael HoShue, who served as treasurer of the JCA ,was acknowledged for his splendid work at the Club. The club's four championship achievements in 1980, 81, 88 and 89 were attributed to a solid batting order and a bowling attack that was very potent. Their batsmen were explosive, always attacking led by William Cole at the top of the order. The exciting Carlton Carter was a nightmare to opposing teams; he was always attacking the best of bowlers with scorching boundary shots and big six hits. Wally Baugh the former Jamaica youth, West Indies youth, and Jamaica national senior player father of West Indies wicket-keeper batsman Carlton Baugh Jr. was one of the most exciting young batsmen in the country; his repertoire of shot making was amazing. It was disappointing that it took so long for him to have been included in the Melbourne team on a regular basis.

The veteran Arthur Barrett, the former West Indies leg spinner, and very competent with the bat, was the captain of the 1980 and 1981 teams; he played a key role during their golden run. Colin Fletcher at the top of the order was always consistent and usually held the batting together for imposing team totals. Mark Neita, considered one of the team top batsmen, was a very good batting prospect from his early teenage years. He was expected by most to have become an international player of repute and one of the younger Jamaican batsmen that the selectors anticipated to have led the national batting in the absence of Rowe, Austin, Mattis and Chang. Neita as captain led the dynamic Melbourne Club to championship honours in 1988.

Earl Melbourne, a touch player of exquisite stroke playing was expected to do well enough to be a national senior player before migrating to North America. Steve Gordon, a well-organized batsman who was expected to have started his senior cup career with Saint Catherine Cricket Club having trained with the Saints team the week before, turned out for the Melbourne Cricket Club. He was expected to have gained his national senior cap much earlier than his belated debut. Odelmo Peters started with Saint Catherine Cricket Club while a schoolboy at Vere Technical High School. When I was the Saints captain, he changed his allegiance to the Melbourne Cricket Club. Peters was a consistent run getter. He possessed the inherent mindset to bat for long periods. He scored his runs with controlled and timely executed shots and his defense was unruffled.

Aubrey Wollaston was an attacking left-handed young batsman with an array of pleasing strokes on either side of the wicket. The talented Paul Palmer, a former national youth player, was good enough to gain national senior representation but never had the backing of the full selection panel. Palmer must have been most disappointed to have missed selection after an innings of ninety plus in the final trial match at Kensington Park and hours after to listen to the announcement of the national squad minus his name. There were the teenagers Robert Samuels and Carlton Carter Jr. who were selected to the national team while they were schoolboys at Kingston College and Campion College, respectively. Samuels later represented the West Indies and was left out unceremoniously before age twenty-six after six test matches with one century and an average of 37.20. Surely Robert Samuels should have been given more opportunities at the test level; it certainly was baffling to most when he was dropped from the team.

Young Carter migrated to the USA at an age when he was eligible for two more years at the regional youth tournament. He was offered a soccer scholarship to the University of St. Johns in New York and that brought an end to the career of an excellent young cricketer destined for greater accomplishments nationally and probably internationally. There were the Ebanks brothers Kirk and Dillon. Kirk was a left arm spinner and very useful with the bat; he represented the national youth and senior teams. Dillon was a very exciting young batsman with a wide range of strokes on either side of the wicket and was particularly very aggressive against the quicker bowlers. The allrounder Deron Dixon, a former Jamaica youth captain and West Indies youth player and a national senior player, was the club captain in 1989. A lot was expected of the gifted Dixon and he was set back by injuries and studies at the University of the West Indies.

Ray Stewart aka Blue, a very young talented batting all-rounder, had the making of a national senior player. He performed splendidly at the school competitions representing Wolmers; he and his boyhood friend Gareth Breese had a record partnership exceeding 450 runs against Campion College in a Sunlight cup game. His contribution was 287 and Breese 299. I also remember with admiration Stewart as a fifteen-year-old brilliant innings of seventy plus in a Sunlight final against Kingston College at Sabina Park. Stewart's performances at the regional under 19 competition was pivotal to Jamaica's 1995 championship achievement. His innings of 109 was the tournament highest individual score. Ray Stewart just missed touring with the West Indies team twin tours to Pakistan and Bangladesh in 1995. He was a reserve player, as the manager of the team, and his presence would have helped significantly. He continued to impress at the senior cup level with his all-round game and was called to the national trials before my departure to the USA.

Marlon Samuels, who I first saw at age fourteen in a Tappin Cup game batting for his school Kingston College against Excelsior at the Elliston Road ground, was impressive. In ten minutes at the wicket, he got to seventeen runs undefeated when his team total surpassed Excelsior's below par score. Marlon's batting in the short period showed early glimpses of his wonderful talent that had an impact on me. I was impressed with the way he batted facing up to the leg spinner Andrew Gayle, brother of the champion batsman Chris Gayle. Andrew having represented the national youth team successfully the year before and continuing to bowl well in the Sunlight Cup competition, was considered a certainty for that year's regional youth tournament. As a leg spinner, he spun the ball appreciably and had excellent control. Samuels, facing up to Gayle, had three boundaries in his short undefeated innings of 17, two brilliantly driven to the long on boundary and the other a classical cover drive that kept going away from the chasing fielder to the boundary. After the game I got permission from the Kingston College coach Roy McLean for a talk with the fourteen-year-old Samuels.

In my capacity as chairman of the youth selection committee, we talked for approximately ten minutes and I learnt that he was a member of the Melbourne minor cup team, I invited Samuels to the under 19 youth training at Sabina Park on the Saturday a couple days later. He explained that his bigger brother Robert Samuels would have had concern about him getting hurt against the older age fast bowlers. I reassured him that I would have a talk with Robert. When I spoke with Robert, he was hesitant and was been protective of Marlon in not wanting him exposed too early to the fast bowlers in the group; however, he agreed for him to attend the training.

On that Saturday of the training, I was being interviewed on the future of Jamaica's youth cricket by Straton Palmer from the JBC TV station on the ground floor of the Kingston Cricket Club, when Junior Bennett who was supervising the training session interrupted the interview and asked that I have a chat with the fourteen-year-old youngster that I added to the squad as he refused to bat when asked to. Accompanied by Palmer and his camera man, I walked across the field to the practice nets. I enquired of Marlon why he never wanted to bat. His explanation was that big brother Robert was worried about him getting hurt.

"Do you want to bat?"

"Yes, sir," he responded.

He was provided with a batting helmet and that was the end of my interview, an interview that was interrupted and resumed days after. The fourteen-year-old Marlon Samuels displayed a batting treat that left the trial invitees in awe; the experienced coach Junior Bennett, Straton Palmer, his camera man and me were impressed.

It was the beginning of the buzz around the name of the gifted Marlon Samuels as a future batting star. After my departure from Jamaica in the mid 90's, the Melbourne Cricket Club continued to provide the atmosphere of attraction to aspiring young cricketers and provided for them meaningful guidance towards their zest for national representation. The central location of the club was and continues to be an irresistible attraction for membership, a club that is an ideal place for socializing after a day at the workplace. As a former player and selector, there were times I questioned myself the non-selection of certain players; players by their consistency and the quality of their game did not make it to the senior national team.

Junior Hall was one such player from a line of very outstanding fast bowlers who represented the Melbourne Club. He possessed remarkable attributes as a fast bowler. He was proportionally built and sustained his quick pace in lengthy spells; his control of length and line was remarkable with a very good bouncer. He was always among the leading senior cup wicket takers and deserved national senior representation. During his career at Melbourne, there were opportune times for his national selection but he was overlooked and failed to get the full support of the selectors.

The other senior cup clubs were well represented by talented players from Kingston Club with Jimmy Adams, Terrence Corke, Jeffrey Dujon, Larry Cunningham, Hopeton Barrett, Franz Cunningham, Raymond Ferguson, Wayne Sutherland, Michael Millwood, Rohan Chambers, Dereck Francis, John Gordon, Mario Ventura, Valentino Ventura, Dwayne Budhoo, Ray Wynter, Nehemiah Perry, John Gordon, The Constabulary Police team with Arthur Brown, Aaron Daley, Percy Tomlinson, Dixieth Palmer, Carlton Moore, Arthur Brown, Lucas Club showcased Chris Gayle, Andrew Gayle, Alford Givance, Ricardo Bramwell, Lyndon Johnson, Marlon Tucker, Delroy Morgan, Gareth Breese, O'Neil Cruikshank, Brian Murphy, Frederick Redwood, Wayne Billings, Nigel Kennedy, Patrick Barrett, Mark English Boys Town's Linden Wright, Courtney O'Conner, Paul Ellis, Alexander Morgan, Leroy Gordon, Michael Laing, Saint Catherine Cricket Club, Courtney Francis, Milton Thomas, Tamar Lambert, Gregory Brown, Andrew Greenwood,

Clifton Folkes, Ephraim Mcleod, Alie Thomas, Randy Nelson, Ransford Evans, Tony Powell, JDF's Robert Clarke, and Medroy Williams.

The national team was well represented by a preponderance of talented individuals in the department of their specialty. In the department of fast and medium to fast bowlers, Jamaica had a variety of skillful individuals headed by the incomparable Michael Holding, Courtney Walsh, Patrick Patterson, Kenneth McLeod, Ray Wynter, Aaron Daley, Dwight Meikle, Rohan Taylor, Hopeton Barrett, Joseph Grant, Brenton McKenzie, Denville McKenzie, Clem Thompson, Percival Thompson, Clive Banton, Shimei Burton, and the medium to fast Laurie Williams.

The national spinners with Robert Haynes leading the way, cunning with remarkable accuracy and variations of leg and top spinning deliveries; Nehemiah Perry the off spinner, was very impressive with his control of varied length and was able to extract unusual bounce that created uncertainty in the minds of most batsmen. The remarkable pair of Haynes and Perry in tandem was inspiring; their exceptional talent and consistency made them a winning combination and virtually closed the door for other spinners' inclusion to the national team. There were other spinners like Errol Wilson the off spinner, Donavon Malcolm left arm spin, Colin Gordon right spin, John Gordon right arm leg spin, Marlon Gibbs off spin, and Alford Givance off spin, all of whom were exceptionally talented but limited to regular appearances.

The wicketkeepers were extremely competent headed by the spectacular and incomparable Jeffrey Dujon. He was considered among the best to have represented the West Indies and there were others including Prince Francis, Patrick Gayle, Anthony Campbell, Shane Ford, and Andre Coley, all of whom represented the national team with distinction. It was a period that defined excellent glove work by our national wicketkeepers. In earlier years of the mid-sixties into the seventies, we had the great Jackie Hendricks who was excellent and considered the very best in the Caribbean, particularly to the spinners. Desmond Lewis was sound and reliable and so was Hume Parris in his limited appearances. There were other very competent wicket keepers including Renford Pinnock, Fitzroy Nangle, Victor Hunter, Junior Powell, Herbert Gordon aka Dago, and Roy Paul; as efficient as they were, the door was closed for their inclusion.

The city senior cup clubs continued to attract a number of young talented rural players to their clubs. The influx of players competing for clubs undoubtedly improved their game. While the city clubs benefited from those players, there were still many more very good rural players who for a variety of reasons such as geographical and financial never made it to the senior cup clubs, including St. Mary's Keith McCrae, Andel Morand, Ralston Samuels, Vincent Dixon, and Garfield Silvera. It was for that reason, I lobbied incessantly for the replacement of the then senior cup competition.

Figure 103 Len Chambers receiving prize for most catches in Machado Sponsored competition for Senior Cup Cricket Clubs

Figure 104 Jamaica National Senior Team Basil Williams (Captain)

Figure 105 Junior Hall – Melbourne Cricket Club fast bowler

Figure 106 Leonard Chambers and Gareth Breese at Sabina Park

The Affable Courtney Walsh

Courtney Walsh, the newly appointed Jamaica captain, came to the job with a lot of experience garnered from his boyhood years at the famous Melbourne Cricket Club, a club that tutored the making of the great Michael Holding.

Walsh first represented Jamaica in 1983 and the West Indies and Gloucestershire in 1984. Throughout his amazing career, he was regarded as one of the most beloved and respected team players in the world of cricket. Like Michael Holding his club mate at the famous Jamaican Melbourne Cricket Club, Courtney Walsh as a Jamaican is extremely respected for his deeds on the playing fields and beyond. The remarkable Jamaican speedster never forget his roots. The young aspiring boys from the neighborhood of Walsh's beloved Melbourne Cricket Club were given his attention, attention that was symbolic of his background during the formative years. There were a few names to be remembered who were there for the great Courtney Walsh. The likes of Ruddy Marzouca, Ruddy Williams, Michael HoShue, and Monica Williams, now Mrs. HoShue ,were compassionate in the shaping of the champion Jamaican Courtney Walsh OJ.

I recall one morning driving on the Causeway to my home in Independence City and in the opposite direction there was flashing head lights coming from Walsh's car. We pulled up on either side for a chat. At the time, Walsh was a mainstay in the West Indies team. In the car were three youngsters, Ray Stewart, Edward Wollaston brother of Aubrey Wollaston, and Donavan Samuels brother of Robert and Marlon Samuels the former West Indies test players. Ray Stewart went on to represent Jamaica's national youth team and was one of three reserves named for the West Indies youth tour of Pakistan and Bangladesh in1995, Donavan Samuels was called to the youth trials in later years. In our conversation, Walsh told me that he took the youngsters for a drive out and was heading back to the Melbourne Cricket Club where the homes of the youngsters were close by, just like it was for Walsh in the earlier years. There are so many related stories associated with Courtney

Walsh, a true Jamaican hero who loves Jamaica and West Indies cricket passionately.

The Jamaica Cricket Association, on the recommendation of the selectors Chester Watson, Roy Paul, and I, appointed Walsh to the captaincy of the Jamaica team, replacing the successful Marlon Tucker who retired from the game months after the 1990 cricket season. As selectors, our first meeting with Walsh the new captain was to name the squad of thirteen; it was traditionally, a privilege extended to the captain when naming the squad.

The selected squad had several players, including Walsh, who were regular members during the successful run by Marlon Tucker. Included in the squad was the newcomer Joseph Grant from the parish of Westmoreland and recently returned from England where he was spotted by Reggie Scarlett the former West Indies player, who asked that the selectors have a look at him. Grant was also recommended to the selectors by the well-known Osmond Erskine, President of the St. James Cricket Association. Erskine was recognized locally for his attacking style of batting and was the owner of the La Mirage Hotel in Montego Bay where Grant was an employee.

Conforming to procedure, the players and their employers were notified by letter through the JCA Secretariat. In the circumstances of Grant and his employer, I suggested to Chester Watson chairman of the selectors, that I would personally drive to Montego Bay and deliver the letter of invitation to Grant and his employer. I explained my reason for wanting to see what the young Joseph Grant looked like; it was a long drive to see the young man and it was worth it.

The scenery along the journey was spectacular and still is that most Jamaicans have come to appreciate. Starting from Spanish Town in the parish of Saint Catherine through the parishes of St. Ann, Trelawney and St. James along the coastline was enchanting. I have always found driving through the districts and frequent stops at irresistible aroma jerk pork and jerk chicken booths and interacting with wonderful and garrulous rural folks an experience of lingering fulfillment. When I got to my destination in Montego Bay, I was stopped at the gate to the hotel by the attendant. I asked if I could see Mr. Erskine; he answered that Erskine was not in and was not expected to be back until later that evening. I asked about Joseph Grant the cricketer, if he knew of him. He replied that he was the individual. I asked of him what his pace was like and how effective he was in the St. James local competitions. His response was that he was very quick and had figures that supported his effectiveness as a very good fast bowler. I further asked him what next in terms of his future in the game.

"Play for Jamaica, Sir," he responded.

It was then that I introduced myself and mentioned the purpose of my visit. He was apologetic talking about himself and I let him know that it was fine and that nothing was wrong with the revelation about himself. I let him know that my purpose of the long drive from Kingston was the opportunity to know about him. I gave him the letters, one for himself and the other for Mr. Erskine. With a congratulatory handshake, I wished him the very best in the trials and started my home journey back to Independence City in St. Catherine.

Interestingly, on the longish return drive of approximately three hours with a stop at the very popular Jerk Centre in Ocho Rios, I wanted Joseph Grant to do well at the trials and be in contention for inclusion to the national squad. In our conversation, I was impressed with his candor, the passion and love for the game. His elation at being invited to national trials without being seen in action by any of the selectors and for one of the selectors to have hand delivered the letter was echoed graciously by the young Joseph Grant. The discernable glee from his eyes was persuasive that he would be well pre-pared for the trials and indeed he was. His bowling impressed captain elect Courtney Walsh who, during the trial matches, gave his impression of the players to the selectors. At the end of the last trial, Joseph Grant the fast bow-ler from Montego Bay was selected to the touring squad, a selection that was deserving and pleasing to the rural followers of the game.

Reggie Scarlett and Osmond Erskine, two knowledgeable cricket minds rec-ommendations to the selectors was vindicated. Before the team boarded the plane for the opening game against Trinidad and while sitting and talking with a confident skipper Courtney Walsh in the departure lounge of the Nor-man Manley Airport in Kingston:

"It is a great honour to be the captain of Jamaica and I will do my very best to keep the team together in the traditional expectation of team morale on and off the field and the team is well balanced to do well," said a very confident Walsh.

"Good luck, Skipper," was my response.

During that period, Allan Rae, Roy Paul, Rex Fennell, Jackie Hendricks, Alf Grant, and I were the accredited members of the JCA welcoming party to meet and see off home and visiting teams at the Norman Manley Airport.

In the opening game against Trinidad, Jamaica led on first innings with Brian Lara dominating in majestic style with scores of 122 not out and 87. It was a one-man show by the great Lara in his team first innings total of 225; he flayed our attack and masterminded his team's eventual first innings total. His control of the batting was spectacular. Patrick Patterson and captain Walsh picked up 3 wickets each but could not stem the flow of runs from the free scoring batting maestro. Our first innings total of 157 was disappointing from a team parading an imposing batting line up with the likes of Wayne Lewis, Delroy Morgan, Jimmy Adams, Jeffrey Dujon, Cleveland Davidson, Robert Samuels, and Robert Haynes. Trinidad declared in their second turn at the wicket with 239 for 4 wickets. Lara again was in tremendous form with a scintillating display of shot making. Jamaica had a better showing in their second knock ending with 157 for four wickets chasing 307 for maximum points. Lewis played well for an attractive 57 and Adams 35 not out. The game ended in a draw with first innings points going to Trinidad.

For the second game we were at home to Guyana. Dujon top scored with 75, batting in his usual elegant style in a first innings team total of 242. Guyana replied with 217. Mark Harper 57, penetrative bowling by skipper Walsh and Patterson 3 wickets each restricted the Guyana batting for 217. In our second turn at the wicket, Dujon again topped the batting with an undefeated 77 and Morgan 38 from a total of 249 for 9 declared. Guyana were 192 for 6 chasing 274 for victory, Jamaica earned first innings points in a match that ended in a draw.

The third game was away from home against the Windward Islands at Rousseau's. Our first innings was again unconvincing with only Jimmy Adams showing his class with a lovely knock of 71 and Dixieth Palmer with 27 in a paltry team total of 177. Nehemiah Perry's penetrative off spin was too much for the opposition as they fell 27 runs short of the Jamaica total when they were dismissed for 150. We did a little better in our second innings total of

221 for 8, Robert Samuels 72, Delroy Morgan 31, Allen 3 for 53. Windward Islands chasing a target of 245 for an outright victory finished with 187 for 3. John 62 and Lewis 59, the Jamaicans came away with first innings lead in yet another drawn game for the Jamaica team.

The penultimate game against the Vivian Richards-led Leeward Islands at Warner Park was the end of our championship aspiration. Our first innings total of 268, Jimmy Adams with a wonderful 87, Robert Haynes an attractive 54, and Delroy Morgan a stylish knock of 42 against the brilliant fast bowling effort by Winston Benjamin 7 for 51. The remarkable Viv Richards with a dazzling 112, Hamish Anthony the young fast bowling all-rounder 82, and Richie Richardson 64 were the main contributors in the formidable Leeward Islands total of 317. Patrick Patterson bowled with a lot of pace to finish with 5 for 57 and got support from Perry 2 for 76 and Robert Haynes 2 for 115. Both Perry and Haynes got their wickets at a high cost; they were unable to contain the free scoring Richards, Anthony, and Richardson. The trio were circumspect facing the hostility from the pace of Patrick Patterson.

Jamaica was bundled out for an embarrassing second innings total of 113. Samuels 22 and Walsh were the top scorers as Anthony showed his promising quality of a top-class all-rounder in the making. His sustained pace was remarkable with some deliveries unbelievably fiery that rewarded him the impressive figures of 5 for 23. Eldine Baptiste finished with the respectable figures of 3 for 44. Leeward Islands were left with the mere formality of scoring 64 for maximum points; they finished with 65 for 3, Keith Atherton 32, Patterson 2 for 6.

The final game played at Sabina Park was a dismal failure for our batsmen as Barbados won convincingly. Barbados batting first ran up the impressive first innings score of 410 for 9 wickets declared with the Wes Indies opener Desmond Haynes scoring a superb 146; Henderson Springer 53, Patterson 3 for 50, and Perry 2 for 80 were the main wicket takers for Jamaica. In our second innings, the batting disappointed to be bowled out for a demoralizing score of 169. Robert Haynes and Cleveland Davidson were joint top scorers with 51. Ezra Moseley 5 for 48 and Otis Gibson 3 for 55 bowled with sustained pace to be the destroyers of the wobbling Jamaica batting. Barbados, in their second turn at the wicket declared at 127 for 4 leaving Jamaica to get 368 for an outright win. The pace of Cummings and Moseley was too much to handle and Jamaica fell away miserably for a second innings total of 146; Adams with a well-played 56 was the only batsman who lived up to the task of scoring freely.

A tournament with great expectation of a showing that would see our team highly competitive and to have performed poorly was a let down by the batsmen. The inconsistency of our leading batsmen was untenable and created too much pressure on the bowlers. No batsman was able to score a century; the highest was 87 by Adams and an innings in the 70's. Dujon had two innings in the 70's and one by Robert Samuels. As captain, Walsh tried his very best to inspire the team, but the ineffectiveness of our batsmen to perform consistently was a setback to his efforts. Courtney Walsh the great Jamaican son, and former great West Indies fast bowler, played 132 test matches finishing with 519 wickets a record for a West Indian bowler and 227 wickets in 205 ODI games. He was captain of the test team for 22 matches.

Walsh represented the English county Gloucestershire from 1984 to 1998 with remarkable success; he was also a bowling coach with the Bangladesh team and the West Indies women's team. The remarkable Courtney Walsh was the recipient of several awards including Order of Jamaica, ICC Cricket Hall of Fame, Jamaica Sportsman of the year.

One of Wisden five cricketers of the year, West Indies Cricketer of the year, The Honourable Courtney Walsh was inducted to the USA Cricket Hall of Fame in Connecticut. The Connecticut-based organization was the first of its kind with the insignia Cricket Hall of Fame that recognized the contribution of Players, Umpires, and Administrators locally in the USA and Internationally. Courtney Walsh, earlier in his career, was embellished by Pakistan locals for his refusal to run out a Pakistan batsman who was backing up while he was in his bowling strides to deliver the final ball of the match with Pakistan needing two runs for victory. Not running out the batsman allowed the opposition to score the required two runs for victory and qualify for the 1987 ODI World Cup.

Courtney Walsh OJ, never allowed his accomplishments globally to overshadow his journey, a journey that included individuals who were helpful in his development towards stardom, and so it was on the night of his Induction to Cricket Hall of Fame in Connecticut. In his acknowledgement speech, he identified Clem Thompson, his very good friend and bowling partner as representatives of Jamaica's senior team and I as secretary to Jamaica's selection committee when he was selected to the national youth team and as a senior selector when he became the national captain. He asked Clem and I to stand. He then lavished praises on us for being participants with him on the amazing journey to that Saturday night of October 05, 2013, at the Hilton Hotel in Hartford, Connecticut.

Figure 107 Courtney Walsh

Home Pressure 1983, 1987, **and** 1991

An experience I have had with regional youth tournaments was the pressure of playing at home. Not to say that the senior team did not encounter needling; because of age, maturity, and mental toughness they were able to have withstood the vile comments coming at them. At the youth level, I remember the experience of Jimmy Adams in the 1983 tournament at the Kensington ground. The insults went unabated while he was on the field and continued after the game. The harsh criticism was the selection of Adams to the squad ahead of the community favourite Rohan Britton. Adams was targeted as the one who was selected ahead of him which was not so. Adams' selection was guaranteed by his outstanding bowling and batting in the trials after a successful Sunlight Cup season. Both Adams and Britton were similar in style; they batted and bowled left-handed. The difference was that Adams did well in the Sunlight competition to be followed with consistent performances in the trials, whereas Britton failed to impress.

Britton represented the youth team in1982 without any success with the bat or ball; despite his failures, he was expected to do enough in the trials for selection to the 1983 squad and was unable to do so. The harassment by a particular group in the crowd was unbecoming and had an effect on the young fifteen-year-old Adams whose selection to the team had no challenger.

There was the case of Maurice Cole whose selection to the squad was unjustifiably questioned leading into the opening of the 1983 tournament. Although Cole bowled well in the trials, it was not reflected in the number of wickets taken; however, the selectors backed his ability with the support of the fielders. Cole was a success, finishing as Jamaica's top wicket-taker and second in the competition to Milton Small, the Barbadian who finished with most wickets. Cole also performed well with the bat getting a crucial half century in one of the three matches. His all-round performances justified in no small way his selection to the thirteen-man squad. Selectors were harassed time after time from uninformed fans; the Cole and Adams situation were tangible evidence. The 1983 four-man selection panel was chaired by Jackie Hendricks the former West Indies wicket keeper with Maurice Foster the former West Indies player, Carlton Forbes the former Nottingham county cricketer and me; there was the case of Perry Jennings' selection to the squad of fourteen for the 1984 Barbados tournament but who was later omitted.

Before 1984, the regional squad for all the teams consisted of thirteen players and at a meeting of the JCA before the naming of Jamaica's squad, I was in my capacity as chairman of the selection committee, told by the secretary Rex Fennel that an increase from thirteen to fourteen players for each squad was approved by Cricket West Indies. It was on that premise the selectors named fourteen players. I was later advised by Fennell at a board meeting of the JCA that Cricket West Indies rescinded on their earlier decision and that a player had to be left out. Perry Jennings was distraught by the development and so were other members of the squad.

Perry Jennings' family members expressed their disappointment in few words:

"Leonard Chambers, we are family members of Perry Jennings."

The occasion was a couple days after those not selected left camp and I went by the Road Runner Ice Cream shop situated in the vicinity of the Regal Cinema parking area and after purchasing ice cream as a treat to the squad members who were still in camp, I heard the words coming from a parked car nearby. The expression of the family was justifiable; they never abused me verbally but were obviously disappointed.

Selection of players at the national level is done and confirmed by the selection committee and not by one person. The chairman, like other members, discussed the merit of players and arrived at a consensus. During my chairmanship, this was the format: if there was an uneven voting, the Chairman was constitutionally empowered to make the casting vote. Uninformed individuals not familiar with the selection system were often times disgruntled and hurled insolent remarks at the Chairman of the selection committee. Thanks to the experienced Allan Rae and Jackie Hendricks, both of whom served in that capacity at the senior level for many years, I was guided how to handle adversities of similar circumstances.

Jamaica, for the 1991 regional youth tournament, was very confident in defense of the title and so was the expectation of the Jamaican fans. From the winning 1990 squad, six players were eligible for selection including captain Rohan Chambers, Carlton Carter Jr., Alvin Bent, Franklyn Rose, Valentino Ventura ,and Tony Powell; the six were certain starters barring injuries or unforeseen situations. Of the six, captain Rohan Chambers and vice-captain Valentino Ventura were experiencing their fourth season at the youth level. Carlton Carter the talented bowling all-rounder, Tony Powell a dynamic batsman with enormous skills as demonstrated the year before against the potent Australians bowling attack led by the incomparable Shane Warne; the other two players were the strongly built fast bowlers Alvin Bent and Franklyn Rose, both of whom were pacey and expected to get early wickets up front. There were others on the fringe that the selectors knew of from the previous year including Alford Givance, Mario Ventura, Rohan Alexander, and Robert Manning, all of whom were seen as front runners for selection. A guideline I established at the beginning of every youth selection meeting was, "Without fear or favour let's respect each other's point of view and discuss." It was my experience over the years that selectors favoured players on performance and commitment to the norms of the game; it was the template to selection that ultimately justified the outcome. Before the regular training camp at Up Park Camp for the 1991 tournament, the JCA announced that Rohan Kanhai would be resuming his coaching assignment.

Kanhai was contracted by the JCA in 1984 to be the coach of our youth team for an extended period ending in 1991. He did not accompany the team to Barbados that year 1984, as only a manager was allowed. As manager, I was given added responsibility as the coach.

Rohan Kanhai, the great West Indian batsman and former West Indies captain, started his contract   as coach with the Jamaica youth team at the regional tournaments in 1985 to 1991 but for the years 1989 and 1990. For unavoidable reasons, he was absent from the 1989 and 1991 tournaments and was replaced by the remarkable Renford Pinnock in 1989 and the exceptional coaching skills of Jerry Reid in 1990.

The return of Kanhai as coach on the premise of his contract was understandable. It was disappointment for Jerry Reid; his success with the 1990 winning team demonstrated his coaching ability to motivate the players to perform at their very best. As Chairman of the selection committee and a JCA member, I assured him that I would use my influence for his return as the successor to Kanhai for the 1992 tournament in Guyana. There was a colossal setback to the selection panel when we learned of Carlton Carter's unavailability for the 1991 tournament. As chairman of the selection committee, he informed me that he was offered a football (Soccer) scholarship to four USA Universities, one of which was St John's University in Queens New York.

It was an opportunity that he could not forego after consultation with his dad Carlton Carter Snr., who was a terrific club cricketer at the Melbourne Cricket Club and was now a resident of the Borough Queens not far from the St. Johns University, the choice of his son. Young Carter was keen on playing the first two matches before honouring the scholarship. Being conversant with the tournament rules, I let him know it was not permissible. Not having the dynamic Carter who was pivotal to our success the year before was a setback of great significance in our quest for back-to-back championship honours. Carter was considered one of the better spinners in the region. His attacking left arm variation wicket taking deliveries supported by his batting ability and his effectiveness in the field meant that we were least formidable; it was difficult replacing a player of his quality.

Before the start of the tournament, the very experienced Barbados manager Jeff Bromes, said to me, "Len, not having Carter would open the door for the Barbados team to win the championship." The team that benefited most from Carter's absences was the Trinidadians; they were the 1991 champions. The three weeks at camp was eagerly awaited and when it got started, it was buzzing with excitement as there was never a stronger coaching staff to any Jamaican youth team. The quality of the coaches headed by the immortal Rohan Kanhai, the great Michael Holding, former Jamaica cricketers Renford Pinnock, Len Levy, and the skills-set of Jerry Reid a former National Colts player could not have been more formidable.

Robert Samuels at age nineteen was no longer eligible for selection. He was the team's most feared batsman for the past four tournaments. His presence and consistency masterminded our batting that inspired other batsmen to have done well, beginning with his first year in 1987 when he demonstrated his enormous batting talent with absolute confidence in scoring two magnificent centuries, and along with Brian Lara were the two batsmen of the tournament. Captain Rohan Chambers in his fourth year, Vice-captain Valentino Ventura also in his fourth year, Mario Ventura, Roger Neil, Kirk Forrest, and Tony Powell after his brilliant century against the Australian youth team were the ones expected to be the mainstay of our batting. At the trials, players were mindful of the many openings; they trained with the resolve to perform and impress the selectors.

As bowlers and batsmen, they adjusted creditably with praiseworthy performances that were recognized by the selectors. There was not much to differentiate between the wicketkeepers Maurice Pinnock and Wayne Cuff. Going into the final trial match it was crunch time, a time for most of the players to lift their performances and send a message to the selectors: "Don't forget me." Of the twenty-two players in the final trials match, five had previously played at the regional tournament the year before, and by performances and experience were automatic choices for selection.

It was not difficult to imagine what it was like for the other seventeen players who, by resolute intent, strived purposefully for inclusion to the squad. The last of the 3-day trials was played at the Melbourne Cricket ground. Shortly after the game started, I left for May Pen where I collected a cheque for the sponsorship of that ongoing trial game from Richard Chen, manager of the Super Plus Supermarket. On my way back, I stopped at Sherwin Williams Paints situated in Central Village where I collected a cheque for the sponsorship of the team blazers from Roy Holness, General Manager of the very popular paint company. Holness was my very good friend, a friend that I encouraged to be supportive of the sponsorship that lasted for four years before my departure to the USA. His marvelous gesture to have had his company's contribution was commendable and appreciated by the JCA. The Super Plus chain of Supermarkets headed by Wayne Chen, an ardent sports fan, and his brother Richard Chen, readily supported the idea of sponsorship of that particular trial match and there were other support provided to the youth teams by the civic- minded supermarket operators during my tenure as chairman of the youth selection committee. The Super Plus branch in May Pen, managed by Richard Chen, and the Christiana branch by Wayne Chen, were two of my clients while I was employed to Wray and Nephew Group of Companies. As chairman of the youth selection committee from 1983 to

1996, I was a one-man sponsorship committee for team Track Suits, Blazers, Blazers emblems, Caps, friendly matches outside of Up Park Camp. I was also instrumental in the placement of several young cricketers to the institutions of educational learning and job/ employment. The JCA acknowledged the contribution of all the sponsors for their continued generosity through the years.

By the time I got back to the Melbourne ground which was in the dying hours of the day's play, Rohan Kanhai met me just after I got out of my car and remarked, " Robinson is not a good enough batsman to be considered for the squad." I asked of him why was he not good enough. Kanhai went on to say he scored a century that had a lot of blemishes and that he should not be considered for the squad ahead of others who were consistently scoring thirties and forties. My first reaction was that he was good enough to be one of the best twenty-eight under nineteen youth cricketers in the country named by the selectors; this I reminded the coach of. I further reminded the great Rohan Kanhai that Julian Robinson, a powerfully built all-rounder, had batting qualities and having scored, "A century at trials, be it at the senior or youth level, is a feat of considerable accomplishment and should not go unnoticed" was my final comment to Rohan Kanhai before the game ended.

The conclusion of the day's play marked the end of the 1991 trials. The selectors convened for the naming of the fourteen-member squad. We were pleased at the efforts of the players throughout the three-week camp; they trained with admirable intent. We looked at the fitness of the players and any proven to be unfit would not be considered for selection (an unwavering principle as stipulated by the Jamaica Cricket Association). Rohan Belight, a favorite for selection, was regrettably, ruled out for selection because of injury known to the players, coaches, and selectors. It would have been a travesty to the selection process; selecting him with the hope that he would sufficiently recovered was not worth the risk.

Belight's non-selection caused an uproar from his fans in the parish of Clarendon. At eighteen years old, he was one of the Parish senior team opening bowlers and his selection to the team was anticipated as a certainty. Understandably, they wanted to have seen him perform during the 1991 home tournament. The players selected got the unanimous backing of the selectors with some time spent on two players Wayne Cuff and Maurice Pinnock the wicketkeepers. There was not much difference with the standard of their wicket keeping and both were reasonable with the bat; in the end, Pinnock was preferred to do the glove work.

The non-selection of Julian Robinson was strongly argued for and against. It was, on the face of it, a strong argument for his inclusion having scored a century in that last trial match. It was said that his century was a one-off effort and that too much credence should not be placed on that innings. I never subscribed to that concept;, an innings of substance could be the turning point in a player's career. The debate of comparison with other batsmen scoring 30's and 40's consistently was essential to a meaningful outcome and sadly, the non-selection of Robinson was heartfelt by some.

At the level of Jamaica national representation, so many players through the years who have had setbacks of non- selection worked their way back, not only to the youth team, but to the senior team as well. An example of that philosophy was proven by a number of players including Perry Jennings, Nemiah Perry, Cleveland Davidson, Odelmo Peters and Wayne Cuff.

The eventual selection of the1991 squad was Rohan Chambers (captain), Valentino Ventura, Tony Powell, Roger Neill, Kirk Forrest, Franklyn Rose, Alvin Bent, Robert Manning, Mario Ventura, Rohan Alexander, Alford Givance, and Maurice Pinnock, Ridley Hinds, Edison Edwards, Rohan Kanhai as coach, and I as the manager. From the opening game of the tournament, the Jamaicans were ready to compete for back-to-back defense of their title. Unfortunately, a number of our matches were affected by inclement weather that curtailed our pursuit for outright results. There were excellent performances by fast bowler Franklyn Rose, who in the open game against Guyana at Melbourne Park had the fantastic bowling performance of eight wickets in one of the innings. He should have had the ninth when a chance was spilled. Guyana lost only 9 wickets batting one short due to an injury inflicted on one of their batsmen.

Rose, like most fast bowlers, tended to be at their very best during the last of their years at this level. He was on top of his game starting in the opening fixture demonstrating the special talent of his craft. It was an encouraging start for the local team; their performance heightened speculation that they were on course for championship honours. There were other good bowling efforts by our bowlers. Robert Manning, the left arm spinner who bowled well within himself, was consistent in not allowing the opposition batsmen the ascendency. Alvin Bent, the six feet tall and proportionately built fast bowler was not at his best when compared with the year before when he was so effective; he unfortunately, sustained an injury that affected his usual smooth rhythm and pacey deliveries. It would have been advantageous to our team totals if our batsmen who had good starts to their innings were able to have capitalized with bigger scores. The vice-captain Captain Valentino Ventura with a century and another half century batted with authority and was always unruffled at the wicket. I was impressed with his mindset; he paced himself well with his runs scoring ability and was always effective with the execution of shot selection supported by a very solid defense. A truly admirable young man whose work ethics was excellent, he served the national youth team with unquestionable commitment from 1988 to 1991.

Captain Rohan Chambers, Tony Powell, Rohan Alexander, and Mario Ventura, younger brother of Valentino, had good performances in specific games but lacked consistency in their attempt to have compiled sizeable scores. Alford Givance impacted with his batting and bowling that argued well for him in later tournaments. Another batsman who had promising starts was Roger Neil, the younger brother of Gary Neil, a dashing left-handed batsman who represented the national youth team in Trinidad 1986. Roger was expected to have improved on the starts he had but was unable to do so when well set. The wicket keeper Maurice Pinnock, son of the former Jamaica batsman Renford Pinnock, was competent with his glove work. His returns with the bat was a disappointment to his assured batting skills.

The remaining squad members Ridley Hinds, Kirk Forrest, and Edison Edwards' playing opportunities were limited. Edwards, notwithstanding his limited appearances, was called to the senior trials later on and was also selected under the Victoria Mutual Building Society sponsored yearly three-month cricket programme to England. At the end of the rain-affected 1991 tournament, we again occupied a position as runners-up that was familiar with our youth teams over the last ten years but for 1990 when we were champions of the coveted trophy.

The Jamaica team played in the true spirit of the game and represented the country in the traditional manner just like earlier youth teams.

Figure 108 Carlton Carter Jr. & Carton Carter Sr - Father and Son -Two Dynamic Cricketers

Figure 109 Franklin Rose

Youth Tournament Guyana 1992

Reviewing the 1992 youth tournament held in Guyana, a number of matches were ruined by intermittent rain, which was very infuriating not only to the players, but also the fans who were very supportive by their excellent attendance at the matches.

Members of the team were Rohan Chambers Captain, Alford Givance, Tony Powell, Roger Neil, Andre Coley, Brian Murphy, Rohan Belight, Mario Ventura, Alvin Bent, Rohan Alexander, Andrew Davis, David Hoilette, Winston Heron, and Chris Miller; the coach was Jerry Reid with me as the manager.

When the Jamaicans played against the Trinidadians at Linden, the first of the three days was unplayable; the pitch was saturated because of inadequate covers after heavy rain the day before. The ineptness of the local authorities to have adequate tarpaulin was inexcusable and left much to be desired; the outfield was dry enough for the game to have started sometime before tea on the first day.

Trinidad having won the toss on the second day's play, elected to bowl on a pitch that was not quite ready for the start of play when it did. It had that dark-brown look, an indication that it needed some more time for the drying process before we started. Throughout our innings, the fast bowlers Marlon Black, Mervyn Dillon, and the wily wrist spinner Dinanath Ramanarine, exploited the helpful conditions that created uncertainties for the batsmen, especially during the pre-lunch session.

On that gloomy day at Mckenzie, the community of Linden in the country of Guyana, Tony Powell defied the odds and again defined his batting talent with a magnificent century. His belligerent style of batting destroyed the opposition bowlers. In an exhibition of control aggression and skillful defense against the fast bowlers Marlon Black and Mervyn Dillon, who had their deliveries lifting disconcertingly from awkward lengths, were contemptuously and expertly dispatched to the boundaries and when Dinanath Ramnarine the wily wrist spinner was introduced in the attack, his deliveries were struck disdainfully to the boundaries and beyond. When Powell expertly defended lifting deliveries before getting into double figures, Andre Coley, one of his teammates, was sitting next to me when I remarked, "Tony will get a century today."

"Manage, you can't be serious," was Coley's response.

My assertion was positive and Tony Powell vindicated my optimism. When I made the prediction, it was not in desperation; I momentarily had a flashback of the splendid century he scored against the very strong bowling attack of the young Australian headed by the crafty Shane Warne and other excellent innings against bowling attacks of repute. Tony Powell's superb century will long be remembered by the players, managers, and coaches of both teams, and so will the fans. The Trinidad young bowlers Black, Deleon, and Ramnarine progressed to their national senior team and later the senior West Indies team. I am sure all three will long remember that day at McKenzie in Guyana, when the batting skills of Tony Powell were superbly displayed.

The 1993 Youth Tournament

The experience of having served as secretary of Jamaica's senior selection committee with Gerry Alexander as Chairman and as a selector with Jackie Hendricks as chairman, prepared me adequately for my role during the fourteen years as Chairman of the Youth Selection Committee. As chief selector, it was incumbent on me at the beginning of each schoolboy season to have an early meeting with the selectors and accentuate the importance of our responsibility as a committee. The key obligation was to have watched as many matches as possible at the Headley and Sunlight competitions, and most importantly, the Kingston Wharves competitions.

Having decided on the fixed number of 28 players for the camp and the eventual squad selection, there were instances of disapproval on the non-selection of individuals from parents, schoolboy coaches, and clubs; their interest in most circumstances was marginalized for self-satisfaction.

A number of school coaches considered having a player or players called from their institution to the trials would enhance their status; they single-mindedly argued for their selection to me and so it was with some senior cup club members.

Some mothers of unselected players to the squad were more circumspect with their dissatisfaction than the fathers who expressed vehemently the non-selection of their sons. At the national youth level, Rohan Chambers was not with the youth team for the regional tournament in St. Kitts 1993; after five years representing the team starting in Barbados 1988 and ended in Guyana 1992, he was no longer eligible for selection going into his 20th birthday. He came to the captaincy of the national youth team in 1990 with the experience as the incumbent captain of his school Wolmers' Sunlight team. His captaincy experienced included the leadership of his school's Under fourteen, Colts and Sunlight teams of the same year in 1987; additionally, he was a member of the youth teams of 1988 and 1989. He showed remarkable shrewdness in his captaincy; his astuteness in handling on the field decisions was remarkable. He had the respect and support of the players and coaches just like the other captains Chris Harris 1983 and 1984, Deron Dixon 19885 and 1986, Jimmy Adams 1987, Michael Millwood 1988, Richard Staple 1989, Alford Givance 1993 and Gareth Breese 1994 and 1995 and Wavell Hinds 1996.

When Rohan Chambers was appointed captain in 1990, there was a small group who thought that Robert Samuels should have been the one to lead the team and that as his father and as Chairman of the selection committee and a member of the Jamaica Cricket Association, my influence was a deciding factor for his elevation to the captaincy; that was certainly not so. It is to be noted that Michael Holding, Maurice Foster, and Chester Watson, all former West Indies test players were the other members of the 1990 selection committee. I recall the day that the four of us unanimously decided on Rohan's recommendation to the JCA for the captaincy. We were walking towards the stairway to the top floor of the Board Room at Sabina Park when Holding asked why should we walk the dreaded steps to the top floor just to arrive at a consensus when Rohan Chambers was the logical choice for the captaincy. Foster agreed and was supported by Watson. Foster then asked, "What says you, Vijay?" (I was called and continue to be call Vijay by several people) "I agree with the three of you," was my reply.

The international wisdom of the three as former West Indies test players with the prerequisites of captaincy was highly respected by the Jamaica cricket fraternity because of the depth of their knowledge on cricket, locally and internationally. The recommendation of Rohan Chambers as captain to the Board was unanimously approved. I respected the views of support for Robert Samuels who was captain of his school team Kingston College for the first time in his last year at school and the overwhelming support was more favourable to Rohan as the captain. Starting with Patrick Harris 1983 and ending with Wavell Hinds in 1996, all the captains of Jamaica's youth teams were unanimously recommended by the selection panel and confirmed by the JCA without a challenger and so was the appointment of Alford Givance for the 1993 tournament.

Givance was waiting in the wings under Rohan Chambers' captaincy at Wolmers Boys School and the national youth teams; his appointment was richly deserved. At the end of the trials, the selectors named a formidable squad of fourteen players including Alford Givance as captain, Andre Coley, David Hoilette, Mario Ventura, Christopher Miller, Gareth Breese, Delroy Taylor, Richard Hoilette, Shimei Burton, Denville McKenzie, Mark Madan, Andrew Gayle, Mark Gray, and Ray Stewart.

As captain, Givance's leadership was inspirational; his assertiveness won the admiration of the players which was an integral component of his leadership. Like all our captains through the years at the under nineteen level, he was well prepared for the job. The pitches at the grounds of St. Kitts offered assistance to the bowlers but were not difficult for the batsmen who were of the mindset to dig in and score with undue risks. Mario Ventura adjusted to the conditions expertly; his repertoire off stroke playing was wide range on the front and back foot. His defense was impenetrable.

The consistency of Mario's runs scoring defined the quality of his batting on pitches that in most situations were very friendly to the spinners. For his tournament performances, the talented Mario Ventura was selected to the 1993 West Indies youth team tour of England. Mario is in the group of a number of gifted Jamaican teenage batsmen to have represented the national senior team; his impressive performance at the youth level impacted his early selection. The fluency of his stroke play and a structured defense was an early indication of his talent that had the making of an international player. Injuries was a factor that slowed his development and derailed the progress of the gifted Mario Ventura that so much was expected of.

Batsmen Christopher Miller, Mark Gray, Delroy Taylor, and Ray Stewart showed glimpses of their natural talent. The flow of wonderful stroke play as batsmen during instances when they batted argued well for the development of their game. Andrew Gayle, the leg spinner, bowled with very good control and developed as the tournament progressed and was reassuring for him to have continued his development for the following year 1994 tournament in Barbados. After the Barbados tournament, he was in consideration for selection to the West Indies youth team against the 1995 Young England team but missed out as Dinanath Ramnarine and Rawl Lewis were the preferred leg spinners (Lewis and Ramnarine were exceptional bowlers at the regional under nineteen tournaments). The fast bowlers Denville Mc Kenzie, Shimei Burton, and Mark Madan were quicks that showed remarkable promise. They demonstrated their ability and keenness to improve their game. Denville McKenzie had another two years at the youth level whereas Shimei and Mark Madan, having reached the age of nineteen, were not eligible for another tournament.

Shimei Burton, as a left arm fast bowler, swung the ball both ways and had a lovely yorker with pace. His early promise after the youth tournament was recognized by the senior selectors when he was invited to the trials. His performances won favour with the choosers of our national teams when he made his debut at age twenty-one against the Windward Islands at Sabina Park in1995. His mentors included Brother Casious Burton, who was a fast bowler of interest to the senior selectors when he represented Lucas Cricket club at the senior cup level and later playing for St Elizabeth. Big brother Casious coached and guided his younger brother through the formative years, not only with his bowling, but valued principles related to the sport. Shimei's progress was ruined by injuries to his knees that prevented him being the bowler he was earlier; the severity of the injury put an end to his first-class cricket career at an age when his game was moving forward.

It was Pat Anderson, former president of Jamaica Football Association, Jamaica Amateur Athletic Association, and a top Jamaica Cricket Association Administrator for several years who called me from the comfort of his Manchester home late one night a week before the commencement of the 1993 youth trials and   recommended young Shimei as a prospect for the youth team. Pat Anderson explained the talent of the youngster and requested of me as chairman of the selection committee to consider him for inclusion to the trials and predicted that the youngster would be selected to the squad for St. Kitts. Like so many, I respected the balanced knowledge of Pat Anderson a former club cricketer at Boys Town and at the Parish level for Manchester. Pat Anderson's assessment of Shimei was vindicated by his expectation. Shimei Burton performed impressively at the trials and was named to the squad of fourteen for St. Kitts. The glove work of Andre Coley was reassuring; his efficiency was inspirational to the bowlers and a motivating factor to the high standard of our fielders. Coley's proficiency behind the stumps was remarkable and was noted by the West Indies youth selectors Andy Roberts, William Bourne, and I when he was selected along with his Jamaican teammates Alford Givance and Mario Ventura for the West Indies youth tour of England 1993.

Gareth Breese, on his first appearance at the regional youth tournament, showed early evidence of his doggedness when confronted with difficulties. His batting was praiseworthy; he batted with absolute unmatched courage that sent a message to a number of his teammates the way to bat through adversities. In one of his innings after being hit painfully, I accompanied him to the hospital for medical attention and was advised by the Medics that he should take no further part in the match. Breese having returned to the ground and seeing his teammates floundering and the team heading towards defeat, with stark grimaces, he pleaded with Coach Jerry Reid and I for his return to the wicket. Reluctantly, Jerry and I acceded to his relentless pleas and through pain and discomfort, he batted defiantly to save the game. Breese's heroics got overwhelming commendation from his teammates; the compliments were heartening and riveting. Jerry Reid and I were extremely pleased with Breese's commitment to the team motto of "One for all and All for one."

Alford Givance had a dream tournament with the ball. The off-spinning all-rounder bagged 33 wickets which was the most by any Jamaican bowler surpassing Clifton Folkes' record breaking 32 wickets in Trinidad 1990. The leadership qualities of Givance were recognized by the West Indies youth selectors Andy Roberts as chairman, William Bourne the former Barbados and Warwickshire fast bowler and I when we named him as Vice-Captain of the West Indies under nineteen tour of England. He joined his Jamaican teammates Andre Coley and Mario Ventura as members of the 1993 West Indies youth team led by the promising bowling all-rounder Ian Bradshaw of Barbados. Givance was an emerging star with bat and ball. He had the natural talent to have furthered his game at the national level for some time. His early departure for the USA was a loss to the game, not only at his local club Lucas, but also at the national senior level. His departure from Jamaica while I was in the USA was as told to me by Givance, that the obstinate Easton McMorris chairman of the national senior selection panel acted indifferently to him as a player and was a factor in his decision to migrate to the USA. Of note, both Givance and McMorris were members of the Lucas Cricket Club. In the annals of Jamaica's cricket, there is no doubt about McMorris credentials as a batsman. He was among the very best to have represented his country but was well known at the local level for his unbridled arrogance to some players that left much to be desired. Givance, now a resident of Atlanta, was the captain of Atlanta's Tropical Cricket Club and ascended to the Presidency of the very popular club.

Givance and Breese attended Wolmers Boys School, one of the premier schools in Jamaica, and with Andre Coley were very good friends and that continues to be so to this day. All three shared the same household with Gareth's father Brian Breese who was a father figure to the affable Alford Givance and the soft-spoken Coley. Brian Breese was an administrator of the popular Lucas Cricket Club and a key member of the Jamaica Cricket Association; he served the game at the administrative level with approbation.

Throughout the years at club and parish levels, there were so many individuals who played the substitute big brother and father figure to many of our cricketers. There were the likes of Sydney Gapour and Errol Subratie of Saint Catherine Cricket Club, Osmond Erskine of St, James, Mikey Matthews, George Watson aka Soro of Lucas Cricket Club, Basil Williams and Maurice Chong of Kensington Cricket Club, Ruddy Williams and Ruddy Marzouca of Melbourne Cricket Club, Dr. Donovan Bennett and Junior Bennet and Horton Dolphin of St. Elizabeth, Pat Anderson of Manchester and Noel McLean of Westmoreland. They were known and recognized for their contribution to the development of so many of our young cricketers who soared to stardom. I would imagine there were other individuals who throughout the years contributed amicably to our young cricketers. Brian Breese of Lucas Cricket Club was a tower of strength to several youngsters in different aspects of their lives and recognized as one of the unsung heroes of Jamaica's cricket fraternity.

The players showed gratitude and never failed to recognize and talk about their experience and appreciation to those extraordinary individuals. The remarkable kindness of those who were able to help the numerous youngsters should long be remembered; their human kindness was mirrored on those players becoming a symbol of recognition in their environment, an environment of adulation that motivated others to become achievers of acknowledged quality.

Figure 110 Mario Ventura receiving Player of the Youth Tournament

Youth Tournament Barbados 1994 – Grenada 1995

Gareth Breese in 1994, was elevated to the captaincy of Jamaica's national youth team succeeding his friend and former teammate at Wolmers Boys Schools Alford Givance. Breese was the leading contender for the position. His all-round ability as a reliable batsman and very useful with his off-spin bowling and the experience as captain of his school team made him the obvious choice for the job. The selected squad was Gareth Breese captain, Delroy Taylor, Ray Stewart, Andre Coley, Andrew Gayle, Keron Baker, Karl McDonald, Mark Madan, Audley Sanson, Denville McKenzie, Wavell Hinds, Marlon Kennedy, Julian Royal, Merrick Couseley, Junior Bennett coach, and I as the manager. The players were upbeat after a successful three-week training programme at Up Park Camp where they were well prepared by the coaches Jerry Reid and Leonard Levy.

During the camp, several players were impressive in the trials, which created optimism of championship honours. The squad was well balanced with a blend of fast bowlers, spinners, and batsmen who were in splendid form. The batting headed by captain Breese got good support from Delroy Taylor, Wavell Hinds, Merrick Couseley, Keron Baker, Karl McDonald, and the batting all-rounder Ray Stewart. Captain Breese batting was outstanding; his stroke play was exceptional with crisp drives on both sides of the wicket and looked as good as any during the tournament.

Wavell Hinds, the gangly lefthander, batted positively and looked assured and composed at top of the order; his attacking style of batting inspired confidence in the other batsmen. Delroy Taylor, a well-organized and attractive batsman, had the makings of transition to Jamaica's senior level. The knowledgeable former Jamaica and West Indies batsman Easton McMorris in his capacity as chairman of the national senior selection committee and I were watching Delroy Taylor at the wicket with Delroy Morgan in an arranged JCA practice match at Sabina Park. Taylor was unruffled with wonderful eye-catching stroke play when McMorris uttered the words, "Len, Morgan certainly is exceptional, so organized and lovely to look at. His drives and pulls are amazing." I replied, "Easton, it is Delroy Taylor on strike and not Morgan."

"Why is he not in the West Indies youth squad to play against England?" asked McMorris.

"He is one of three reserves," was my reply as manager of the West Indies youth team.

Delroy was later called to the young West Indies team as a replacement for a player who was injured in the first game. He played in five of the six matches against the England team that was on tour for a series of three 1-dayers and three 3-day games. There were instances during the 1994 West Indies youth tournament when he threatened to score heavily and was dismissed when well set. Taylor had the misfortune of knee injuries that circumscribed to his limited appearances at the club level that hampered his progression to the national senior team.

Merrick Couseley was easy on the eye. He was a touch player and looked in command every time at the wicket. He possessed the natural batting talent that many thought would have earned him national senior selection at an early age. Unfortunately, the gifted batting talent of Couseley was short-lived; he left the game at an early age in pursuit of other objectives. Keron Baker, like Couseley, was one who charmed with his exquisite stroke play and looked the part. Jeffrey Dujon, the former West Indies wicket keeper batsman who was involved with the Jamaica youth system, was impressed with Baker's batting and predicted that "Fox" as he was called by his friends, would go a far way in Jamaica's cricket and potentially the West Indies team. It was a remarkable comment from the experienced Jamaica and West Indies great, a testament to the treasured value of Baker's batting.

Ray Stewart, the batting all-rounder, had a reasonable tournament with bat and ball. His medium pace bowling was very effective. The fast-bowling unit was spearheaded by the strongly built Denville McKenzie who bowled at a lively pace with wonderful control and got good support from his other two quicks Mark Madan and Audley Sanson, both of whom were athletically built at over six feet tall and at times menacing with their pace and variable bounce from the traditional pacey pitches in Barbados. The experienced wicketkeeper Andre Coley the West Indies under-nineteen player, as to be expected, was very competent with his glove work and was of significant help to his very good friend and captain Breese regarding strategies while on the field of play. The two main spinners Julian Royal and Andrew Gayle bowled well in tandem. Andrew, brother of the great Jamaican and West Indian champion batsman Chris Gayle, was a leg spinner who spun the ball prodigiously with a well-disguised googly. He was used shrewdly by captain Gareth Breese who was always proactive in his bowling changes; both Breese and Andrew Gayle were members of the Lucas Cricket Club senior cup team.

Julian Royal, the off spinner, also played in the senior cup competition representing Kensington Cricket Club; he possessed remarkable skills of control and variations and took a lot of watching from the opposition batsmen. As an off spinner myself at the national senior level and manager of the team, I spent time watching him from the middle at practice sessions and was able to offer hints to him just like I did with previous youth off spinners including Maurice Cole 1983, Paul Beckett 1984 and 1985, Nehemiah Perry 1986 and 1987, Vivian Sailsman 1988 and 1989, Marlon Gibbs 1990, Alford Givance 1991, 1992 and 1993 and Gareth Breese 1993, 1994 and 1995. The team was well served by Jamaica's most successful schoolboy coach Junior Bennett who was truly amazing with his wide knowledge of how to effectively communicate with the youngsters.

Junior Bennett succeeded the former Jamaica Colts player Jerry Reid who served as coach 1990, 1992, and 1993. Bennett's effective coaching method was remarkable and well received   by the players. As manager, I was impressed with the St. Elizabeth Technical High School and Jamaica's most successful schoolboy cricket coach. He has been and still is humble about his successes as a coach at all levels of Jamaica's cricket from St. Elizabeth Technical High School to the national youth and senior teams. The affable Junior Bennett demonstrated total commitment to the game. He is an amazing individual that is loved by so many players, administrators, and fans. The 1994 youth tournament in Guyana was the first of his many years as Jamaica's coach of the under-nineteen team, and it was a success for him when Jamaica and the host country Guyana were joint championship winners.

For the 1995 regional youth tournament, Junior Bennet, Gareth Breese, and I were returned in our respective roles for the tournament in Grenada. The team was well-prepared with the usual three weeks at Up Park Camp where the physical and net training was satisfactory; the young players were physically and mentally ready for the trial matches. The selectors were impressed with the showing of the players selected; their performances in the trials were consistent and suggested that the team was well prepared to go one better and be the outright champions for 1995.

The players selected were Gareth Breese captain, Leon Garrick, Sheldon Gordon, Julian Royal, O'Neil Richards, Marlon Kennedy, Merrick Couseley, Keron Baker, Carl Wright, Ray Stewart, Wavell Hinds, Denville McKenzie, Andrew Gayle, and Garsha Blair. The performances of the previous year enhanced the optimism of the selectors and those close to the team going into the 1995 season. The eligibility of eight players from the previous season's winning team and the impressive performances by the incoming players in the trials gave optimism to the overwhelming confidence. From the very first game of the tournament, the players exhibited the quality of a team that was unified. Their successes were defined by the resolve shown; in a couple of matches, they came from behind to have the better of their opponents.

Captain Breese was shrewd with the handling of his bowlers and imaginative in his field placing; the players responded superbly to his leadership. The bowling was a varied combination of three genuine quicks in Denville McKenzie, O'Neil Richards, and the left arm medium to fast swing of Garsha Blair supported by Ray Stewart the medium pace all-rounder. The spinning department was headed by Andrew Gayle the right arm leg spinner, Julian Royal off spin and Gareth Breese who was much improved over the tournament before; all three spinners were members of the winning squad the year before. The batting headed by the captain Breese and vice-captain Wavell Hinds led the way with consistency. There was significant support from Carl Wright the wicketkeeper batsman whose attacking approach was a feature of his batting. Keron Baker, Merrick Couseley, Leon Garrick, Sheldon Gordon, and Marlon Kennedy adjusted themselves fittingly when included in a strong batting line up.

There were signs of Leon Garrick, a prodigious type of talent seen in most great Jamaican batsmen from their early teens; he was most certainly in that revered group. I recall a youth trial match played at Mona Bowl in1996 with

Chris Gayle and Leon Garrick batting together in a partnership of graceful stroke play when rain interrupted the game. As customary during my tenure as Chairman of the youth selectors, I used every opportunity to have former national representatives addressing our youth players. Present at the Mona Bowl game was the former Boys Town, Jamaica youth and senior player, Linden Wright. He acceded to my request for a talk with the players. In his address, he expressed confidence in what he had seen of the batsmen before the premature ending of the day's play. He did not single out any player but privately said to me how he was impressed with the batting of Gayle and Garrick. He was pleased with the elegance of Gayle's stroke play on the front foot between extra cover and midwicket and the sureness of his square cut and pulls. He mentioned the classical style of Leon Garrick that reminded him of the controlled aggression of former Jamaica top batsman Sam Morgan and the elegance of the former international Lawrence Rowe.

I had the opportunity of seeing Garrick at age seventeen after he was recommended to me by his school coach Derrick Azan who described him as a batting sensation in the making and asked me to have him included in a group of 24 players for a pre-trial match at the popular Vineyard ground in St Elizabeth. The pitch at the ground had areas of green grass and rolled perfectly for the fast bowlers, offering extraordinary pace and variable bounce. Garrick joined the team bus at around 7: 30 AM in May Pen, Clarendon, and after fifteen minutes of driving, breakfast was served to the players at a "Rest Stop" in nearby Clarendon Park.

All the players, but for Garrick, showed a penchant for the scrumptious dishes of Ackee and Saltfish with boiled yam, bananas, boiled, and fried dumplings. Like the other members, Garrick never had breakfast before joining the team. I encouraged him after I was told that, unlike the other members, he was not eating. I reminded him that next meal would be between innings at the venue of the game and that a meal would be served between the innings, which was a long way off. One of the players handed him a glass of orange juice. Garrick, with a smile, thanked the player.

"Manage, he is shy," said the player.

When we got to the ground, we immediately got the game started; his team led by Gareth Breese, batted first with him down to bat at number three. The openers Kennedy and Cousely were unsettled by the speed and awkwardness of the deliveries from the fast bowlers; they were ducking and taking evasive actions and absorbing body blows. Breese the captain of the batting team, left the confines of the players' enclosure to advise me that Garrick, who was down to bat at the fall of a wicket, was standing with bat and gloves in hand and no pads on. Having approached Garrick, I asked him if he were going to bat without pads?

"Yes Sir, I don't have a pair," said the soft-spoken Garrick.

He was then provided with a pair of batting pads but refused wearing a helmet. When the gifted Garrick got to the wicket, he showed no fear of been unsettled by the hostility and awkward bounce that the fast bowlers generated that caused uneasiness for the openers with balls rearing head height. The talented Garrick attacked the bowling without being troubled by the wicket conditions; he was unruffled and pulled the first two deliveries over the midwicket boundaries viciously and batted brilliantly for a respectable score. That day, a day when he was seen for the first time by a majority of the players and watched by coach Junior Bennett, selectors Len Levy and me, the consensus was that we were seeing the emergence of a young batting star. He was at first very reticent in embracing the usual exuberance of his age group; shortly after, he became very confident and expressed his thoughts with lucidity. Leon Garrick went on to represent the national youth team, the West Indies youth team, Jamaica's senior team, and the West Indies senior team. The West Indies senior selectors were obviously impressed with his early performances at the regional level and included him in the test squad before his debut game but he was dropped after one test appearance.

As a national selector for the many years that I was, there were reasons why players were overlooked for selection. It could have been medical and disciplinary issues that the fans were not aware of. Like so many fans, I am not sure why the gifted young batsman was limited to just one test. The extraordinary batting talent of Leon Garrick's splendid 200 in an unbroken opening stand of 425 with the renowned world champion batsman Chris Gayle 208 is a first-class record in West Indies cricket. Garrick was expected to have had a lengthy first- class and international career displaying his majestic batting skills at venues regionally and internationally; sadly, the much talked about son of the tourist attractive parish St. Ann was not realized. Garrick now resides in the USA. He expressed to me how much he needed someone who would have understood his upbringing and that I would have been that person to help him through times of instability.

Gareth Breese's leadership was remarkable; the players performed as a cohesive unit in 1995 as they did in 1994 when he again led the team to championship honours. The quality of Breese's batting and leadership made him the obvious choice as captain of the West Indies youth team to Pakistan and Bangladesh later that year 1995; the team included three other Jamaicans: Wavell Hinds, Denville McKenzie, and O'Neil Richards.

Figure 111 Leonard Chambers with Leon Garrick and Wavell Hinds at Sabina Park

Perception of Administrators and Players

As I reflected on the years 1983 to 1996, a period I served as a national selector at both the under-nineteen and senior levels, there were times at the senior level, especially during the latter half, that were disappointing. It was disconcerting to me knowing that there were selectors who lacked the awareness of players' suitability to have been invited to the national trials. As a player involved with Parish and Sugar Estate Cricket, I have seen so many talented players who performed consistently and who were denied recognition by the selection process. The selectors had not seen the players because of their nonappearance at rural matches. It was obligatory for selectors to have watched rural cricket consistently and not to have assumed the ability of players on hearsay from individuals who lacked acceptable cricket acumen.

As a selector, I continued to believe in the concept of seeing the players in a match set up as often as possible, which allowed for better assessment of their ability. I also believed and trusted recommendations from well-informed and impartial individuals. At a senior selection meeting chaired by Easton McMorris to name invitees to the national trials, I reiterated strongly my objection to George Sterling, a member of the committee who mentioned a player to be invited. Sterling had not seen the player in any game, so I asked him what was the premise of his recommendation. Surprisingly, his answer was, "I heard that the player was a good fielder," This to me was unacceptable.

I happened to have known a lot about the player; he came to the youth trials in his final year and performed poorly. After that experience, he struggled to create attention for senior national recognition, and surprisingly, was called to the trials. It was inconceivable that a national selector's perception of who should be qualified to the trials was so superficial. There was absolutely no way a player whose strength was neither as a bowler or batsman

301

should be considered for the trials; the exception would be a wicketkeeper. I emphasized to McMorris and Sterling that it was incumbent on them to watch more local games, especially in the rural areas of the country, and that it was a disservice to those players. McMorris and George Sterling were obviously unprepared of my admonition.

The following year at a JCA Board meeting, the appointment of the senior selectors was postponed as both McMorris and Sterling, after being nominated, declined after I was confirmed. It was agreed that at the next Board meeting, the committee would again try to confirm the selection committee. On that day of the Board meeting, as chairman of the youth selection committee, I decided to attend a very crucial schoolboy game between the two top rural schools St. Elizabeth Technical and Holmwood Technical at the Alpart Cricket ground in St Elizabeth. As a selector and chairman of the youth selection committee, it was imperative for me to have been at that important fixture with the prospect of identifying players in preparation for the youth camp of that year. It was in that Alpart game that I first saw the batting talent of a very young Ricardo Powell.

I was told by two senior Board members Chester Watson and Roy Paul to forego watching the match and attend the board meeting. They advised me that McMorris and Sterling were seeking support of the members not to have me as a senior selector. Both Watson and Paul explained, "If you are present, no one would have the audacity to vote against you."

Needless to say, I was immersed with the youth level of our cricket. I explained to Watson and Paul that I was duty bound to be at Alpart and that McMorris and Sterling should have no influence on the members not voting for me as senior selector. I was obviously disappointed with the Board members' fragility in succumbing to Sterling and McMorris' influences that led to my non-appointment to the selection committee of that year.

There were members who voted for me, including Rex Fennell, Jackie Hendricks, Maurice Foster, Chester Watson, Dr. David Crawford, Keith Brown, and Roy Paul. Hendricks, Foster, Watson and Paul served with me as selectors previously with Hendricks and Foster as my teammate at the national level. Fennell, Brown, Paul, and Crawford knew my value through the years and always supported me as a selector at both levels. The members who succumbed to the whims of McMorris and Sterling and did not support my retention was a surprise to most, including the former President Allan Rae. The following year, I was reinstated to the committee and continued my duties as I knew best.

In retrospect, as I observed and assessed the game administered by the city clubs and the performances of the players throughout the years, a number of clubs stood out. The 1992 Cricket season was yet another successful season for the Melbourne Cricket Club under the leadership of the experienced Mark Neita. The attractive brand of cricket displayed by the 1992 championship team was deserving of the coveted trophy. The Melbourne Cricket Club has been one of if not the most flourishing of the senior cup clubs, from the early years located at Elliston Road to its current residence. The club's centralized location at uptown Kingston is accessible to members of different age groups, from the playing field to indoor activities of table tennis, billiards, dominoes, cards, and the availability of hot meals were an added attraction to the club membership. The atmosphere was always vivacious by the presence of male member's spouses, some of whom were members of the club.

Several young cricketers were attracted to the legendary club, a club with the ever presence of past international, national and other club cricketers who were helpful to the development of their game. Former and present players at the time included Ruddy Williams, Ruddy Marzouca, Gerald Wollaston, Bruce Wellington, Arthur Barrett, Keith Reese and George Sterling; they inculcated the principles and accepted culture of club life and team spirit. The conducive club environment and the opportunity presented for aspiring youngsters, including the greats Michael Holding and Courtney Walsh. There were other wonderful players such as the internationals Arthur Barrett, Marlon Samuels, and his brother Robert Samuels, Donavan Pagon, and Carlton Baugh Jr. Others like Mark Neita and Odelmo Peters as Cricket West Indies List "A" players benefited immensely and there were others before and after I migrated to the USA. The club administration was expertly organized through the years by outstanding Presidents such as Ivan Herron, George Sterling, Tony Becca, Teddy Griffiths and Ralph Holding.

Through the years from the 50s to the mid-90s, a cadre of outstanding fast bowlers have represented the Melbourne club and progressed to national and international status and there was a group that performed exceptionally at the club level but missed out on selection, There was the case of the young-ster Errol Nolan; his progress was closely followed after his performances in the 1989 regional tournament in Guyana. He bowled brilliantly; his pace troubled most of the batsmen, including the Barbados opener Sherwin Campbell who was the tournament leading runs scorer with three magnifi-cent Hundreds. Campbell found the pace of Nolan very difficult to handle and was bowled in both innings for zero. He was bemused by the hostility and effectiveness of the fiery deliveries of the gangling pacer. Nolan's superb bowling efforts impressed the selectors and that led to his selection to the West Indies Youth team tour of Canada.

He continued to bowl effectively and in a local senior cup game against Po-lice played at Elletson Road, the young pacer had the marvelous bowling figures of 9 wickets for 27 runs in a fiery spell of 15 consecutive overs in the Police team second innings. His meticulous training habits mirrored his physical attributes as an exceptional fit athlete. The selectors, of which I was one, had him at age 22, on a short list of fast bowlers from which to be chosen to the Jamaica team. He was destined to have made his national senior debut that year 1992. Unexpectedly, the young speedster got married to his early childhood girlfriend Althea Brown, and as a couple relocated to Houston, Texas where he currently resides and works as Pre-Owned Director of sales at BMW of West Houston. Errol Nolan is a family man and the proud dad of four children, two boys and two girls, all grownups; he is also a grandad.

From Jamaica's perspective, selectors at the senior level have consistently shown an interest in the performances of players at the most recent youth regional tournament. As manager and as a selector at both levels, I was often asked about the ones who should be considered for our national senior trials. Naturally, the merit for inclusion would be assessed on consistent perfor-mances; there were players with the ability and so often one or two missed out. The inconsistency of known players was not an unfamiliar passage of our cricket. There were so many players at school and club levels who were on the fringe and just missed invitation to the national youth and senior tri-als, and there were players who performed extremely well in local competi-tions and fizzled out at the trials; their performance was a shadow of their true potential.

Figure 112 Errol Nolan

West Indies Youth Manager at Home

At the end of the 1994 regional youth tournament, Cricket West Indies appointed a youth selection committee of three with David Holford as chairman; the other members were Pat Legal from Guyana and me. We were assigned the responsibility of naming a squad and reserves for three 3-dayers and three fifty over matches against England's under-nineteens. The matches were played in Trinidad, Barbados, Guyana, St. Kitts and St. Vincent. I was later named manager of the team by Cricket West Indies at a meeting held in Guyana.

Maurice Foster, one of Jamaica's two members of the CWI, first told me of my appointment in an early morning call from Guyana to me in Jamaica. I was later officially notified by CWI Secretary Steve Camacho of my selection. Like Maurice Foster, Steve Camacho was pleased with my choice as manager and I was indeed appreciative of their compliments. Having played regional cricket against the Guyanese, Steve Camacho and my relationship with the Jamaican Foster at the local club and regional level and as members of the Jamaica Cricket Association was comforting.

To be named manager of the West Indies under-19 youth team was marvelous. It was an appointment of recognition for my several years as manager of the Jamaica national youth team at the regional level. I was indeed exceptionally thrilled of the honour. The squad assembled in Trinidad for a week of training before the first of the three-day matches with the first at the Queens Park Oval, the second in St. Kitts, and the third in Guyana. For each game, there was a different coach. This was not an ideal situation for symmetry; each coach had his method and could create confusion on the minds of the youngsters. I was not aware of the unusual situation until the last day of the Trinidad game when Cricket West Indies Assistant Secretary Andrew

Sealy advised me.

The selected squad included Andre Percival Captain, Rawl Lewis Vice-Captain, Dinanath Ramnarine, Andre Coley, Nicholas DeGroot, Marlon Black, Gareth Breese, Reon King, Adrian Murphy, Dennis Rampersad, Balty Watt, Lincoln Roberts, and Ricky Christopher. An injury to Nicholas de Groot ,the Guyanese right-handed stroke player resulted in replacement by the elegant stroke player Jamaican opener Delroy Taylor who just missed selection to the original fourteen-member squad; he was one of the three reserves named. The coach for the first game was Trinidadian Debideen Manick who was unknown to me. Having seen and being familiar with coaches of regional youth and senior teams over a period of fourteen years, I was expecting someone like William Bourne of Barbados to have been given the coaching job. In the truncated stint as coach and unfamiliar with the players, Manick did an exceptional job. His systematic style was impressive. The players listened attentively to his skills set and responded positively with a wonderful sense of purpose to their game. I provided him useful information on each player and we both shared ideas regarding strategies germane to match situations. Leading up to the first game, Chairman David Holford, while in Barbados kept in touch with me on the squad physical and net preparation. The administration of the Trinidad Cricket Board throughout our one-week preparation and for the first three-day game played at the historic and beautiful Queens Park ground was excellent.

Of the group named Dinanath Ramnarine the right arm leg spinner, Rawl Lewis right arm leg spinner who was no novice with the bat, Gareth Breese batsman and off spinner, Lincoln Roberts a lovely stroke playing batsman, Marlon Black the strongly built fast bowler, and Reon King the fast bowler who reminded me of the great Michael Holding with his lovely look alike rhythm, were all selected to their regional senior team shortly after before representing West Indies senior team later on during their careers. There were others from the squad who went on to represent their country's senior team including Trinidad's Dennis Rampersad, a free scoring batsman with a very good technique, Ricky Christopher fast bowler to the Leeward Islands, Balty Watt a right handed batsman who batted aggressively with a sound defense to the Windward Islands, Andre Percival a left handed stroke player to his native Guyana, Andre Coley the wicket keeper who was brilliant with the gloves and very useful with the bat was selected to Jamaica's senior team early after leaving the youth ranks. Coley was considered by the Jamaica national selectors as talented with the ideal attitude to succeed at the national senior level and someday becoming an international player. Coley later became a national Jamaica and West Indies international senior coach. Nicholas de Groot as an opener demonstrated in the regional youth tournament that he possessed the natural talent to become a regular to Guyana's senior team. His boyhood dream was realized when he eventually got into the team. He later migrated to Canada where he represented that country internationally in ODI'S.

During the matches against their English counterparts, the West Indies youth players were intent on doing well as a team and individually they performed remarkably with encouraging performances. The matches were enthralling and gave the fans hope that the exposure gained would help them individually for national and international recognition. The first of the three-day games played at the Queens Park Oval in Trinidad ended in a draw, scores England 317 and 194 for 4 declared, and West Indies 168 and 152 for 7. The West Indies with resolute batting in their second innings prevented their opponents victory. England batted first and amassed a good first innings total with Chris Schofield top scoring with a lovely 83. Anthony McGrath an attacking 79, and David Sales a well-paced 70. Bowling for the West Indies Reon King 4 for 49, Dinanath Ramnarine 4 for 74 and Marlon Black 2 for 60. King was impressive with his accuracy and bowled at a lively pace; his fast-bowling partner Marlon Black bowled at a lively pace in his early overs and looked like finishing with more than his two wickets. Ramnarine, with his varying mixture of leg breaks and googlies was always a threat to the batsmen who were bemused by his variations. Our batsmen found it difficult to handle Flintoff's swing and lively pace and fell apart with a modest first innings reply of 168. Adrian Murphy at the top of the order played a workmanlike innings to top scorer with 52 followed by the captain Andre Percival with 33 and Nicholas de Groot 27. Andrew Flintoff 5 for 39 and David Thompson 2 for 43. England in their second innings declared at199 for 4 with Trescothick scoring freely for a delightful century (106) followed by Vikram Solanki with 40; bowling for the West Indies Black and King each picked up 2 wickets. The home team was under pressure to avoid defeat; in the end they held on for a draw with Murphy finishing with 49, Lincoln Roberts 37 and Gareth Breese 23, Vikram Solanki 4 for 50 and David

Thompson 2 for 41 were England leading bowlers.

The second game at Warner Park, St. Kitts, ended with the West Indies team securing a wonderful victory in a closely contested game; scores were West Indies 176 and 240, England 195 and 187. In a low scoring game, the wicket was conducive to the West Indies two wrist spinners Dinanath Ramnarine and Rawl Lewis. West Indies had first strike scoring 176; Adrian Murphy 44, Dinanath Ramnarine 27 and Lincoln Roberts 22 were the main contributors, bowling for England Vikram Solanki 3 for 10, Matthew Diamond 3 for 39, and Andrew Flintoff 2 for 47. In reply, England gained a first innings lead of 19 runs having been dismissed for 195 with worthwhile contributions of 49 from Alex Morris, 35 from Anurag Singh and 30 from Anthony McGrath. Bowling for the West Indies, Dinanath Ramnarine 4 for 63, Rawl Lewis 3 for 30 and Marlon Black 2 for 40.

The West Indies improved on their first innings total with 240, Lincoln Roberts 45, Gareth Breese 42, captain Andre Percival 39, Andre Coley 26 and Marlon Black 22, bowling for England Mathew Diamond reaped 5 for 70, and Vikram Solanki 3 for 50. England were set a target of 229 for victory and fell short having been dismissed for 187 with Anurag Singh scoring a workmanlike 52 and Anthony McGrath 31 as the leading scorers. Ramnarine and Lewis created uncertainties among their batsmen on a pitch that suited their wrist spinning deliveries. Ramnarine had the remarkable figures of 7 for 73 in the first innings to finish with a match haul of 11 for 136 and Lewis 2 for 66 with match figures of 5 for 96. Lewis' figures did not reflect on how well he bowled; he could have had more wickets for least number of runs. A significant percentage of the runs scored of his bowling were streaky.

The third and final game was played at Bourda ground in Guyana and ended in a draw. It was an outcome that gave the West Indies team the satisfaction of winning the three-match series. The players were delighted with their achievement against an opposition with many first-class players, players who were English county cricketers and very experienced. The West Indies batsmen collectively found their best form with the bat and it was a revelation to see the batting talent of our young hopefuls on display. The batting of Lincoln Roberts and Denis Rampersad in a partnership exhibited total dominance against a varied and potent English attack. Roberts' brilliant century of attacking and attractive stroke-play, and Rampersad's half century with precise and exquisite drives on either side of the wicket were delightful entertainment for the fans. The supporting knocks by captain Andre Percival, Rawl Lewis, Adrian Murphy, and Delroy Taylor in this the last of the three-day matches were indeed impressive.

The overall batting talent of the young West Indians augmented their aspirations for development as future national senior representatives, players like Denis Rampersad, Lincoln Roberts, Gareth Breese, Adrian Murphy, Andre Percival, and Delroy Taylor appeared to be special talent. The bowling of the leg spinners Dinanath Ramnarine and Rawl Lewis was a revelation of internationals in the making; their controlled accuracy with consistent variations was marvelous. The outstanding talented fast bowlers Reon King and Marlon Black bowled with sustained hostility and created indecision for most of the English batsmen. For the fans looking on, it was inspirational watching the two in tandem; as ardent West Indies supporters, they would have been impressed with the promise shown by the two.

Andre Coley, the wicket keeper, was a seasoned campaigner having represented the West Indies under-19 on tour of England in 1993. He was very impressive with his glove work. It came as no surprise that so many from the squad achieved National and International status. It was disappointing that Adrian Murphy was not able to make it to the Barbados senior team after performing reasonably well and was impressive on a subsequent West Indies youth tour of Pakistan and Bangladesh.

The England players, some of whom were professionals, showed maturity and a challenge for the West Indians. There were outstanding performances by batsmen Marcus Trescothick, Anthony McGrath, Chris Schofield, All-rounders David Sales, Vikram Solanki and Andrew Flintoff; bowlers David Thompson and Matthew Diamond were impressive with the ball.

For the third and final three-day game in Guyana, it was surprising to me as manager when I was introduced to the coach. I was not aware of his coaching credentials regionally at the youth or senior levels nor as a regional player; he was unknown to the players excluding the two Guyanese Andre Percival and Reon King. I was surprised when he asked me to conduct the fielding practice as he had a permanent frailty with one of his arms and could not grip the bat firmly to knock the ball. The naming of the eleven for this important game never had his input; his lack of knowledge on the players meant I had no alternative but to tell him what the starting eleven was. His response was favourable. He did not stay around for our team meetings after each day's play, and surprisingly, changed the batting order as was discussed and agreed on at our meeting the evening before. I made it known to him that we had a set formula that worked well throughout the series and that it would have been prudent for him to have consulted with me before; he was not defiant in any way and was apologetic. The drawn result of the third and last game meant that we were winners of the three-match series.

Scores in the game were West Indies 277: Rawl Lewis 75, Andre Percival 37, Lincoln Roberts 32 Marlon Black 31 and Delroy Taylor 26. Alex Morris 3 for 66, Mathew Diamond 2 for 46, Andrew Flintoff 2 for 57 and 334 Lincoln Roberts 114, Denis Rampersad 64, Andre Percival 35, Adrian Murphy 35. Jason Searle 3 for 56, Vikram Solanki 3 for 73. England 267: Anthony McGrath 133, Vikram Solanki 34, Ismail Dawood 20, Reon King 7 for 97, and Dinanath Ramnarine 2 for 54.

At the end of each three-day game, I conveyed to the host countries the overwhelming appreciation for the hospitality extended to both teams. There was no doubt the warmth of the fans to the players of both teams in each territory, their meaningful conversation with the players at the end of a day's play and the encouragement given especially to the West Indies youngsters was uplifting.

For the three ODI'S, one change was made to the squad with wicket keeper batsman Rondette Yearwood from Barbados, who was one of the reserves, replaced Andre Coley. Coley was considered the better of the two with the gloves, but Yearwood with his attacking style of batting was ideally suited for this version of the game.

The first and second of the three ODI'S were played at the picturesque Arnos Vale ground in St. Vincent. The sounds of aircraft landing and taking off at the nearby Airport and the activity of the waves and serenity of the adjacent Caribbean ocean blending with the energetic chattering of the cricket loving fans in the open stands was captivating. This was my second visit to one of the paradise islands of the Caribbean. The first time I visited the island was as a player in a regional match in the nineteen seventies against the Windward Islands during my in and out of the Jamaica regional team over a nine-year span. I was impressed with the upgrade of the facilities; the additional stands were imposing and stood out in reshaping the beauty of the ground.

When Michael Findlay the former West Indies player accompanied me to the grounds a day before the first game, Findlay, who was the liaison to our team, was no stranger to me and understood my interest in wanting to see the ground and the structural development and what the playing area was like. Findlay, a son of the St. Vincent island, was and is still highly respected and revered for his contribution to West Indies cricket. Findlay was the first player from the region of the Leeward and Windward islands to have represented the West Indies in test cricket. Findlay, on behalf of the Windward Board, extended exceptional courtesy to our team during that leg of the tour. A very pleasant individual with an attribute of calmness that personified his eminence as one who would make a good leader of Cricket West Indies.

The young players adapted satisfactorily to the 50 overs version of the game. From England's perspective, Markus Trescothick, Anurag Singh and Vikram Solanki with the bat and Andrew Flintoff the fast-bowling all-rounder and for the West Indies Adrian Murphy, Gareth Breese, Delroy Taylor as batsmen, Reon King, Marlon Black and Ricky Christopher as fast bowlers and Rawl Lewis the leg spinning all-rounder.

England won the ODI series two games to one after both teams entered the final game having won one game each. Scores in the first game England 178 Anurag Singh 40, McGrath 40, Flintoff 32 and Vikram Solanki 23, Rawl Lewis 3 for 18, Ricky Christopher 2 for 40. West Indies 179 for 7 Adrian Murphy 67, Gareth Breese 52 Flintoff 2 for 18 and Searle 2 for 23. West Indies won by 3 wickets. Excellent bowling figures by Lewis and Christopher and two lovely knocks by Murphy and Breese took the honours in a West Indies victory that was most deserving. The second game, at different stages ,the balance shifted. In the end England triumphed. Scores England 215, led by a brilliant 88 from Marcus Trescothick and a timely 40 from Vikram Solanki with support from Alex Morris 30. Reon King bowled superbly with sustained hostility and accuracy ended with 4 for 36. West Indies found the target hard to overcome and fell short, finishing with 172 losing by 43 runs. Batting for the West Indies Denis Rampersad 25, Adrian Murphy 24, Rawl Lewis 24 and Marlon Black 24 were the main contributors, Alex Morris 2 for 14, Marcus

Trescothick 2 for 34 and Jason Sealers 2 for 38 restricted the West Indies batsmen in their quest for victory.

In the final game to decide the winners of the three-match series, England demonstrated supremacy at the limited overs version with a convincing 90 runs victory, scores England 278 for 6, Anurag Singh 130, David Sales 50, Christopher Schofield 35, bowling for the West Indies Gareth Breese 2 for 43, Marlon Black, Ricky Christopher and Rawl Lewis each picked up a wicket. West Indies 188, Delroy Taylor 61, Rawl Lewis 41, Reon King 26 and Dennis Rampersad 24.

Preparation for Inaugural Regional Under Fifteen Competition

The long-awaited West Indies regional under-15 tournament was finally agreed on and played during the first half of the 1996 cricket calendar year in Trinidad. A committee of three from the Jamaica Cricket Association headed by the youth committee Chairman Jackie Hendricks, Secretary Brian Breese, and I were appointed to start the process leading to the selection of the squad and later a recommendation of the manager and coach. As chairman of the youth selection committee, I recognized from experience with the under-19 teams the enormous task ahead in getting the best group of players together from which the squad was selected. At the age group of fifteen and under, very little was known of the players and so much was dependent on coaches and knowledgeable individuals from the schools. Coaches Dennis Miller and Junior Bennett, himself a National Youth selector along with Rohan Kanhai, who joined the programme much later, were mentioned and agreed by the JCA to conduct the training as soon as a manageable group was identified.

As chairman of the youth selection committee and the other selectors, we were able to identify an initial group numbering approximately fifty, and as the weeks went by, we were able to reduce the numbers, and while doing so we were adding new ones. I asked of and welcome recommendations from knowledgeable school coaches of individual players who were considered during the early stages of gathering the group from which the squad was selected. At one of my addresses to the youngsters at Sabina Park before they took to the field for Calisthenics, Odelmo Peters the former Jamaica and "West Indies A player" brought to my attention two youngsters that he thought were good enough to be in the group.

Peters as a schoolboy played for the Saint Catherine Cricket Club senior cup team while I was the captain. I trusted his recommendation and suggested that the two could join the group the following day. Peters indicated that he brought along the players and that they were sitting in his motor car behind the player's enclosure. He confessed that he knew that I would have trusted his judgement of the players and went on to say, "I was confident that you would accept my assessment of the two and they have with them their cricket gear ready to join the group." I smiled and acceded to his compelling presentation of the two youngsters.

The names of the two were Donavan Pagan and Carlton Baugh Jr. Pagan was a batsman and Baugh was a batsman who could keep the wicket. Peters knew the ability of the two as he was conducting a coaching seminar of youngsters at the Melbourne Cricket Club Annual youth camp. I introduced the two youngsters to the coaches Bennett and Miller as added players to the group.

Pagan and Baugh confirmed the confidence of Peters in their skills, and despite not making the touring squad that year, they later went on to be included in the under-nineteen, national senior Jamaica teams and then to the West Indies senior team; a remarkable assessment of the two by Peters.

There was one other player added to the group for continued training before the touring squad was named; his name was Derwyn Hillock. I saw him after conducting a coaching session in St. Mary at the request of youth club organizer Keith Leslie, popularly known as Piggy. Keith Leslie was a club cricketer in the parish and was closely connected with the St. Mary Cricket Association. For five consecutive years, at his invitation, I addressed aspiring young cricketers in around the parish of St. Mary at a designated club environment. I was invited in my capacity as chairman of the Jamaica Youth selectors and as someone who was familiar with youth clubs, having spent my early years actively involved with youth clubs in Spanish Town.

The day before that particular day of coaching, Keith Leslie called me before my yearly address to the youngsters of the Parish that was started four years before and advised me that unlike previous years, I would be required to coach a group of youngsters numbering about fifty and that I should make it there by mid- afternoon. The previous years, I was required to address the youngsters indoors at a clubhouse starting at 5: PM. I reminded Leslie that I was not a coach and that it was an enormous group for one person to coach in one afternoon session. Keith Leslie confidently assured me that I played the game and as one who played nationally, I was qualified to do the job.

Keith Leslie, the energetic organizer for the young cricketers of the parish worked tirelessly for their development through the years and served as a conduit to the St. Mary Cricket Association youth programme. I did not want to let him down on his commitment to the youngsters who themselves would have been terribly disappointed if I were unable to conduct the coaching session. We both admired each other for our contribution to youth clubs and my better instincts guided me to say, "Rest assured, my friend, I will be there."

I was able to have Tony Powell, who at the time was a national senior player accompany me to the Sugar Cane and Banana producing Parish of St. Mary to assist with the coaching after my initial welcome address to the enthusiastic youngsters. There were two players that caught the attention of Tony and me. One was Warren Medwynter, a twenty-two-year-old fast bowler who swung the ball both ways and bowled in cutters at a lively pace, and a fourteen-year-old left arm spinner by the name of Derwyn Hillocks. Hillocks spun the ball appreciably with good control and impressed as one for the future; that led to his invitation to the under-fifteen training group, and Warren Medwynter as a prospect for the national senior trials was later selected to the national senior team. Looking at the national under-fifteen age group going through the early stages of preparation for the regional tournament was a process that needed the selector's meticulous attention, separating the ones with the visible ability and readiness for the occasion.

Unlike the under-nineteens who were more advanced in the development stages of their game, the age group was in the infancy of learning the basics. I took it unto myself to be ever present on a daily basis to address and watch the youngsters go through the routine of calisthenics and net sessions. As the weeks went by, the selectors along with the coaches, were beginning to see a number of the players displaying themselves as worthy contenders to be in the final group from which the touring squad was to be selected.

While the Jamaica under-fifteen trial invitees were preparing for the inaugural tournament, a West Indies Youth Team was selected for tours of Pakistan and Bangladesh with me as the manager and Gus Logie as the coach. A date was also confirmed for the team to gather in Trinidad for a week of training preceding departure for the sub-continent tours. I was absolutely delighted to have been named as manager and with Gus Logie the former West Indies player as coach. The players selected was a formidable unit, well balanced with talented players. I was familiar with the players who earlier participated in the regional youth tournament and were rewarded by their impressive performances.

Before leaving for Trinidad, I continued my role on a daily basis of monitoring the progress of the under-fifteen preparation at Sabina Park,. On one of the days while I was at Sabina Park, Mr. Rex Fennell, President of the JCA and a Director of Cricket West Indies visited me. He asked how the preparation was progressing with the young group and also congratulated me on my appointment as manager for the Asian tours. Fennell mentioned that I could be paid in advance for the tour by the Jamaica Cricket Association before I left for Trinidad. I reminded Fennell that earlier that year as manager of the West Indies youth team during the young England tour of the West Indies, I was paid for the tour just before the first game in Trinidad after been there for a week and that I was in no hurry to be paid. Fennell explained that he was experiencing a temporary cash flow in a "Dog Food Business" that he recently started with his son Herman Fennell and asked if I could help him by getting the advance from the JCA to settle an immediate financial cash flow issue. He went on to explain that in a matter of days he would be able to sort out his cash flow problem and return the funds representing the amount given to me by the JCA treasurer Verley Harrison with a satisfactory explanation. As friends and one who I greatly respected from my teenage years as a Sugar Estate cricketer, the friendship that we enjoyed as members of the Jamaica Cricket Association and the years of support given to me while he was Secretary and continued through his Presidency, I acceded to his call for assistance with the understanding that the issue would have been settled locally and that I would await payment from Cricket West Indies at a later date while I was in Pakistan. I got the advance the same day from the JCA treasurer and cashed it and handed the full amount to Mr. Fennell. Later that day, without trepidation, I saw the issue as settled.

Before leaving for Trinidad in preparation for the tours to Pakistan and Bangladesh, I gave my blessings to those in charge of the under- fifteen programme and that I would be back for the final period of its preparation.

Pakistan and Bangladesh Tours

Along with the four Jamaicans Gareth Breese, Wavell Hinds, O'Neil Richards and Denville McKenzie selected for the Asian tours, we arrived in Trinidad for a period of training with the other players. The squad of players selected was based on their splendid performances during the 1995 regional youth tournament. A number of the players who played earlier that year against the England under-nineteens and eligible for selection had an impact on their selection to the squad for the historic sub-continent tours.

The touring squad was Gareth Breese Captain, Nicholas De Groot Vice-Captain, Sylvester Joseph. Adrian Murphy, Reon King, Raymond Casimir, Amarnath Basedo, Tyrone Greenaway, Ryan Hurley, Mahendra Nagamootoo, Vishal Nagamootoo, Shirley Clarke, Denville McKenzie, Wavell Hinds, and O'Neill Richards, with Gus Logie as coach and me as manager. Logie, due to his youthful look and demeanor had an early impact of acceptance on the players; the youthful players responded enthusiastically to his system of preparation at the net sessions, team meetings and his remarkable talent as a coach. Before leaving Trinidad for the twin tours of Pakistan and Bangladesh, Cricket West Indies appointed two former West Indies cricketers Steve Camacho, who at the time was Secretary of the Board, and the great Sir Wesley Hall, manager of the West Indies team, to brief both Logie and I on our respective roles while on the sub-continent tours. Steve Camacho, the former Guyana and West Indies opening batsman, and Sir Wesley Hall, one of the great West Indies fast bowlers from Barbados were vastly experienced West Indies team managers. The meeting was informative and valuable to me as manager away from the Caribbean.

Logie's vast experience as a former West Indies player was of immense value to the young players and to me as manager. His previous visits as a senior West Indies player was advantageous to the team in many ways. His preparation of the players set the tone for what was to be expected of pitch conditions, togetherness as team players, acceptance, and respect of umpires decisions; his training methods were clearly uncomplicated and articulated with positive effect.

The Trinidad Board was very accommodating during our one week stay, ensuring that the training facilities were of an acceptable standard, and briefs by professionals regarding ethics oration was greatly appreciated. It came as no surprise to me the efficiency of the Trinidad Board, as earlier in the year against England under-nineteens throughout our one-week preparation before the opening game at the Queens Park Oval, the administration provided similar arrangements that were of immense value to the young West Indies players. The preparation went well. Coach Logie and I were impressed with the zest shown by the players during practice sessions, and they certainly looked ready for the task ahead and to be on that plane for England *enroute* to Pakistan for the first leg of the sub-continent tours.

Arriving at Gatwick Airport, we were met and welcomed by a party of two officials on behalf of Cricket West Indies. They were very cordial and ensured that all arrangements were in place before our departure for Pakistan, including hotel accommodation nearby to the airport. The players were two to a room with Ryan Hurley and Vishal Nagamootoo sharing. It was surprising that shortly after the players went to their respective rooms, Vishal Nagamootoo reported to me and Logie that Hurley, his designated roommate was uncomfortable sharing the room with him because of his Indian background. We immediately had a meeting with both youngsters and explained what it meant representing the West Indies as one nation. Hurley assured both Logie and I that he would conform to what was required of him followed by handshakes with Vishal.

After leaving London, we made a short stop in Paris *enroute* to Pakistan. The players were thrilled when the plane touched down at Charles de Gaulle Airport in the French capital known for its amazing attraction as a tourist destination.

On arrival at the Karachi Airport, we were met by Officials of the Pakistan Board and introduced to our Liaison who was with us throughout the Pakistan leg of the tour. He was a current club cricketer at the time and was very helpful to the team in adapting to our new and unfamiliar surroundings.

The players were eager to start their preparation for the next six weeks. The experience of Gus Logie was exceptional in having them well-prepared leading into the first game against a very strong Karachi team. They showed early signs of adaptation at the Southend Cricket Club Ground which ended in a tame draw. Batting first, the West Indies 345 for 9 wickets with Ryan Hurley showing early form scoring a brilliant level 100, Mahendra Nagamootoo 61, Gareth Breese 60 ,Nicholas de Groot 54. Shahid Afridi 4 for 133. Karachi 294 Masood Ali 108, Fahood Usmar 51.Nagamootoo 6 for 95, O'Neill Richards 3 for 30. West Indies in their second innings 76 for 3 Wavell Hinds 46.

The West Indies batting guided by Hurley's splendid century was very entertaining and the Karachi fans showed their appreciation on an innings laced with majestic stroke play on either side of the wicket. There were wonderful supporting roles played by Nagamootoo, Breese, de Groot, and Hinds. The bowling of leg spinner Nagamootoo with his control and variation and the fiery pace of O'Neil Richards were inspiring for the young West Indians. Masood Ali's century and Fahad Usmar's half century and with Afridi's bowling were good signs for the Karachi youngsters. Shahid Afridi's leg spin bowling was impressive in his marathon spells and he looked competent with the bat. All matches on the tour were supposed to have been competed by players 19 and under; that's how it was perceived and agreed on by both countries. We later learned when Afridi announced his retirement from international cricket that he was four years older than the world of cricket thought he was. He was at age twenty and not sixteen when the teams met in that first game in Karachi. The drawn game was a good result for both teams with plusses for a number of our batsmen and the effectiveness of our bowlers led by Mahendra Nagamootoo and O'Neil Richards meant that we were off to an inspiring start.

Before leaving Karachi for our next game, I got a call from Andrew Sealy the Assistant Secretary of the West Indies Cricket Board regarding payment of my tour fees. I suggested to him that he should send it to Roy Paul who was the secretary of the JCA and a very close friend. I immediately contacted Paul that Sealy would be calling him and that he should make the lodgment to my Nova Scotia Bank account that I had given to him earlier. I assumed the call from Sealy meant that Mr. Fennell honoured the arrangement he made with me before I left for Trinidad for the one-week team preparation before departure to Pakistan.

Our next game was against Multan in Sahiwal at the Montgomery Cricket Club Ground. The teams travelled in separate buses which was a long drive to the province. It was prearranged by the PBC that the teams would have lunch at separate sections of a designated restaurant. As we were walking to the entrance of the building, an attendant directed the players to their respective enclosed dining area. There was one player on the Pakistan team who was of Jamaican parentage and looked like a young Vivian Richards, the great West Indian cricketer. He was directed to our area and it took a while of sustained persuasion by the Pakistan players before the attendant accepted that the youngster was a Pakistani.

The Montgomery Ground was an ideal venue for the players. From our chalets, we walked unhindered onto the playing field, a distance the length of a cricket pitch. The ground was contiguous to the Montgomery Flour & General Mills Limited that manufactured Confectioneries, Vegetable Vanaspati and Cooking Oils. At the end of a remarkable match and an enjoyable four days in the beautiful surroundings, both teams were presented with packages of Assorted Biscuits and Soaps. The managing Director of the company, Mr. Basharat Shafi and owner of the multilayered complex was a known cricket enthusiast; he extended his influence in no small measure for us to make the event a memorable experience of comfort.

I remember during the course of a day's play, he invited me to his private box and the experienced Gus Logie said to me, "Manage, should he invite you in having a drink, let him know a cup of tea would be fine?" In Pakistan, alcoholic beverage was not allowed openly.

The four-day game ended in a draw, scores West Indies first innings 174: Wavell Hinds 35, Denville McKenzie 24 not out, Adrian Murphy 22, Ryan Hurley 21, Zubair Ayub 6 for 65 Mohammad Riaz 4 for 54, Multan eleven 228, Rashid Khan 38, Magid Inayal 39, Mohammad Riaz 34, Sadaqat Hussain 32, Raymond Casimir 4 for 38, Ryan Hurley 2 for 72, Gareth Breese 2 for 29. West Indies second innings 416: Ryan Hurley 154, Adrian Murphy 125, Raymond Casimir 44, Riaz 3 for 100, Azhar 4 for 103.

The West Indies pushed hard for victory, but was denied by Mohammad Riaz and Zubair Ayub with defiant knocks in the last session of the game.

The batting of Hurley and Murphy was admirable. The two batted with assurance and were never troubled by the varied Multan bowling attack. Their remarkable partnership placed the young West Indians in an impregnable position and set the stage for our bowlers to attack the opposition batsmen, and in the end ,we were only able to get seven wickets. It was a truly enjoyable five days of our visit to the beautiful surroundings of the Montgomery Complex and the hospitality extended.

The third game, the first of three so called test matches against the Pakistan team at the under-19 level was played at the National Stadium in Faisalabad; it was a thriller. The West Indies won by 5 wickets, scores Pakistan 116 Zeeshan Pervez 39, Faha Usman 25, Masood Ali 25, Reon King 5 for 37, Mahendra Nagamootoo 3 for 34. West Indies 132 Mahendra Nagamootoo 40, Shirley Clarke 17, Mohammad Zahid 6 for 48, Naved-ul Hasan 3 for 54, Pakistan second innings 132, Adil Nisar 34 , Shahid Afridi 30, Fihad Usman 24, Mahendra Nagamootoo 5 for 29 and Denville McKenzie 3 for 24. West Indies second innings 119 for 5, Ryan Hurley 29, Adrian Murphy 19, Nicholas de Groot 17, Naved -ul -Hassan 3 for 36.

The game was played on a bowler's friendly pitch that offered significant assistance to the pacers and spinners. The batsmen on both sides struggled to gain any form of ascendency. In the end, the West Indies came out with a comfortable victory that could have gone either way at different periods of the game. Mahendra Nagamootoo had a good game with bat and ball. The fast bowlers Reon King and Denville McKenzie bowled with pace and were rewarded with good figures.

The fourth game was the second test played at the Khan Research Laboratories Ground in Rawalpindi and ended in a draw. The West Indies batted first scoring 187, heading the batting was Mahendra Nagamootoo 54, Gareth Breese 38, Nicholas de Groot 31 and Adrian Murphy 24, bowling for Pakistan Naved –ul –Hassan 5 for 48 and Mohammad Zahid 4 for 46, Pakistan 388. Majid Inayah 95, Mohammad Riaz 83, Adil Nisan 60, Shadab Kabir 52, O'Neill Richards 3 for 85, Tyrone Greenway 2 for 67. West Indies second innings 257 for 6, Gareth Breese 64,Wavell Hinds 47, Mahendra Nagamootoo 37, Nicholas de Groot 24, Naveed –ul Hassan 2 for 52, Afridi 2 for 55.The West Indians Breese, Nagamootoo, Hinds and de Groot batted resolutely that denied a Pakistan victory.

Our stay in Rawalpindi, the capital of the remarkable cricket-loving country of Pakistan, was satisfactory. The match venue was picturesque with the main pavilion and dressing room facilities adequately suitable and appreciated by both teams. The fans were very receptive; they cheered when a boundary was hit by both teams. The brilliance of the fielding by either side got their acclamation.

Our next game, the fifth of the tour was against Lahore at Lahore City Cricket Association Ground. The game ended in a draw, Scores Lahore 212, Adil Nishan 12, Aamer Munir 25, Mahendra Nagamootoo 4 for 43, Denville McKenzie 2 for 28 and Tyrone Greenway 2 for 48. West Indies 132, Vishal Nagamootoo 38, Shirley Clarke 27 and Raymond Casimir 20, Babar Ali 7 for 49, Lahore second innings 86 for 6, Babar Ali 31, Greenway 2 for 19 and Casimir 2 for 20, West Indies 2nd innings 75 for 2, Wavell Hinds 41, Sheraz 1 for 16 and Babar Ali 1 for 19.

It was a low scoring game; only Adil Nisan, who batted attractively for 121, showed mastery on a pitch that the other batsmen on both teams found runs scoring difficult to come by. During Nisan's time at the wicket, he played in a manner as if he were batting on a different pitch, his dominance over the bowlers was remarkable and his teammate Babar Ali was outstanding with bowling figures of 7 for 49. Of the West Indies batsmen, only Vishal Nagamootoo the wicketkeeper and younger brother of Mahendra Nagamootoo batted fluently with a lovely innings of 38 that showed up the inept batting of his top order teammates in the first innings, in our second turn at the wicket, Wavell Hinds batted well for his 41.

The 6th game was the third and last of the three match test series played at the Railway Stadium in Lahore. It was a game of close matching totals that was tense to the last Pakistan wicket fell giving the West Indies victory by 14 runs. Scores, West Indies 147, Gareth Breese 40, Vishal Nagamootoo 23, Shirley Clarke 20, Adrian Murphy 19, Shahid Afridi 4 for 53 and Naved-ul Hassan 2 for 14. Pakistan 141 Salman Fazal 36, Zeeshan Perez 48, O'Neil Richards 3 for 16, Mahendra Nagamootoo 3 for 68, Ryan Hurley 2 for 20 and Reon King 2 for 30. West Indies 2nd innings 183, Wavell Hinds 45, Shirley Clarke 30, Ryan Hurley 29, Breese 22, Salman Fazal 5 for 44, Hassan 3 for 47 and Mohammad Zahid 2 for 8. Pakistan 2nd innings 175, Shadab Kabir 61 not out, Fahad Usman 40, O'Neil Richards 4 for 33, Manhendra Nagamootoo 3 for 66 and Breese 2 for 5.

The narrow first innings lead of 6 runs by the West Indies set the stage for a keen tussle for ascendancy in the second innings. The batsmen on either side fought gallantly for victory on a pitch that favoured the bowlers. Fortunes grippingly fluctuated either way as the youngsters competed with unswerving intensity to gain the advantage for their country with the West Indies emerging the victors. For the West Indies, batsmen Breese and Clarke in both innings, Hinds and Hurley in the second innings ,played responsibly to set the stage for a remarkable match. The West Indies ended the test match series as champions having won two matches with the other ending in a draw.

The first of the ODI'S was played at the Jinnah Stadium in Sialkot, a very lovely cricket community where the passion for the game was like other areas of Pakistan. The fans turned up in large numbers to see the emerging young players from both countries competing in a game where cricket was a populace obsession. Scores in the game, West Indies 223 for 6 wickets, Sylvester Josephs 78, Mahendra Nagamootoo 44, Wavell Hinds 23, Gareth Breese 21, Ul Aasan 2 for 45. Pakistan 157, Adil Nisar 54, Breese 2 for 25, Mahendra Nagamootoo 3 for 22, Reon King 2 for 36, and Tyrone Greenway 2 for 47. It was a wonderful win by the West Indies led by Joseph's brilliant batting and well supported by Mahendra Nagamootoo's consistency with the bat. Mahendra Nagamootoo demonstrated his enormous all-round ability and value to the team that won the praises of his teammates.

The second ODI played at Lahore City Cricket Association Ground was won by Pakistan, scores Pakistan 192, Pervez 81, Ul- Hasan 26, O'Neil Richards 3 for 27, Mahendra Nagamootoo 3 for 53. West Indies 121 Shirley Clarke 31, Vishal Nagamootoo 29, Nicholas de Groot 25, Salman 6 for 29, Babar Ali 4 for 25.

The Pakistan total, although not imposing, became a struggle for the West Indies batsmen to have surpassed; only Shirley Clarke, Vishal Nagamootoo, and Nicholas de Groot batted with assurance and the intent to surpass the Pakistan total of 192. Richards bowled with pace and control for his rewards. Nagamootoo bowled without luck; his figures did not reflect how well he baffled the batsmen with his mixture of leg breaks, arm balls, and straight ones.

With both teams having won one game apiece, each went into the third and final game determined to win and finish an historical tour with glory. The match was played at Sheikhupura Stadium in the community of Sheikhupura. Like most of the games, the final one was well attended by adoring hometown fans enthusiastically applauding every wicket taken and runs scored by their young Pakistan cricketers. Scores West Indies 163, Wavell Hinds 53, Adrian Murphy 24, Mahendra Nagamootoo 22 and Shirley Clarke 19, Ul- Hasan 4 for 43, Zahid 2 for 19 and Ali 2 for 31.

Pakistan 166 for 6, Ul Hasan 40, Adil Nisan 35, Tyrone Greenway 3 for 16 and Mahendra Nagamootoo 2 for 29. The Pakistan team had the better of our team and won the series two games to one. It was a wonderful series played in an atmosphere of very good sportsmanship by the youngsters of both teams; they garnered tremendous experience from the exposure that enhanced their game in the years that followed. The talent of the West Indies players on the first leg of the twin tours impressed coach Logie with the confidence that several of them would represent the senior team in years to come.

Wavell Hinds, Gareth Breese, Reon King, Mahendra Nagamootoo, Sylvester Josephs, and Ryan Hurley went on to represent the senior West Indies team, and most of the others gained selection to their regional senior teams. Hurley's brilliant form with the bat, two centuries in the first two matches was remarkable; he was a special batting talent and his ability as an off spinner argued favourably for him progressing to the West Indies senior team. It was a disappointment to the team management that after the first game of the tour, he showed little or no interest in playing in a number of the matches, with unacceptable excuses. The unendurable attitude of the gifted Hurley had an effect on team morale that left the team management no choice but to inform Cricket West Indies of our decision to send him home. Logie and I reminded him of his enormous talent that could serve him well moving forward if he were to embrace and exhibit the disciplines of team sport. Sending him home was the right call for team unanimity and a reminder to the young players of pitfalls that could be detrimental to the dreams and progress as they continued their journey as cricketers.

The Pakistan leg of the twin tours lingers; the warmth of the administrators and fans was exceptional. The customs of their lives varies from ours in many ways. I recall being with the Secretary of the Pakistan Board at the Karachi Stadium discussing the Pakistan tour when the manager of the hotel that the West Indies players were at in preparation for the following day departure to Bangladesh contacted me and suggested that I return to the hotel as quickly as I could, as there was a problem that needed my immediate attention.

When I got back to the hotel, I was taken aback by the manager's disclosure that there were Pakistan Airline trainees (all women) occupying the same floor as the West Indies players and that they were uncomfortable seeing the players dressed only in shorts and no tops. The Hotel manager, an Englishman, understood the situation of the West Indies players' culture dressed as they were and moving from one player's room to another on the same floor for chit chat. The young ladies were culturally not exposed to seeing the almost nakedness of the opposite sex; the young West Indies cricketers understandable apologized for the uneasiness that they may have caused to the trainees.

The Bangladesh leg was a history-making tour for the young West Indies players. It was the very first tour for a West Indies youth team to the cricket-loving country of Bangladesh. We were met on arrival by administrators of the Bangladesh Board with commendable courtesies and then to our hotel where we were greeted by the hotel staff in the finest Bangladeshi tradition. We learned throughout that leg of the tour the tremendous outpour of love and respect for West Indies cricket. The hospitality was overwhelming. Our young players were like "Rock Stars." They were likened to the great names of past and present West Indies test players.

The presence of our coach, the affable Gus Logie as a former player with the recent past greats of West Indies Cricket, amplified attention of cordiality to our young players. On match days, after disembarking from the bus at the Dhaka National Stadium Ground, the venue of all three matches, the players were greeted with hand clapping and shouts of "West Indies!" The players warmed to the adulation with smiles and the bowing of heads. Our Liaison, like the one we had in Pakistan, was an active club cricketer and a member of the Bangladesh Cricket Board. He was amiable and of tremendous help to coach Logie and I throughout or stay in a country that loves the sport of cricket fervently. As the twin tours progressed, there were instances at team meetings when the affable Gus Logie shared his invaluable experience as a member of the great West Indies team under the leadership of the majestic Clive Lloyd. The cheerfulness in his expression was enthralling to the players as they listened intently with admiration. Logie, who played 52 test and 152 ODI matches during the greatest period of West Indies cricket ,was adored by the West Indies young aspirants. His masterful perception of what it meant representing, not only the regional islands back home, but the esteemed honor to represent collectively the islands of the West Indies cricket nations. Logie's universal knowledge of the game was amazing; the players could not have had a more qualified individual as coach to strengthen the basic fundamentals of their game. It certainly was a wonderful experience for me to have had the opportunity to see him interacting with the youngsters.

The hospitality extended by the management and staff at the Sheraton Hotel where we stayed while in Bangladesh was of the highest quality. They all showed a noticeable passion for the game, a passion that was emblematic of the Bangladesh population. For those employees at the Hotel who planned to attend the matches, we extended complimentary passes that they accepted elatedly.

The matches played under lights in front of 30,000 fans was exhilarating; the type of turnout and playing under lights was a new experience for the young West Indians.

The fans filled the Bangabandhu National Stadium for the three games with remarkable enthusiasm. They cheered every run scored by the local batsmen. It was a scene of spectacular happenings for the home team. We were very dissatisfied at the ages of our opponents, some of whom were players well over the age of nineteen. I addressed the disparity of the age differences to the Bangladesh Cricket Board, not as a protest, but that the contest was favourable to the Bangladesh team. That aside, it was a memorable tour enjoyed by the players and fans alike and indeed satisfactory to the Bangladesh Cricket Board at the packed attendances at the three games.

Scores in the matches starting with the first game against the Bangladesh under 23: West Indies batted first having won the toss scoring 185, Wavell Hinds 44, Shirley Clarke 39, Adrian Murphy 32, and Mahendra Nagamootoo

19. Salim Shahid 2 for 26 Sharfuddoula 2 for 29. Bangladesh Youth Eleven 186 for 4, Jared Omar 79, Salim Shahid 28 not out, Mohammad Rafique 21, bowling for the West Indies, Reon King, Denville McKenzie, Tyrone Greenaway and Mahendra Nagamootoo picked up one wicket each. The game was won by the home team highlighted by the brilliant batting of Javed Omar knock of 79; his stroke play was dazzling. The second game was closely contested with the home team as the winners, again watched by a capacity crowd exceeding 30,000 just like the first game. The West Indies, after winning the toss and elected to bat first scored 196, Mahendra Nagamootoo 36, Vishal Nagamootoo 31 not out, Wavell Hinds 28, Nicholas de Groot 27 and Shirley Clarke 24, Bowling for Bangladesh under 19, Nairmur Rahman took 3 for 18 and Hasibul Hossain 2 for 46. Bangladesh replied with 198 for 8 wickets, Mohammad Mostadir 45, All Sahariar 40 and Nairmur Rahman 29 not out. Bowling for West Indies, Reon King 3 for 40 and Mahendra Nagamootoo 2 for 22.

The third game was gripping with the Bangladesh Cricket Board eleven winning with four balls to spare. Scores West Indies again batted first after winning the toss and finished with a score of 181 for 9 wickets, Adrian Murphy 51, Nicholas de Groot 43, and Shirley Clarke 24. Bowling for Bangladesh Naimur Rahman 4 for 26, Salim Shahid 3 for 25. Bangladesh in reply 182 for 6 wickets, Khaled Mashud scoring 42 and Naimur Rahman 32, bowling for the West Indies, Reon King, Tyrone Greenaway, Mahendra Nagamootoo, Raymond Casimir, O'Neil Richards and Gareth Breese each picked up a wicket.

Figure 113 Joyous moment after WI Youth Team defeated Pakistan at Railway Stadium - Lahore, Pakistan 1995

Figure 114 O'Neil Richards receiving Man of the Match Award on West Indies Youth Team Tour of Pakistan 1995

Figure 115 Wavell Hinds

The Inaugural Year of the Regional Under Fifteen Tournaments

Returning from the twin tours of Pakistan and Bangladesh and arriving back home in Jamaica on November 22, 1995, I was given a briefing on the progress of the under-fifteen preparation by Brian Breese, secretary of the youth selection committee, and was later updated with the performances of the players by coaches Rohan Kanhai, Junior Bennett, and Dennis Miller. After a squad of fourteen was selected with Tamar Lambert as captain, I presented the list of the players selected to Roy Paul secretary of the JCA, which was the standard practice. The squad was Tamar Lambert, Barrington Bartley, Mel Wint, Kamal Dennis, Roveen Woolcock, Abraham Huges, Kerneil Irving, Rashard Marshall, Andre Dwyer, David Bernard Jr., Marlon Samuels, Andrew Richardson, Kamar Duncan; the Manager was Horton Dolphin with Dennis Miller as Coach.

So much work was done during the inaugural year of the competition, recognizing the over fifty players named initially and the process of reducing the number for the trials, and ultimately the squad selection was a challenging task. Before the initial year of the competition, the major assignment for the youth selection committee was the process of naming the under-nineteens for the regional tournaments and periodically for matches against visiting under-nineteen international teams. The players were selected from the Headley Cup, Sunlight Cup, and the Kingston Wharves competitions. Very little attention was placed on the schools under-fifteen competitions.

The support of school coaches was invaluable in the early process of identifying the large number of under-fifteen players from which the selectors were able to have had a representative group of twenty-four for the final trial matches. The trials was the first for the young players; they prepared and endured the intense training programme with gusto. Before the commencement of the final trial match, I addressed the players to perform at level that would have had an impact for their selection to the squad. Congratulations were in order for the selected group. As individuals, they performed encouragingly; that rewarded their selection. For the ones left out , I expressed encouragement for their effort and reminded them that from their failures would come success in later years as they developed.

At the tournament, the team performance was brilliant in winning four of the five matches played and they became champions of the inaugural year of the competition. The team was superbly led by Tamar Lambert who was the first player to have been notified about selection to the early group training at Sabina Park. He was lauded with praises for his leadership acumen by team manager Horton Dolphin. Dolphin apprised me of the individual performances of the players and the ones who contributed significantly to our championship honours.

"Tamar Lambert, the captain, was an amazing leader. No surprise that he continued in this vein up to the first-class level," said the champion team manager Horton Dolphin. "Marlon Samuels performed outstandingly throughout the competition and so was Ryan Hinds of Barbados. Rashard Marshall and Kamal Dennis were also top performers," said manager Dolphin. Continuing his views on the competition and the players, Dolphin highlighted Marlon Samuels as the first player from the inaugural tournament to have been selected to the West Indies senior team, to be followed by Ryan Hinds, Devon Smith and David Bernard Jr. I must mention that as chairman of the selection committee, Dolphin was not my first choice for the job as manager; Renford Pinnock the former Jamaica Player was.

There was no doubt about Dolphin's managerial ability. He was manager and coach of Munro College Headley Cup team for several years and was a first-class cricketer who understood the game strategically. His leadership qualities contributed significantly to having the youngsters focused on teamwork and factors germane to the game that led to Jamaica as first holders of the prestigious trophy. Horton Dolphin, in later years, became a perpetual manager of the Combined Colleges team in the West Indies regional first-class tournament. Commendation must also be extended to Dennis Miller, the coach who in tandem with manager Horton Dolphin motivated the youngsters on the monumental achievement as champions.

Figure 116 Jamaica Caribbean Cement Regional U-15 Champions 1996 Standing L-R: Barrington Bartley Jr., Mel Wint, Kamal Dennis, Roveen Woolcock, Azard Ali, (Liaison Offer), Abraham Hughes, Keneil Irving, Rashard Marshall, Andre Dwyer. Sitting L-R: David Bernard Jr.

Figure 117 Tamar Lambert driving through the covers

The Joy And Disappointment of the 1990S

The Jamaica National Senior Team, having won the 1988 and 1989 regional championship titles, began the defense of their title in 1990 impressively with an outright victory in the first game and first innings points in the second; however, the inclement weather was disastrous to the team's chances of a three-peat as the next two matches were abandoned without a ball being bowled and that ended the nations overly anticipated championship expectations. Notwithstanding the results, the impressive showing of the team during the first two games in defense of their title was gratifying to the Jamaican supporters.

At the under-nineteen level like previous years, the 1990 squad was very confident that it would be the year for championship honours. It was never loose talk by the players; they delivered by winning the title impressively. In previous years with strong teams, we were denied winning the title when well positioned to do so. The disappointment of previous youth teams year after year, the heartbreak and tears of the players not having a hold on the coveted title was disheartening; the 1990 season was a turnaround from championship failures to success.

During the early part of the training programme leading into the commencement of the trials, I watched a match between Headley Cup champion school team St. Elizabeth Technical High and Holmwood Technical High at the spacious and beautifully surroundings of the St. Elizabeth team home ground in Santa Cruz. Only one over was bowled before torrential rain ended the game for the day. In that over, there were two impressive revelations to me; the over was bowled by Franklyn Rose at extreme pace and the competence and surety of glove work by wicketkeeper Orville Pennant, and the two were not among the list of players invited to the trials. I was convinced by what I saw of the two that they were good enough to be at the trials.

At the ground, were two of the most dedicated mentors of schoolboy cricket in the island: Dr. Donavan Bennett manager of the St. Elizabeth team and Robert Lewis manager and coach of the Holmwood team; their candor was exceptional. I let them know how impressed I was by the two youngsters and that they were now added to the group in training. Lewis was overjoyed by my disclosure, knowing that two of his charges would be in the trials and there was the possibility both could be included in the touring party. Schoolboy players making it to the national trials was a booster to the school coaches and more so, when they make it to the national team, it gives recognition and elevated their ratings.

After getting back to Kingston that night, I communicated to Foster and Watson, two of my fellow selectors, the quality of Rose and Pennant and that they looked a sure bet for selection to the squad. I further suggested with the high number of fast bowlers in the training group the weakest of the lot could make way for the impressive Rose. The group in training at the Seprod cricket ground was being supervised by Michael Holding, the other member of the quartet of youth selectors. I got the consent from both Foster and Watson that Holding make the decision on which of the quickies to be left out; unfortunately, Porteous from Mannings High, the quickest of the speedsters was left out. Holding contended that much work needed to be done with Porteous' inconsistent control and should be the one omitted for Rose's inclusion.

During the last of the trial matches, Clifton Folkes was not among the top wicket takers and he was concerned about his selection to the squad. I reassured him that he bowled impressively and that the way he troubled the batsmen in the trials was an indication that he would perform successfully in the tournament. I further told him that the experience of playing the previous year's tournament was in his favour. His brilliant bowling was significant to Jamaica winning the 1990 tournament and for his achievement, he was named the most valuable player of the tournament.

As manager, the 1990 youth success was the first of three championship achievements during the first half of the nineteen nineties before I was replaced by Derron Dixon in 1996. The 1996 season was the last of my fourteen years as chairman of the youth selection committee and twelve years as a senior selector before my departure to the USA in 1996.

At the club level, the Saints celebrated championship honours in 1993 and

1995; the achievement was felt by fans of the capital parish Spanish Town and its environs. The celebration was shared by former players and ardent fans at different locations outside of Jamaica. I was manager of the Championship 1993 team and experienced the joy of the players and the exuberance of the many across the sphere of St Catherine and neighbouring parishes. I was actively engaged with the club as a VP and was unavailable to have been the team manager because of national and international cricket duties away from Jamaica periodically. I was, however, as a club member wrapped in the glory of the players' accomplishment.

The 1993 team at the beginning of the season was a team of young hopefuls and seasoned campaigners led by a young captain Milton Thomas. Having the experienced Renford Pinnock as a selector with me as the chairman and team manager, a lot of work needed to be done for a good season and much more to become champions. As two veterans of past outstanding Saint Catherine Club teams, Pinnock and I were able to give the type of support needed by the captain who skillfully guided his young squad successfully on their journey throughout the season. It was a season that the captain thrived as a leader and got good support from his most experienced players Randy Nelson, Ephraim McLeod, Ransford Evans, Tony Powell, Melbourne Austin, and Courtney Francis.

Captain Milton Thomas featured prominently with the bat that set the tone for respectable team totals. There were other top performers with the bat, including the dynamic left-handed Tony Powell the former Jamaica youth and senior Jamaica national representative. Tony went on to represent the West Indies A team on tour of Sri Lanka; Randy Nelson, the tall, lean an elegant stroke player and a former Jamaica national youth player; Courtney Francis a sound reliable top order batsman and a former Jamaica youth player; and Ransford Evans the opener who also was one of the opening bowlers. The bowling was impressive with the very experienced leg spinner Ephraim McLeod bowling effectively with rewarding success. The talented fast bowler Clifton Folkes, who was an outstanding player on Jamaica's regional youth cup winning team in 1990 and was named man of that tournament having taken 32 wickets, went on to represent Jamaica's national senior team before migrating to England at an early age. His penetrative bowling was pivotal to the Saints championship achievement. Melbourne Austin the medium pacer and very useful with the bat and an outstanding fielder contributed significantly. Austin later migrated to England where he was very active in the weekend cricket leagues. The less experienced players, Delroy Barron, an off spinner, had the attributes to have become a bowling all-rounder of known quality. Steve Nelson was quick with a very good bouncer that lifted awkwardly and was of concern to most batsmen. He was one who with proper guidance could have become a national senior player. Colin Buchanan, leg spinning all-rounder, Dwight Williams, a medium pacer and very good outfielder, and Lloyd Rattray a medium pacer who could bat, showed promise of becoming a more than useful all-rounder. The valued quality of Thomas's leadership was an attribute that served the team magnificently in their successful run for championship honours. It was celebration time for the wonderful players, players who brought to the confines of their domain prolonged joyfulness; no wonder the euphoria.

The club was again senior cup winners in 1995 under the captaincy of Ransford Evans. Evans' leadership was inspirational and was a motivating component of the team success. The players responded admirably with match-winning performances that allowed them deservingly to cuddle the coveted senior cup. Having won the cup in 1993, the club failed in its pursuit to defend the title in 1994, but the 1995 squad led by Ransford Evans, who was most resolute in his leadership acumen, led the team expertly in recapturing the cup. As captain, Evans masterminded the batting and bowling efforts with remarkable success leading from the front as one of the opening bowlers and also as one of the opening batsmen. In his earlier years as a senior cup batting allrounder, he showed signs of developing to be a contender for national senior selection.

As in 1993, the cup winning achievement of 1995 returned joyous feelings of celebration to the capital Spanish Town and the neighbouring communities and beyond. The successes of Saint Catherine Cricket Club, Jamaica's under-19, and the West Indies under-nineteens in the Caribbean and the twin tours of Pakistan and Bangladesh to that point was a satisfactory period of my contribution to the different levels of the game in the 1990s. I was now looking forward to be returned as the 1996 Jamaica under-nineteen manager for the regional tournament and as the West Indies youth manager for the Pakistan youth team visit to the Caribbean before my impending departure as a resident of the USA later that year.

The standard of Jamaica's cricket from 1990 to 1996 was an encouraging period, specifically at the age group level. The under-nineteens were regional champions in 1990, 1994, and 1995, and the under-fifteens were champions in the inaugural year of the competition in 1996. Before the championship achievements of the under-fifteens during the Easter month of 1996, Jamaica hosted the first test match between the West Indies and India March 6th to March 10th. On one of the match days while watching the run of play from the JCA Board Room, President Rex Fennell hand motioned me to join him by the entrance door. We then walked along the hallway.

"Len, I am apologizing for not letting you know that I did not follow through with the arrangement I agreed to regarding your payment by the Jamaica Cricket Association for the tours of Pakistan and Bangladesh. Please, look at this fax message," said Fennell.

It was a message from Cricket West Indies stating that I was paid by their organization for the Pakistan and Bangladesh tours when I was already paid by the Jamaica Cricket Association. I was stunned and asked Fennell why he allowed me to have believed he honoured the arrangement.

"You should have contacted me of your inability to follow through with the agreed arrangement before I left for Trinidad or while been there in Trinidad or the early weeks of the Pakistan tour."

I could see the sadness in Fennell's eyes with tears flowing down his cheek with uncontrolled emotion.

"Rex, I am hurt more than you are. It will be an embarrassment to me. I am truly hurt. This is a brutal situation for me. I will have to explain as it happened."

Fennell asked that since I would be leaving to settle in the USA, I should say it was a misunderstanding when I accepted payment from Cricket West Indies. I responded, "Rex, I will have to address your role in the sordid issue to exonerate me from guilt of knowingly accepted the double payment. If I were to accede to your request, it would make me guilty of the double payment." He again explained that he was still experiencing a cash flow in the business with his son Herman and that he would make every effort to pay me back. I found myself considering the options I had. Should I explain to the Jamaica Cricket Association and Cricket West Indies exactly what happened at the different stages or to protect Fennell as he wanted me to?

I pondered on the choice for a week, days of discussions with Fennell who kept apologizing with remorse for the ineptness that caused embarrassment to me. It was a period that left me in doubt of people's perceived intentions. How could someone of Fennell's standing be so irrational? I also tried to rationalize why it took so long a time for Jamaica Cricket Association treasurer to have notified Cricket West Indies of the payment to me; surely, if this were done months earlier, Sealy would not have contacted me on the issue of my contractual arrangement while I was in Pakistan. I eventually agreed to Fennell's request that I knew would be questionable and perceived as irresponsible on my part and damaging without a satisfactory explanation.

In the end, I paid back to the JCA the full amount that was given to me with minimal help from Fennell. It was surprising to me and other members of the Jamaica Cricket Association at the Biannual meeting of that year when Verley Harrison commented disparagingly the circumstances of the transaction; the fact that the money was paid back, there was no need for the subject to have been enunciated at the meeting. It was Mr. Vincent Wong President of Kensington Cricket Club who asked, "Was the money paid back?"

"Yes," answered Fennell.

"Well, that should be the end of the issue," said Mr. Wong.

"Agreed. Let's move on, gentlemen," replied President Fennell.

After the meeting, Dudley Bryan in a one-on-one conversation with Fennell asked why would Chambers knowingly accept double payments that would later be held against him and was told by Fennell it was a misunderstanding. At that point in time, I never revealed to anyone that Fennell was fundamentally complicated in the reprehensible transaction that was so harmful to me. I protected him as President of the Jamaica Cricket Association and as a Director of Cricket West Indies. He was a friend who I met from my teenage years, a friend I held in high esteem throughout the years. I stayed loyal to Fennell knowing that I would be leaving for the USA months after.

It was a couple years after Fennell's retirement from the JCA and CWI that I mentioned the facts to a couple of close friends including Basil Williams, Lawrence Rowe, Sydney Bennett, Samuel McFarlane and much later Ronnie

Burnett, all of whom were at that point in time residents of the USA just as I was.

Fennell, on a visit to one of his daughters living in Maryland, returned to me a nominal part of the amount I had given to him. It was Ronnie Burnett, a longtime friend of Fennell, who invited me for the drive to Maryland minutes before I finished a midnight to 8:AM work schedule from my job at the Mount Sinai Hospital on Maddison Avenue in Manhattan. Earl Daley, the former Saint Catherine and Melbourne Cricket Club player and USA cricketer was with us on that Saturday morning drive.

Last Assignment as Manager and Selector

My last assignment as chairman of the youth selection committee was for the 1996 under-nineteen regional tournament held in Jamaica from July 27th to just after mid-August. A squad of fourteen was named with Wavell Hinds as captain, the other players were Xavier Gilbert, Dwayne Cooper, Ryan Cunningham, Keith Wilby, Wade Allen, Ricardo Powell, Llewelyn Meggs, Orlando Baker, Carl Wright, Christopher Gayle, Paul Tomlinson, Leon Garrick, and Julian Royal. The 1996 tournament was the first time since 1983 that I was not the manager of our national under-19 team. I made myself unavailable for consideration after the payment debacle, but continued as chairman of the selection committee. As chairman, I was happy to see my nominee Deron Dixon confirmed by the Jamaica Cricket Association to be my replacement as manager and Junior Bennett returning as coach.

The matches were played at different parish venues in Kingston, Saint Catherine, and Manchester with large crowd attendances, especially at the rural venues. The Jamaica team was endowed with enormous talent and led by a very shrewd captain in Wavell Hinds. The team with so many debutants performed marvelously but missed out on retaining championship honours by being the runners-up to the eventual winners Barbados. Leon Garrick batting was exceptional with two magnificent hundreds; the first 152 at Sabina Park against Guyana was a dazzling display of breathtaking stroke play and the second was his master class 174 against Barbados at Chedwin Park. Leon Garrick was exceptional among the tournament batsmen. His batting skills showed a wide range from backward point to long leg; his repertoire was amazing. Captain Wavell Hinds was in awe of his remarkable batting skills. Chris Gayle and Orlando Baker were the other Jamaican batsman among the runs in this their first year at the youth level. Batsmen Leon Garrick, Wavell Hinds, Chris Gayle, Orlando Baker, and the bowlers. Left arm spinner Ryan

Cunningham and fast bowler Paul Tomlinson bowled impressively. Tomlinson was very effective. He bowled a good line and length at pace with consistent accuracy. His performances were noted by the selectors and along with Leon Garrick, Wavell Hinds, and Christopher Gayle, he was selected to the West Indies under-nineteen squad against the touring Pakistan under-nineteens early during the month of September 1996.

The Pakistan opening game of the tour was against their Jamaican counterparts at Sabina Park August 30-September 1, 1996. The selection of the Jamaica team was my last assignment as a national youth selector before I migrated to the USA. The Jamaica team was Wavell Hinds as captain, Leon Garrick, Chris Gayle, Marlon Samuels, Keith Wilby, Keith Hibbert, Orlando Baker, Julian Royal, Paul Tomlinson, Ryan Cunningham, and Dwight Mais.

The match ended in a draw; scores Pakistan 357 for 8 declared Kasif Ibraim 113. Ahmer 106, Paul Thompson 3 for 50, Wilby, Royal and Samuels had a wicket apiece, Jamaica 186, Marlon Samuels 89, Leon Garrick 58,, Fahad Khan 5 for 65, Tafeek Badaruddin 2 for 39, Pakistan 208 for 5 declared, Shahid Quambrani 52, Mohammad Saleem 40, Keith Wilby 3 for 27, Jamaica 170 for 6, Samuels 42, Gayle 42, Garrick 28., Baker 28, Taufeeq Badaruddin 2 for 31, Fahad Khan 2 for 56.

Marlon Samuels, who earlier missed the preparation process leading to selection of Jamaica's squad for the 1996 regional under-nineteen tournament because of school assignment, was named for the first time to the national youth team.

Marlon demonstrated in the Pakistan game his wide range of attractive stroke play seldom seen at his age group; the fans and teammates were left in admiration of the fifteen-year-old's marvelous skills. Marlon Samuels, having done so well against Pakistan with scores of 89 and 42, never had a realistic chance for selection to the West Indies youth team of that year; the squad was already selected earlier on the performances of the players during the regional under-nineteen tournament that Marlon missed.

Figure 118 Chris Gayle

Figure 119 Marlon Samuels

Services to the Game

As I continued my multiple responsibilities at the Saint Catherine Cricket Club and that of the Jamaica Cricket Association, I continued with fervor to do my very best for an outcome of success. The responsibility with Saint Catherine as a VP, club captain, manager, and chairman of the club selection committee was a priority of conscious involvement for me. At the club level, Saint Catherine was like most senior cup clubs and Parish Associations had their challenges and were able to overcome adversities by the quality of leadership in their ranks; so, it was with the Jamaica Cricket Association as a national body.

In the earlier years, senior cup clubs like Kingston, Kensington, Lucas, Saint Georges Old Boys, and Melbourne were well financed by an affluent club membership; the members supported their financial coffers with mandatory dues payment and fraternizing at the club bar. Additionally, their membership included influential members with connections to corporate Jamaica. St. Georges Old Boys was an exception without the asset of a bar, but amongst their membership was a strong alliance of entrepreneurs. The other senior cup participants, Jamaica Defense Force and Police were recipients of Grants from within their institutions. Jamaica Public Service and the All Bauxites were adequately financed by their respective companies. Boys Town, with the influential Father Sherlock and other Directors of the famous institution along with the senior membership was able to sustained viability. Saint Catherine Cricket Club was, up to the late sixties, exclusively buoyed by Bernard Sugar Estate while their home ground was at the Lime Tree Oval before moving to Chedwin Park and continued by a vibrant club membership.

The success of the clubs, Parishes, and cricket-affiliated institutions was served by dedicated administrators, administrators whose contribution to the sport of this wonderful game should be enshrined in the chronicles of Jamaica's cricket. The names are of individuals related to my time as a player to that of an administrator with the Jamaica Cricket Association from age 31 to 54 ending in 1996 when I took up residence in the USA.

At the senior cup clubs, the names of the amazing group mentioned should long be remembered: Donald Lacy, Allan Rae, Bobby Nunez, Errol Zadie Alva Anderson of Kingston Cricket Club, Laker Levers, Ruddy Marzouca, Monica Williams Hoshue, Ruddy Williams, Keith Reese, Tony Becca, George Sterling, Michael HoShue of Melbourne Cricket Club, Arthur McLean, George Prescod, Errol Mudie, George Watson aka Soro, Roy Paul, Brian Breese, Percy Lindo, Easton McMorris, E B King, Mickey Matthews, Keith Wedderburn of Lucas Cricket Club, Noel Silvera, JK Holt Jr. Vincent Wong, Chester Watson, Oscar Hamilton, Dave Cameron, Maurice Chong, Alf Grant, Eddie Bailey, Silburn Mitchel of Kensington Cricket Club, Frankie Lewis, Vinnie Binns, Alan Alberga, , Ronnie Nasralla, Louis Teape, Arthur McKenzie Snr. of St. Georges Old Boys, Father Hugh Sherlock. Cannon R. O.C King, Carl Goodison, Gladstone Robinson, Locksley Comrie, Leonard Levy, Victor Hunter, John Maxwel, Linden Wright, Conrad Ball of Boys Town, Cliff Lashley, Roy McNaughton, Dave Roberts, Sydney Bennett, Hopeton Robertson, Renford Pinnock, Louis Goldson, Ariel Dwyer, Sydney Gapour, Adolph Bacchus, and Winston Rhoden of Saint Catherine Cricket Club.

The Sugar Estates that operated in the Parishes were a reliable source of support to the viability of most Parish Associations. Additionally, the Clubs and Parishes had in their ranks, members blessed with unmatched passion for the game; they were instrumental in soliciting the necessary assistance to run their cricket programmes and worked assiduously for the procurement of school scholarships and employment of young aspiring cricketers. The years from the ending of the 1950s to the mid-1990s were glorious years in cricket administration for the parishes with the likes of Aston Spence, Noel McLean, Danny Keddo from Westmoreland, Dennis Dewar, Orrette Symister from Hanover, Owen Davis, Paul Williams, Dr. David Crawford, Vincent Dixon, Errol Lynch, Keith Leslie aka Piggy from St. Mary, Dr. Lenworth Jacobs, Howard Bembridge, Leslie Talboet, Dennis Latchman, Bobby Marsh of St Ann, Neville Hammond, Mark Campbell from Trelawney, Howard Cooke Snr., Osmond Erskine, Donath Creighton, Cecil Fletcher, Owen Brown, Jerry Reid of Saint James, Dr. Donovan Bennett, Keith Brown, Basil Walker, Horton Dolphin, Clovis McKnight. Junior Bennett of St. Elizabeth, Patrick Anderson, Vinnie Isaacs, Novelyn Ricketts from Manchester, Rex Fennell, Dr.

John Tate, Charlie Lewin, Winston Casanova, Winston Brown, Egbert Williams, Fritz Harris, Fearon Pitterson from Clarendon, Hugh Perry of Portland, Bill Bennet and Phillbert Trenchfield of St, Thomas, Inspector Manley Butler, Ralph Ramdath, Leroy Beckford, Milhando Barker of St. Catherine Parish.

From the city clubs to the Parishes, individuals aforementioned were true champions, blessed with the inherent love for the game matched by administrative richness prevailed and sustained the viability of their respective organizations throughout the years. My apologies for the oversight of others who would have contributed worthily to their respective clubs and parish organizations .The support during the period 1983 to 1996 of school principals and coaches to the Jamaica Cricket Association youth programmes was immeasurable and so were the businesses of Wherry Wharf/Kingston Wharves for the under-nineteen cross country competition; Roy Holness General Manager of Sherwin Williams for under nineteen team blazers; Copeland Samuels Managing Director of Economic Maintenance Products for team track suits; Franz Botec General Manager of Cigarette Company of Jamaica for under-nineteen team transportation; Jamaica Broilers for trial matches; Wayne and Andrew Chin of Super Plus Super Markets for scholarship to University of Technology and sponsorship of under-nineteen trial matches outside of Up Park Camp; Errol Cann of Candon Enterprize for under-nineteen practice matches; Louis Williams Managing Director of Matrix Engineering for scholarships to the University of Technology; Victoria Mutual Building Society for its yearly three-month development programme of two young players to England. The programme lasted for several years. Candon Enterprises Limited of Spanish Town for its sponsorship of under nineteen trial and practice matches, Hand Arnold Jamaica Ltd. for under-nineteen and trial matches; Wray & Nephew Group of Companies to the Clarendon Cricket Association for its youth programmes and score board ;and the Seprod Group of Companies for its funding of the 1990 special one-week training of trial invitees conducted by the world-famous Michael Holding at the Seprod cricket ground.

All the sponsorships but for VMBS, Wherry Wharf, Kingston Wharves, Seprod, and Jamaica Broilers were attained by me personally. An important component of Jamaica's cricket was the Kingston-based Sunday competitions dating back to the early fifties to the mid-nineties. Competitions like

Masterton, Hamilton, Rankine, Carib, Henriques, and Roy Lowe were competitions founded mostly by the ingenuity of individuals such as Messrs. Masterton, Hamilton, Rankine, Roy Lowe, and the Henriques. The Carib Competition was spearheaded by a body from the commercial sector in Kingston and extended to two Spanish Town-based clubs Saint Jago Youths and Crystal Sports. The competitions were extremely competitive with a galaxy of well-known internationals, nationals, senior and junior cup players along with several schoolboy players. The well-organized competitions helped significantly the popularity of the sport at the community level and also at the lower echelon of the more established clubs. The competitiveness of the matches with the participation of highly recognized players was very helpful to the younger players in the process of their development. The founders of the many Sunday competitions were lauded for their creativeness in widening the participation opportunity for cricketers, many of whom were offered job opportunities and other incentives. A number of the teams were community-based with endearing spectator support; the matches in most cases were electrifying. The Jamaica Cricket Association recognized the importance of the competitions, competitions that expanded the growth of the sport for many, including a surfeit of young cricketers.

As for myself, I am ever grateful to my youth club leaders from the institutions of the Spanish Town Boys Club and The St. Jago/ St. Johns Youth Clubs, and the YMCA for the early starts where discipline of team sports and leadership was imbedded in me. Also, to Saint Catherine Cricket Club for the support given to me during the early years as a senior cup cricketer; Captain Mickey Murdock, Renford Pinnock and Herbert Bailey were exceptionally helpful in those early years. At the senior cup level with Mickey Murdock as captain, it was the beginning of a glorious period for the Saints with an almost unchangeable team of talented players led by an astute captain that defined our high standard and effectiveness in winning matches. My second phase with the Saints was more challenging. Having returned as captain with a very experienced group of players to be led, their thought processes was never the same. I was, however, supported respectfully in my leadership decisions.

As I reflect on my life separate and apart from the game, I am ever so grateful to the ones who were very helpful to me in job opportunities that sustained my livelihood before my migration to the USA. Sincere thanks to Roy

Deleon, my teammate at the Saint Catherine Cricket Club, for my employment with the United Fruit Company Shipping Department; to Allan Rae for procuring my job with the Port Authority of Jamaica; to Ludlow Stewart, Managing Director of RS Gamble Shipping Company; and to Tony Burrowes, Sales manager of Wray & Nephew Group of Companies.

My services to the sport of cricket was recognized by the established organizations of Insports of Jamaica, Carreras Foundation, the Spanish Town communities of New York and New Jersey, Parish Associations, Schools, Primrose Cricket Club of New York, Induction to the USA Cricket Hall of Fame in the International Category for my contribution to cricket in Jamaica and the West Indies; the ceremony was held in 2018 at the Hilton Hotel next to the Kennedy Airport in New York. Appreciation to my son Rohan for trips to the 2019 ODI World Cup in England, South Africa for the T20 series in March of 2023 and to Florida for the T20 matches vs India during August 2023.

Figure 120 Leonard Chambers with world famous umpire Steve Bucknor at Lords 2001

Figure 121 Leonard Chambers & Happy Sutherland, Former St. Catherine Football Association President, JFF President & CONCACAF Hall of Famer. Recognized for their contribution to football and cricket in Jamaica by the sporting community of Jamaicans at a ceremony in Queens New York, 2009.

Figure 122 Members of USA Cricket Hall of Fame Inductees – 2018. **L-R:** Richard Staple, Leonard R. Chambers, Jimmy Adams

Figure 123 P Brian Chambers (Grandson) presenting the Cricket Hall of Fame Jacket

Figure 124 Roxanne Chambers (daughter) presenting the Cricket Hall of Fame ring.

Figure 125 Shirley Matthews (President USA CHOF) presenting the Cricket Hall of Fame Induction Certificate

Figure 32 Maurice Foster being Inducted to the USA Cricket Hall of Fame (CHOF) receiving his Certificate from Shirley Mathews, President of CHOF. Foster's daughter Michelle looks on.

Figure 127 Maurie Foster's grandson, Zane Willis, with Dave Cameron & Michael Chambers, Cricket Hall of Fame CEO.

Figure 128 Touring England with Rohan – ODI World Cup, Worcestershire- 2019

Figure 129 Len Chambers & Lawrence Rowe, WI v. India, Ft. Lauderdale, August 2023

Figure 130 Rohan, Leonard, and Chris Gayle – World Cup 2019, Durham, England

England, South Africa, and USA

The England visit was a spectacular experience attending matches and visits to eighteen county grounds. At most of the grounds, we visited the main pavilions and subsidiary stands. Our tour guide to the main pavilion of the world-famous cricket grounds Kennington Oval and Lords was breathtaking; the portraits of some of our great West Indian players on display was inspiring. George Headley's name on the honours list of batsmen to have scored a century 106 and 107 in each innings of the same test match at the famous Lords cricket ground was eminent as indicated by Rohan to the multilateral group. "George Headley was the only non-English batsman to have accomplished the unique feat," emphasized Rohan. Headley's feat drew applause from the diverse gathering when it was underscored by Rohan.

Our visit to Edgbaston was for me nostalgic; it was the first test match ground apart from Sabina Park that I had the honour of playing. Having played at the famous ground some fifty-three years before rekindled the wonderful memories I had with the playing members of the Warwickshire County Cricket Club. The imposing changes of the Edgbastan County ground for the players and the increased capacity and comfort for the fans is indeed laudable.

My visit to South Africa along with my son Rohan in late March of 2023 was for me an historic time filled with unforgettable memories of events on the playing fields, and landmarks of significant settings in the communities of the province of Gauteng, South Africa.

The visit to South Africa with my son Rohan in support of the West Indies cricket team during the three match T20 series in March of 2023 was enthralling, notwithstanding moments of apprehension by turbulence during the fourteen-hour nonstop flight from Newark Airport, New Jersey to O. R. Tambo International Airport in Johannesburg and the return flight of sixteen hours nonstop by a different route. On our journey from the airport in Johannesburg to the Sandon Hotel with Rohan as the driver of the rented car, we drove through the evening hours of long lines of slow-moving vehicles; the slowness was attributed to truncated distribution of electricity at traffic lights in the capital city, Johannesburg.

When we got to the hotel, we were pleasantly surprised to see the top management of the West Indies team, manager Rawl Lewis and coaches Jimmy Adams and Andre Coley sitting in the lobby apparently discussing the T20 matches to come. After going through the formalities as guests of the hotel, the three top management personnel signaled for us to join them with hugs of appreciation and to be there in support of the West Indies team. Jimmy Adams smilingly queried, "Manage, you made it. Are you okay after the long flight?" "Yeah, Jimmy. It was a long flight and I am okay."

We spent a good time exchanging pleasantries before we departed to our respective rooms with high hopes of the West Indies doing well in the series. After watching the players at net sessions, we attended the first game at Super Plus Park, a game that the West Indies won, the second at the same venue won by the very strong South African team and the final game by the West Indies at the Wanderers Stadium. The first match was reduced to 11 overs apiece because of intermittent rain showers; scores South Africa 131 for 8 wickets, West Indies 132 for 7 wickets in 10.3 overs. It was a very exciting finish in the runs chase, led by a brilliant undefeated 42 from captain Rovman Powell, Johnson Charles 28 and Brandon King 23.

In the second game, the West Indies recorded their highest T20 score of 258 for 5 wickets and lost, with the South Africa team attacking our bowling with disdain. At the end of the second over, their total was 42 without loss and they got to 100 in 5.3 overs. Their batsmen relished the going on a pitch that favoured the batsmen. There was no encouragement for the bowlers; it was a batting paradise that produced 517 runs for the loss of only 9 wickets in 38.3 overs with two century makers, two other batsmen with 50's and other useful individual scores. The South Africans won the game with seven balls to spare, replying with 259 for 4 wickets. The West Indies opener Johnson Charles scored a magnificent 118 from 48 balls in the West Indies total of 256 for 5. Charles was at his very best with well-executed boundary shots and smashing sixes well beyond the boundary that entertained the large crowd.

Kyle Mayers batted in entertaining fashion with an attractive well-compiled knock of 51 from 27 balls. The South Africans replied strongly, led by the champion batsman Quin De Kock. He scored briskly during the early stages of his innings and maintained a tempo that our bowlers were unable to have restricted. His brilliant 100 from 43 balls and an open partnership of 152 with Reeza Hendricks who played delightfully for 68 and Captain Aiden Markram with an undefeated 38 surpassed the record-breaking total of 258 for 5 by the West Indies.

The high-scoring match was wonderful entertainment for the fans. Despite losing, the West Indies team never slackened their intent in pushing the South Africans to surpass our total with seven balls to spare. The third and final game played at the Wanderers Stadium emphasized the depth of the West Indies batting at the T20 level. The team looked unlikely to have reached 200, but with self-assuredness, Shepherd and Joseph shared a matching winning ninth wicket partnership of 50 from 24 balls. The two came together at a time when we were backpedaling and looked destined to be short of a par total. The two assessment of the team position was expertly handled with conventional stroke play that allowed the West Indies total to end at 220 for 8 wickets; there were very good contributions by Nicholas Pooran 41 from 19 deliveries and Brandon King 36 from 25. In reply, the home team ended with 213, giving the West Indies victory in the series by 2 games to 1. Our team played marvelously and was acknowledged, not only by the sparse presence of West Indian supporters, but also by majority of the home fans.

The small group of West Indian presence included WIPA secretary Wayne Lewis and his wife Alicia Cargill Lewis, Jamaica Cricket Association director Radcliffe Daley, Raymond Donalson, Wilfred Bassaragh, Grace Bassaragh, my son Rohan Chambers, and I. We enthusiastically expressed overwhelming support to our West Indies team at the three matches. We cheered every run, byes leg byes, wides and runs from the bat of our batsmen. The success of the team was distinguished by their brilliance in the field; the excellent fielding was an inspiration to the bowling unit but for the second game that we lost. The totals we amassed in the three games were very encouraging to the batting potential of our team, a team that was well-prepared and managed by a very good cricket manager Rawl Lewis, coaches Andre Coley, Jimmy Adams, Kenny Benjamin, and the inclusion of Samuel Badree for the

T20 did an excellent job with the successes of our team in the white ball formats.

Having shared the same hotel as the West Indies team, my son Rohan and I were privileged to have interacted regularly with the players, coaches, manager, and supporting staff. I was extremely impressed with the deportment of the group; their civility as representatives of the Caribbean nation was amazing. It was a wonderful experience talking with them one-on-one at different times while at the hotel. They were a well-composed group with the passion to perform successfully for the West Indies. The courteousness of the touring group left Rohan and I with the feeling of recognition and appreciation expressed that we were there as West Indians to support the team. Being a first-class cricketer, manager, and selector at the regional and West youth level was to my benefit, and to have been manager of the West Indies team and the manager of the Jamaica youth teams when Coley and Jimmy Adams played and of the West Indies youth team with Coley and Rawl Lewis as members of the team added value to the recognition given to me.

Rohan played against Rawl Lewis at the regional youth level and as Jamaica's youth captain when Coley first represented the national youth team in1992. Rohan was also a member with Jimmy Adams at the Kingston Cricket Club.

From my experience as a former manager of local teams, Jamaica's youth at the regional tournaments and against Australia and South Africa under-nineteens at home, Jamaica senior teams regionally, West Indies Shell Awards team against New Zealand, West Indies youth teams against young England in the Caribbean and against Pakistan and Bangladesh in the subcontinent, I am aware of the importance of managers and coaches reaching out to the players away from the game. The understanding of a player's journey to where he is at allows for circumspection; the mindfulness allows confidence in an environment of team unity and acceptance to belong. I was of the opinion that this was in evidence with our West Indies team during the T20 format of the South Africa tour of 2023.

Having managed Rawl Lewis at the West Indies youth level and having knowledge of my years as a cricket manager, we talked about player management; his perception of the responsibility as a manager was superbly articulated. He emphasized the importance of a cohesive unit for success.

During our conversation, I listened intently to his vision of seeing the West Indies team the equal of the top teams at the different formats of world cricket. I was impressed with the young manager Rawl Lewis from Grenada who I first saw in Jamaica representing the Windward Islands at the 1991 regional under-19 competition and continued at that level to 1994 and in early 1995 when he represented the West Indies youth team in six matches against young England at five different regional grounds.

As the manager of that West Indies under-nineteen team, my impression of Rawl Lewis the cricketer was that as a young player he showed the potential of becoming a very good leader; his contribution at our team meetings was immeasurable. My critique of him then has been vindicated in his role as West Indies manager at the senior level. He is highly respected by the players, coaches, and supporting staff, an affable individual that is knowledgeable and well prepared as a cricket manager. Rawl Lewis the former West Indies cricketer and now manager, potentially should be a candidate for the leadership of Cricket West Indies if and when he is no longer the West Indies cricket manager. Coach Andre Coley was very inspiring in his methods of coaching and vision for West Indies cricket as articulated in the conversations we had away from the game such as when we had lunch at a restaurant away from the Sandton Towers in Sandton city.

From my perspective, it was surprising when Cricket West Indies replaced Coley the successful interim white ball coach with Daren Sammy as head coach of the ODI and T20 formats. Coley was appointed head coach of the test team only, notwithstanding his successes as head coach of the white ball formats. I believe it was a travesty of justice to Coley's effectiveness with the team by the least experience coaching quality of Daren Sammy. Before Coley's appointment as the interim head Coach for the West Indies tour of South Africa, the two previous head coaches Otis Gibson and Phil Simmonds were appointed as full-time coaches for the three formats. Coley as an interim head coach against South Africa lost the test match series, drew the ODI's one game each, and won the T20 games two to one. The experience and knowledgeable Andre Coley should have had the honour of being appointed as head coach for the three formats.

While in South Africa, our interest in the sport was extended to visits at several cricket grounds in the province of Gauteng. A number of the venues had a cricket museum and a gym. The exhibits at the museums were uplifting, displaying the history of the game through the years at the club, province and international levels, the changes of cricket bats, boots, batting and wicket keeping gloves, team and individual pictures, the changes of the playing area, improved stands for the seating of spectators and remarkable improvement to the players enclosure and the extension of the pitch squares as compared with earlier years. At the grounds, there were numerous nets located beyond the playing area with several practice wickets, with the number of pitches; batsmen had the luxury of batting for long periods with the bowlers interchanging from net to net.

Prior to the start of the second T20 game played at the Wanderers Stadium, my son Rohan and I went to Willomere Park in the district of Benoni in the Province of Gauteng where there are four grounds that are non-playing test match venues. The main ground staged many ODI's and some of the 2023 Women's U19 World Cup matches, it is a lovely ground that is well suited for first-class matches. There are three outer grounds that are dimensionally adequate for the playing of club matches and possibly first-class games. Although lacking the facility of adequate stands as compared with the main ground, the pitches were satisfactorily grassed and so were the outfields. Places of interest visited included Mandela Square, one of the top shopping centres in South Africa with a mall adjacent to the players' Sandton Hotel. It is huge with attractive looking stores and eye-catching modernized brand names for the young and older generation and several choice restaurants. I dined at one of the restaurants that served mainly African type dishes and was asked by two lady servers if I had any Jamaican money with Bob Marley's profile. They were stunned to know that there was no Jamaican currency portraying the great entertainer who they revered like a national hero and likened him to the great Nelson Mandela. They reminded that two of their paper currency; the ten and one hundred rand portrays the picture of Nelson Mandela.

Fort Lauderdale, Florida USA

My first visit to the spacious Central Broward Regional Park Stadium was to watch the WI engage India in two T20 matches played on successive days Saturday August 12th and 13th 2023. I was again accompanied by my son Rohan. We arrived at the Fort Lauderdale Hollywood International Airport a day before the first game and settled in comfortably at a villa not far from the ground. Early that evening, we made contact with Lawrence Rowe and his son Lawrence Rowe Jr., confirming that we had arrived and that we would see each other at the game the following day as we arranged previously. Rohan and Rowe Jr. have been friends from preteen age while attending Wolmers Boys High School. They had represented the school cricket teams Colts and Sunlight together. Young Rowe was a mystery left arm spinner while Rohan as captain was a batting allrounder. They performed consistently during the years at Wolmers and in the 1987 Chester Watson Cup final against Campion College at Melbourne Oval; they performed brilliantly in their school victory. Scores Wolmers 285 all out Rohan Chambers 107 not out, Campion College 117 all out Larry Creighton 34, Julian Robinson 13, Lawrence Rowe Jr. 7 for 26 off 20.3 overs, Chambers 2 for 29 of 14 overs.

The re-union of the four of us over the two days at the stadium was memorable. We shared with pride the West Indies' convincing win in the second game to give us a 3-2 series victory; the first three games were played in the Caribbean. Scores in the matches at Fort Lauderdale were: first game West Indies 178 for 8 Shimron Hetmyer 61, Shai Hope 45, Arshdeep Singh 3 for 38, Kuldeep Yadav 2 for 26, India 179 for 1, Yashasvi Jaiswal 84 not out, Shubman Gill 77, Romario Shepherd 1 for 35. Second game India 165 for 9 Suryakumar Yadav 61, Tilak Varma 27, Romario Shepherd 4 for 31, Akeal Hosein 2 for 24, Jason Holder 2 for 36, West Indies 171 for 2 Brandon King 5 not out, Nicholas Pooran 47. Varma 1 for 17.

It was fun time for the West Indian fans on the last day convincing win that gave our team a lot to celebrate for their series victory.

Figure 131 Celebrating WI series win against SA. Johannesburg, South Africa 2023. from left to right: Major Radcliffe Daley, Wayne Lewis, Wilfred Bassaragh, Grace Bassaragh, Raymond Donaldson, Leonard Chambers and Rohan Chambers, front Alicia Cargill-Lewis

Figure 132 Johannesburg, SA. - Rohan Chambers & Leonard Chambers

Figure 133 Johannesburg, SA. Mandela Square, 2023 - Rohan Chambers & Leonard Chambers

About the Author

Leonard Chambers's' early journey as a cricketer started with the St. Jago Youth Club as a player and then he became captain of the team at the Hamilton and Carib competitions while he was President. He represented Bernard Lodge in the *Sugar Estates Cricket Competitions*. He captained Saint Catherine Cricket Club at the senior cup level for several years; he was also captain of the *All Indian* and *Jaghai's Cricket Teams* in the popular *Rankine competition*. Leonard represented the Jamaica National Colts Cricket team against the English Cavaliers, Australia, and Worcestershire. His impressive performances as a batting all-rounder for the Colts team and the Flagship of Jamaica's cricket competition the senior cup impacted his selection to Warwickshire County, England for a three-month development program. While in England, Leonard represented Warwickshire County Second Division team and Stourbridge Cricket Club in the Birmingham League. In 1966, he made his national debut against Trinidad at the Queens Park Oval, and in 1975 he was appointed player manager of the national team in Cricket West Indies regional tournament. He was later that year named captain of the Jamaica team against Tobago in Tobago.

Leonard was again appointed player manager in 1975 for a special tournament involving the six regional teams in Guyana. At age 31, he was elected a member of the Jamaica Cricket Association for twenty-three years. The first two years he was elected as Assistant treasurer in 1973 and Assistant secretary in 1974. During his twenty-three years as a member of the Jamaica Cricket Association, he served on several committees including the senior selection for twelve years and thirteen years as the youth selection chairman. Leonard served as manager of the Jamaica regional youth team for fourteen years and for matches against England in 1985, Australia 1990 and South Africa 1991, he was manager of the West Indies youth team against England in the Caribbean 1995, Pakistan and Bangladesh away from home 1995. He was a West Indies youth selector for four seasons and was manager of the Regional Awards team against New Zealand at Sabina Park. Leonard was instrumental in the formation of the Wherry Wharf / Kingston Wharves under-nineteen cricket competition. He procured scholarships for a number of former youth cricketers to secondary and tertiary educational institutions and for sponsorship of team blazers, Caps, track suits for the national under-nineteens. He served as the Liaison to regional teams and the touring Indian test team. He represented Primrose Cricket Club in the USA Bronx Cricket League.

Leonard, for his services to the game, is the recipient of several Awards including the Carreras Sports Foundation Award for services to Jamaica's Youth Cricket, Citation from Insports of Jamaica for outstanding service to cricket in Jamaica and the West Indies, Citation from the Consulate General of Jamaica, New York, Citation from Eric Adams President of the Borough Brooklyn for services to cricket in Jamaica and the West Indies, from the Mayor of the city of Hartford, Connecticut for his contribution to Jamaica and West Indies cricket, for outstanding contribution in the field of cricket from New York friends of Spanish Town. From Shirley Matthews President of USA Cricket Hall of Fame for his Induction to USA Cricket Hall of Fame for services to the game in Jamaica and the West Indies.

Made in the USA
Monee, IL
02 September 2024

3eb37a00-9ec6-4a71-9a23-8c7b4bc4bb2dR01